# Cyber Law & FISM Compliance

# ConvoCourses

Copyright 2023 - All rights reserved.

The content contained within this book may not be reproduced, duplicated or transmitted without direct written permission from the author or the publisher. Under no circumstances will any blame or legal responsibility be held against the publisher, or author, for any damages, reparation, or monetary loss due to the information contained within this book, either directly or indirectly.

Legal Notice:

This book is copyright protected. It is only for personal use. You cannot amend, distribute, sell, use, quote or paraphrase any part, or the content within this book, without the consent of the author or publisher.

Disclaimer Notice:

Please note the information contained within this document is for educational and entertainment purposes only. All effort has been executed to present accurate, up to date, reliable, complete information. No warranties of any kind are declared or implied. Readers acknowledge that the author is not engaged in the rendering of legal, financial, medical or professional advice. The content within this book has been derived from various sources. Please consult a licensed professional before attempting any techniques outlined in this book. By reading this document, the reader agrees that under no circumstances is the author responsible for any losses, direct or indirect, that are incurred as a result of the use of the information contained within this document, including, but not limited to, errors, omissions, or inaccuracies.

## Table of Contents:
Join the Community
BOOK #1: Cybersecurity & Privacy Law: Introduction
**Chapter 1: Fundamentals of Cybersecurity and Privacy Laws**
What are Cyber Laws

*Crimes Against People*
*Crimes Against Property*
*Crimes Against Government*

Privacy Laws

*Consent*
*Purpose*
*Disclosure*
*Security Practices*

Privacy Laws Vs. Security Laws
Why Do We Need Security And Privacy Laws?
Impact of Cyber Laws

*Impact On Industry*
*Impact on People*

Intellectual Property
**Chapter 2: Key U.S. Cybersecurity Laws and Regulations**
Federal Information Security Modernization Act (FISMA)

*What is FISMA?*
*Benefits and Penalties*
*Best Practices*

Computer Fraud and Abuse Act (CFAA)
Privacy Act of 1974
Freedom of Information Act
Cybersecurity Information Sharing Act (CISA)

*What is CISA?*

Gramm-Leach-Bliley Act (GLBA)

*What is GLBA?*
*Financial Privacy Rule:*
*Benefits of GLBA*
*Potential GLBA Penalties*
*Best Practices*

California Consumer Privacy Act (CCPA)

*What is CCPA?*
*Exceptions to CCPA*
*Consumer Rights under CCPA*
*Business Obligations*
*Enforcement*

Children's Online Privacy Protection Act (COPPA)

*What is COPPA?*
*Requirements under COPPA*
*Applicability*

Electronic Communications Privacy Act (ECPA)

*What is ECPA?*

**Chapter 3: Understanding the NIST 800 RMF Framework**
What is the NIST RMF Framework?

*Purpose of the RMF*

How to Manage Security and Privacy Risk

*Organization-Wide Risk Management*
*RMF Steps and Structure*
*Information Security and Privacy in RMF*
*System and System Elements*
*Requirements and Controls*
*Security and Privacy Posture*
*Supply-Chain Risk Management (SCRM)*

Executing the RMF
**Chapter 4: Global Cybersecurity Laws and Regulations**
Europe

*Cyber Resilience Act (CRA)*
*General Data Protection Regulation (GDPR)*

Japan

*Act on the Protection of Personal Information (APPI)*

China

*Cyber Security Law*

*Information Security Technology – Personal Information Security Specification*

Singapore

*Cybersecurity Act*
*Personal Data Protection Act (PDPA)*

India

*Information Technology (IT) Act*

**Chapter 5: Industry-Specific Cybersecurity Laws and Regulations**
HealthCare

*Health Insurance Portability and Accountability Act (HIPAA)*
*Health Information Trust (HITRUST) Common Security Framework (CSF)*

Retail

*Payment Card Industry Data Security Standard (PCI-DSS)*

Financial Sector

*Sarbanes-Oxley (SOX) Act*

**Chapter 6: Cybersecurity Laws in Government and Defense**
NASA Cyber Security Policies

*What is NPD 2810?*
*Applicability*
*Responsibilities*

DoD Security Requirements

*Defense Federal Acquisition Regulation Supplement (DFARS)*
*NIST SP 800-171*
*Cybersecurity Maturity Model Certification (CMMC)*

**Chapter 7: How to Implement Cybersecurity Law Compliance in Your Organization**
What Laws To Comply With?
Using the NIST CSF to Ensure Compliance with Laws and Regulations

*Origin and Purpose of NIST CSF*
*Implementation Tiers of NIST CSF*
*Aligning with Laws and Regulations*

Education on Laws and Compliance
Risk Assessments

*Step 1: Catalog Information Assets*
*Step 2: Categorize the Risk*
*Step 3: Analyze the Risk*
*Step 4: Establish Risk Tolerance*

Choosing a Framework
Setting and Updating Policies and Controls
Monitor, Respond, and Iterate
**Chapter 8: Privacy Laws and Their Impact on Cybersecurity**
Privacy Is Not The Same as Security
Common Challenges

*The Complexity of the Environment*

# CYBER LAW & FISMA COMPLIANCE 7

*Sophisticated Threats*
*The Shift of Threat Landscape to Mobile Devices*
*"Big Data" Paradox*
*Compliance Vs. Risk Management*

Impact of Privacy Laws on Organizations
Security and Privacy Together
**Chapter 9: Cybersecurity Laws and System Certifications**
Certifications In the Law

*FISMA*
*NIST SP 800-37 Authorization Process*
*Office of Management and Budget (OMB) Circular A-130*

ISO 27001
Certifications for PCI DSS

*Certification Process*

HIPAA Certification
COPPA Safe Harbor Program
GDPR Certification
**Chapter 10: Future of Cybersecurity Laws**
Cybersecurity for the Internet of Things
Child Privacy Laws
AI Laws
**Conclusion**
Book #2: FISMA Compliance - Understanding US federal information security law
INTRODUCTION TO INFORMATION SECURITY IN THE FEDERAL CONTEXT
CHAPTER 1
FISMA BACKGROUND AND LEGISLATIVE HISTORY
The Sections of FISMA
Key Objectives and Scope of FISMA 2002
Key Objectives and Scope of FISMA 2014
**CHAPTER 2**
**AUTHORITY AND FUNCTIONS UNDER FISMA 2014**
The Role of the Office of Management and Budget (OMB)

*Policy Development and Implementation*
*Budgetary Oversight*
*Compliance and Oversight*
*Facilitating Interagency Coordination*

The Secretary of Homeland Security's Responsibilities

*Enhanced Cybersecurity Framework and Collaboration*
*Technical Assistance and Cybersecurity Services*
*Operational Security Measures and Incident Response*
*Coordination with Critical Infrastructure Sectors*
*Advocacy for Cybersecurity Awareness and Education*
*Policy Development and Legislative Engagement*

Delegation of Authority to the Director of National Intelligence for Specific Systems

*Specific Responsibilities Entrusted to the DNI*
*Risk Management and Security Oversight*
*Coordination with Federal Agencies*
*Information Sharing and Cybersecurity Integration*
*Innovation and Technology Adoption*
*The Importance of the DNI's Role*

## CHAPTER 3
## INFORMATION SECURITY POLICIES AND PRACTICES

Development and Implementation of Agency-specific Policies
Binding Operational Directives and Compliance
Integration with National Institute of Standards and Technology (NIST) Guidelines

*Key Aspects of NIST Integration*

## CHAPTER 4
## FEDERAL INFORMATION SECURITY INCIDENT CENTER (FISIC)

Role and Functions of FISIC

*Centralized Oversight for Cybersecurity*

*Proactive Threat Identification*
*Expertise and Resource Hub*
*Comprehensive Incident Management*
*Collaborative Cybersecurity Ecosystem*
*Cybersecurity Policy Development*
*Training and Awareness Programs*
*Evaluation and Continuous Improvement*

Incident Reporting and Response Coordination

*Enhanced Incident Reporting*
*Strategic Response Coordination*

## CHAPTER 5
## REPORTING AND EVALUATION
Annual Reports on the Effectiveness of Information Security Policies

*Purpose and Importance of Reports & Evaluation*
*Content of the Reports*
*Process and Evaluation*

Independent Evaluation of Agency Information Security Programs

*Purpose and Scope*
*Execution of the Evaluation*
*Outcome and Impact*

Major Incident Reporting Requirements

*Reporting Protocol*
*Accountability and Transparency*

## CHAPTER 6
## ENHANCED SECURITY MEASURES
Integration of Security with Budgetary and Operational Planning
Automated Tools for Security Assessments

*Advantages of Automated Tools:*
*Challenges and Considerations*

Special Provisions for National Security Systems

**CHAPTER 7**
**BREACH NOTIFICATION AND RESPONSE**
Policies for Data Breach Notifications
Roles of Different Government Entities in Breach Response
Reporting Requirements to Congress and Other Authorities

*Immediate Reporting*
*Annual Reporting*

**CHAPTER 8**
**CONTINUOUS DIAGNOSTICS AND MITIGATION**
Implementation of Advanced Security Tools

*Key Components of Advanced Security Tools*
*Challenges and Considerations*
*Strategic Implementation for Enhanced Security*

OMB's Role in Assessing Agency Adoption of Security Technologies

*Enhanced Oversight and Policy Guidance*
*Strategic Resource Allocation*
*Evaluation and Compliance*
*Feedback and Continuous Improvement*
*Collaboration with DHS and Other Stakeholders*

**CHAPTER 9**
**LEGAL AND REGULATORY IMPLICATIONS**
Impact on Existing Laws and Information Security Practices

*Enhanced Risk Management Focus*
*Strengthening Agency Accountability*
*Integration of Continuous Monitoring*
*Collaboration and Information Sharing*
*Revising Compliance and Reporting Mechanisms*

Amendments to Other Related Acts and Policies

*National Institute of Standards and Technology (NIST) Guidelines:*

*Integration with the Cybersecurity Enhancement Act of 2014:*
*Revisions to the Clinger-Cohen Act:*
*Updates to the Privacy Act of 1974:*
*Alignment with the Homeland Security Act of 2002:*

**ORIGINAL TEXT OF THE ACT**

*Title*
*SECTION*
*SEC*
*Open Quotes, Notes, and Annotations*

Public Law 107-347- Federal Information Security Management Act of 2002 (Sample)

Public Law 113-283 Federal Information Security Modernization Act of 2014 (Sample)

**GLOSSARY OF KEY TERMS AND ACRONYMS**
**REFERENCES**

# Join the Community

**Sources and downloadable:**
The main authoritative resource for FISMA is to
https://www.congress.gov/
You can also check out my downloadable at
http://convocourses.com/courses/cyberlaw
**Check us out on:**
*youtube.com/convocourses*
**Contact us:**
contact@convocourses.com

# Cybersecurity and Privacy Law
*Introduction*

# ConvoCourses

# Chapter 1: Fundamentals of Cybersecurity and Privacy Laws

On January 29th, 2015, Anthem Blue Cross Blue Shield admitted to a data breach that affected over 78 million people, employees and their customers included. Anthem reported this breach, where a lot of customer information was leaked. It was reported that one of their database administrators discovered that their credentials were being used without their knowledge and consent. This unauthorized access led to the breach of consumer information, including but not limited to member names, member health identification numbers, dates of birth, Social Security numbers, addresses, telephone numbers, email addresses, employment information, and income data. Because Anthem is a health insurance company, the exposed data directly violated the Health Insurance Portability and Accountability Act (HIPAA). There was a consolidated class-action lawsuit, i.e., a case was made on behalf of many people against Anthem. This class action was settled in 2018 for a sum of $115 million. Anthem collaborated with the FBI and a private security agency to track down the hackers and was able to trace them to a few Chinese nationals. No evidence suggested that the breach had led to identity fraud, and Anthem maintained they were not violating data security laws. This incident almost ten years ago suggests that there has long since been a need for better-defined cybersecurity laws to protect our digital assets.

More data breaches have violated various security and privacy laws in recent years. Notably, the Equifax leak in 2017, where the financial and personal information of more than 150 million people was lost because of a known Apache vulnerability, which was left unpatched. The company had to make massive settlements with the Federal Trade Commission (FTC), the Consumer Financial

Protection Bureau (CFPB), and all 50 U.S. states and territories. All because they were negligent in maintaining and updating their devices and software. Hacks on the Democratic National Party during the 2016 elections were a serious breach of privacy and cybersecurity laws. These are only a few examples of law violations caused by data breaches. Another gross violation of privacy by design occurred when Facebook came under scrutiny for selling user data to the analytics company Cambridge Analytica. While Facebook faced lawsuits and fines by the FTC and SEC. It also raised a lot of ethical questions. The need for better and well-defined laws was deeply felt after this incident in 2018. Along with these laws, a need for better enforcement of said laws, as well as awareness of cyber laws, became an essential part of the path forward.

Over the past decade, as the number of incidents has risen, it has become amply clear that there is a need to regulate how things are handled in the digital world. Users' personal information has become a sought-after entity; we need stricter rules to protect the privacy and security of the customers. As countries recognize this need, there have been numerous Acts and Laws that different governments have implemented to ensure proper security and privacy measures are in place whenever a company handles customer or other sensitive data.

Just like the existence of these laws is important, awareness and proper implementation from the management level to the implementation level are also equally important. This book is written with that in mind. This book aims to make its readers aware of the most important data security and privacy laws in play today and how they apply to different organizations providing different functions in the industry. Accordingly, in the book's first part, we'll discuss the basic principles behind these laws and how they affect the tech industry, introducing readers to standards that help make organizations compliant with cyber law. Standards like the NIST 800 Risk Management Framework. NIST 800 provides a structured approach for managing security and privacy risks within an organization by implementing a continuous monitoring process. We'll also talk about the most common security laws in the US today.

Next, we talk about the different cyber laws across the globe and how, despite the laws being for a different countries, they can also affect data handling practices in other countries. Given how interconnected the online world is, this is a natural consequence. We discuss laws specific to the healthcare industry, the payment card industry, and publicly traded companies. We'll also discuss cyber laws in government organizations like DoD and NASA.

This book will discuss privacy laws and how they can differ from cyber laws. We'll provide practical information on implementing these laws in organizations. We will also cover how certifications for specific laws and regulations can enhance your security posture while at the same time helping organizations abide by the said laws. We hope to provide a comprehensive guide to important cyber and privacy laws, their role in everyday industry functioning, and how to incorporate them into your work to remain compliant while providing the best product or service for your customers.

## What are Cyber Laws

When we think of law enforcement in the digital world, a natural question arises: What are cyber laws? Cyber laws encompass the legal aspects of any activities and interactions that happen in cyberspace. This includes communications and transactions over networked devices and the distribution and storage of data and information. For this book, we only talk about the abstract or "digital" aspect of cybersecurity and not the physical machines and connections where the digital world lives. These laws exist to ensure all actions happening on the internet are ethical and authorized by all parties involved in the action. They are designed to protect both the individual as well as the organization. Cyber laws protect against three types of cybercrime: crimes against people, property, and government.

## Crimes Against People

These are the most common types of cybercrime where the target is to defraud people on the internet and to either cause them harm or gain something from them, or both. These include crimes ranging from cyberbullying, stalking, and harassment to credit card theft, identity theft, and human trafficking.

## Crimes Against Property

Crimes against property are those cyber crimes that target devices on the internet like servers, routers, firewalls, etc. For most hacking activities, crime against property is a byproduct of the actual purpose of the hack, which is usually to disrupt normal function or steal information to inconvenience end-users. Common types of this crime are Denial of Service (DOS) attacks, computer viruses, exploiting network vulnerabilities like the Dyn DNS attack, etc.

## Crimes Against Government

These types of crimes are more specific and target nation-state vectors to disrupt a nation's defense systems to either cause fear and panic, gain confidential national security information, or even facilitate physical attacks.

With comprehensive and well-enforced cyber laws, the idea is to protect against these most commonly seen cyber crimes.

# Privacy Laws

Privacy laws generally fall under cyber laws but deserve to be discussed separately because of how much they affect the entire cyber landscape. Privacy laws predominantly apply to the privacy of individual people on the internet. These laws dictate how a user's personal information is obtained, stored, and used. An important factor is how this information is processed and shared with third-party organizations, which may use this data for marketing, analytics, or something else. As hackers focus on the easier target of user personal information, privacy laws and enforcement of privacy laws become increasingly important. With the rise of new privacy laws, some data collection, processing, and storage fundamentals remain common. These privacy fundamentals include consent, purpose, disclosure, and security practices.

## *Consent*

Consent is at the forefront of privacy laws. It is the process by which end users grant permission for organizations to collect, store, or process their data. This is imperative to ensure that the data collection is transparent and ethical.

**Key Aspects of Consent:**

Explicit Consent: Users must actively give permission, usually via a distinct action like ticking a box. Pre-ticked boxes or any form of assumed consent aren't considered valid in many jurisdictions.

Informed Consent: Users must be provided with clear and comprehensive information about what data will be collected and how it will be used.

Revocability: The users should be able to withdraw their consent at any given time.

## *Purpose*

The purpose of data collection is another pillar of privacy. Data shouldn't be gathered without a clear, predefined reason.

**Key Aspects of Purpose:**

Specificity: The reasons for collecting data should be specific and not overly broad.

Legitimate Reasons: Organizations should only collect personal data for genuine, legitimate purposes and not for malicious intent.

No Excessive Data: Only the necessary data for the expressed purpose should be collected. Superfluous data collection without clear reasoning is frowned upon.

## *Disclosure*

Disclosure revolves around transparency. It emphasizes the importance of organizations being open about their use of personal data.

**Key Aspects of Disclosure:**

Transparency: Organizations must be transparent about how they plan to use the data.

Third-party Sharing: Any intentions to share user data with third-party entities should be clearly stated.

Duration: Organizations should inform users how long they intend to keep their data.

## Security Practices

Information on the security practices and procedures followed by the data collection organization.

Ensuring that collected data is secure is vital. With the rise of cyber threats, robust security practices are a non-negotiable aspect of data privacy.

**Key Aspects of Security Practices:**

Data Encryption: This involves encoding data to prevent unauthorized access. Data should be encrypted both in transit and at rest.

Regular Audits: Organizations should conduct security audits to identify and fix potential vulnerabilities.

Access Control: It is essential to limit who can access the data and ensure that only authorized personnel can view or process it.

Breach Notification: In the event of a data breach, organizations must have procedures in place to notify affected users and relevant authorities promptly.

These fundamental rules are part of most privacy policies applied by organizations as a result of the privacy laws. Like cyber laws, privacy laws also can vary between countries, and based on where the data is stored and handled, privacy laws from a different country may be applied to data in another country.

# Privacy Laws Vs. Security Laws

While it may be that privacy laws fall generally under cyber laws, there are differences. Security laws mainly focus on protecting all the data that an organization has, whereas privacy laws focus on managing personally identifiable information (PII), points of data that can be used to accurately identify a specific person. Security laws dictate how we store, transmit, and maintain data within an organization; this includes whether data is encrypted, different access control measures, etc. Privacy regulations dictate what PII data is collected, how we collect it, how it is being used in the organization, and who we share it with.

As you can see, there is a lot of overlap. One can argue that they can be considered the same, but their approach towards regulations is the biggest difference. Security is data-focused; it will protect whatever data falls under the regulation. Privacy is user-focused to protect real end users online. However, they are deeply interconnected, and one only strengthens the other.

Here is an example to understand the nuanced difference between the two: when a data breach occurs where hackers forcibly access or steal information, we consider security laws violated. But, if information or data is shared voluntarily by an organization without the knowledge of the user whose information is being shared, it would be considered a violation of privacy laws.

## Why Do We Need Security And Privacy Laws?

The internet can be very autonomous, offering little in terms of regulations or behavior guidelines. We interact with people's data and websites from all around the world daily over the internet. Similarly, malicious actors can sit in any corner of the world and affect people. Because of this internet structure, it can be difficult to understand and apply rules and regulations. The internet can seem like a fully virtual space, but with the increasing intersection of the internet with our physical lives, any disruption online can affect our lives seriously. With things like banking, shopping, education, contract agreements, and more happening online, a hack or a data breach can really impact our lives. As cyber-attacks increased and their after-effects became life-altering, a need to demarcate jurisdictions and apply laws for protecting everyday online activities is very real.

As the number of users online and the involvement of citizens in online activities differs from country to country, different governments apply their laws for data protection and handling. Because of differences in culture and mindsets, the strictness of laws, especially privacy laws, can vary quite a bit. With time, it was understood that organizations from different industries interacted differently with data. The social media industry thrived on sharing people's data, whereas the healthcare industry needed strict confidentiality of an individual's data. Looking at this, some new laws were enforced with regulations specific to the industry they were applied to. As laws and regulations became more and more common across the internet, the cybersecurity industry had to adapt.

## Impact of Cyber Laws

### Impact On Industry

Cyber Laws have had a two-sided impact on the tech industry. On the one hand, it provides individuals and organizations a way to seek justice and compensation for damages in a cyber attack. On the other hand, it requires organizations and the industry, in general, to adhere to stricter rules and be more organized in their approach to security.

Because of cyber security laws, industries that deal with sensitive data, like banking, finance, etc., have to uphold higher security standards in following these rules. E-commerce industries have started accessing more sensitive information from their users and are rapidly beginning to fall under the categories where higher security laws need to be followed. The need to follow security laws has introduced the concept of compliance within the tech industry. Having compliance, or being compliant, implies that a company or organization is in a state where it is following all the rules and regulations set upon the industry by the responsible legislative bodies. In many major companies, compliance has become a separate department unto itself to ensure a particular product or service is running in accordance with the established regulations.

Nevertheless, having a compliance department is insufficient to know if a company adheres to the laws, nor does it automatically ensure compliance requirements are met. Because of this, third-party reviews have been introduced to ensure all the regulations are properly followed and implemented. These reviews are called compliance audits conducted by authorized external organizations on companies. The audit reports measure risk management, thoroughness of compliance preparations, user access controls, and so forth based on what type of company it is and what data it gathers, stores, and/or transmits. Apart from these external compliance audits, internal audits are also performed within the company to ensure the organization follows both external and internal guidelines, and these reports can be used to improve a company's compliance posture iteratively.

## *Impact on People*

Cyber laws have also had a social impact on the world. With cybercrime on the rise, more and more people have faced its negative effects and, therefore, have become vigilant about cybercrime and cyber laws. With stricter standards in the industry in general, there has been a shift in how data is collected and used, which has also seen its impact on the people. New rules on password creation, use, recovery, and two-factor authentication have become commonplace, along with various other security standards applied based on the industry. With rising awareness, end-users have also increased the use of security products like anti-virus software and virtual private networks (VPNs). Overall, there has been a shift towards better security practices within the user community.

# Intellectual Property

When discussing cyber laws, it's relevant to discuss intellectual property (IP) law and how it applies to technology. While it doesn't directly correlate to cybersecurity, IP must be protected when discussing cybercrime and online theft. In the digital world, some of the assets where IP rights can be applied are:

## Copyright

> These protect any asset that can be transmitted over the internet, including but not limited to music, movies, books, blogs, etc.

## Patents

> There can be two types of patents in the digital world. It can be either for a new software or business methodology; IP rights protect both.

## Trademarks

> Trademarks are used the same way online as in the physical world and are mostly used to protect websites.

## Domain Disputes

> Domains here refer to the web addresses used by any website, and owners of said domains can invoke IP rights in case of any dispute for the domain.

These are examples of how IP rights are applied in the digital world. Many other digital assets can be protected under IP rights, which are beyond the scope of this book. In case it is unclear whether a particular aspect of the system or business function is covered by IP law, it is best to consult a legal team specializing in cyber and IP law.

# Chapter 2: Key U.S. Cybersecurity Laws and Regulations

To know exactly which control needs to be applied to remain within legal boundaries and in compliance with security and privacy requirements, this chapter focuses on some of the most common cybersecurity and privacy laws in practice in the United States.

## Federal Information Security Modernization Act (FISMA)

### *What is FISMA?*

The Federal Information Security Modernization Act (FISMA) was enacted as a part of the E-Government Act of 2002. It establishes regulations for federal data security standards and guidelines. FISMA requires all federal government agencies, even those not involved in national security, to develop, document, and implement an information security program. This program is designed to protect sensitive data and the information systems supporting agency operations and assets. These requirements extend to assets managed by another agency, third-party vendors, or service providers.

These agencies must also perform annual reviews to determine the efficacy of the implemented data and information system protections. It has since expanded to include state agencies administering federal programs as well.

### *FISMA 2014*

The replacement of FISMA 2002 with FISMA 2014 deserves to be mentioned as it brought to the forefront the need to emphasize data and systems protection within the federal systems. According to the Federal Information Security Modernization Act, this replacement updated the practices by:

- Codifying the Department of Homeland Security (DHS) authority to administer the implementation of information security policies for non-national security federal Executive Branch systems, including providing technical assistance and deploying technologies to such systems;
- Amending and clarifying the Office of Management and Budget's (OMB) oversight authority over federal agency information security practices and by
- Requiring OMB to amend or revise OMB A-130 to "eliminate inefficient and wasteful reporting."

The National Institute of Standards and Technology developed the standards and guidelines for all federal agencies to protect their systems and information.

It works closely with federal agencies to improve their understanding and implementation of FISMA.

*FISMA Requirements*

FISMA determines many organization requirements, but an agency must comply with seven main requirements:

*Information System Inventory*

FISMA requires agencies and third-party vendors to identify all the information systems and maintain an inventory; this includes any interfaces the systems interact with, including those not controlled by the agency itself.

## Risk Categorization

All assets, data, and systems need to be categorized based on the risk they pose and the number of security controls they may need for a range of risk levels.

## Security Controls

FISMA emphasizes the importance of security controls but does not delve into their specifics. Instead, it mandates federal agencies to implement necessary controls, drawing guidance primarily from the National Institute of Standards and Technology (NIST). To aid agencies, NIST's Special Publication 800-53 offers an extensive catalog of potential security and privacy controls. However, agencies are not required to apply all these controls; they are to implement only those deemed essential based on their specific risk assessment and operational needs.

## Risk Assessment

Risk Assessments are a very important aspect of determining an agency's security and privacy posture when we start adding controls. It is even more important to conduct these assessments on an ongoing basis to evaluate the effectiveness of the implemented risk management. Potential cyber threats, cyberattacks, vulnerabilities, exploits, and other common attack vectors must be identified and mapped to controls designed to mitigate them. Then, the risk is determined based on the likelihood and impact of a scenario based on the existing controls.

## System Security Plan (SSP)

FISMA mandates that federal agencies maintain thorough documentation of their security controls. Central to this requirement is the System Security Plan (SSP), which provides a detailed record of the security measures in place for a particular system. The SSP should be regularly reviewed and updated to reflect changes in the system and its environment. It serves not only as a reference for the agency but also as a crucial component during the security assessment and authorization processes. The plan's accuracy and completeness are critical, as it is evaluated against the guidance provided by the NIST to ensure that the chosen and implemented controls adhere to recommended standards and best practices. NIST SP 800-18 describes the content that should be in an SSP.

## Certifications and Accreditations

FISMA underscores the significance of certification and accreditation to validate that security controls are properly implemented and risks are mitigated to an acceptable level. Accreditation is a formal declaration by an agency official, indicating they acknowledge and accept the security postures of their systems, and thus can be held accountable for any breaches or lapses. To facilitate the intricate process of certification and accreditation, NIST Special Publication 800-37 offers a structured framework, providing federal agencies with detailed steps, procedures, and best practices to ensure a thorough and consistent approach.

## Continuous Monitoring

Continuous monitoring is an important requirement of FISMA. Monitoring is to ensure ongoing security and compliance of federal information systems. For a system to be FISMA accredited, it isn't just about initial implementation; the system must be regularly observed, with any significant changes or updates documented. When these modifications occur, they may necessitate a reassessment to guarantee continued adherence to security requirements and to identify potential vulnerabilities. This proactive approach helps in maintaining the system's security posture and in responding swiftly to emerging threats or changes.

Implementing the FISMA requirements across all federal systems relies heavily on the National Institute of Standards and Technology guidelines, which are discussed in greater detail in the next chapter.

## *Benefits and Penalties*

FISMA has significantly improved federal agencies' security and privacy posture and allowed them to eliminate vulnerabilities cost-effectively.

A benefit to private agencies is that FISMA compliance significantly improves their likelihood of getting a federal contract with the side effect of improving their security in the process.

For government agencies and third-party agencies working with them, failing to meet FISMA compliance can result in reduced funding, reputation damage, congressional censure, and government hearings, among other drawbacks.

## *Best Practices*

Some of the best practices to follow to easily obtain and maintain FISMA compliance are:

- Classify information as it is generated to easily identify and prioritize risk mitigation.
- Encrypt sensitive data at rest and in transit.

- Run regular risk assessments.
- Conduct employee training and education.
- Maintain evidence of what your organization is doing to achieve compliance.
- Be up-to-date with the latest changes to rules and regulations.

## Computer Fraud and Abuse Act (CFAA)

The Computer Fraud and Abuse Act (CFAA) is a US federal law created in 1986 to amend the first federal computer fraud law, the 1984 Comprehensive Crime Control Act. The CFAA primarily addresses the issue of hacking or unauthorized access to computers, especially those owned by the federal government and financial institutions. Still, its applications have been broadened over time.

Originally, the CFAA targeted particularly federal computer crimes, such as attacks on government computers. However, its scope has expanded over the years due to various amendments. Now, it covers a wide range of computer activities, which can sometimes encompass seemingly benign activities if they involve unauthorized or exceed authorized access.

The CFAA has attracted criticism and controversy, primarily due to its broad language and the perception that it can be used to prosecute relatively trivial offenses. Critics argue that some of its provisions are overly vague, which can lead to disproportionate penalties for minor infractions.

Violations of the CFAA can lead to both criminal and civil penalties. Criminal penalties range from misdemeanors to felonies, depending on the nature and consequences of the offense. In some circumstances, violators can face substantial fines and imprisonment.

Over the years, the CFAA has been the subject of numerous court cases, and its interpretation has evolved. Some courts have taken a broad view of what constitutes "unauthorized access" or

# CYBER LAW & FISMA COMPLIANCE 33

"exceeding authorized access," while others have adopted a narrower perspective.

The CFAA remains a critical piece of legislation for addressing computer-related crimes in the U.S.. Still, its application and interpretation have been, and continue to be, the subject of debate and litigation.

Some key provisions of the CFAA include:

- **Unauthorized Access to a Computer:** This includes accessing without authorization the computers of the U.S. government, financial institutions, and any computer used in or affecting interstate or foreign commerce.
- **Exceeding Authorized Access:** This means that someone had permission to access the computer, but they went beyond the limits of that permission (for example, by accessing data they weren't supposed to).
- **Transmitting Harmful Code:** It's an offense under the CFAA to knowingly transmit a program, code, or command that causes harm to a computer, its data, or its systems.
- **Fraud:** If someone accesses a computer without (or beyond) authorization and, by doing so, obtains something of value, they can be charged under the CFAA.
- **Trafficking in Passwords:** Knowingly selling or otherwise distributing passwords to a computer can be a violation. This is done a lot on the Dark Web.
- **Damaging a Computer or Information:** This section applies to those who cause damage through unauthorized access or transmitting harmful code.

The Department of Justice (DOJ) has guidelines and policies that federal prosecutors can use when determining whether to bring charges under various statutes, including the CFAA. These are not directly part of the CFAA but are part of the DOJ's broader prosecutorial discretion. They can clarify which cases are prioritized and how the law should be applied in different circumstances (see https://www.justice.gov/ for more).

## Privacy Act of 1974

The US Privacy Act of 1974 allows individuals to access records about themselves. It applies to federal organizations collecting data on people. It restricts the government's ability to collect information about citizens. It controls how they collect information, how it is maintained, used, and published. Its purpose is to give rights to the individuals whose data is collected. It protects individuals against unwarranted invasions of privacy.

Some of the main features of the Privacy Act are:

- Consent of individuals whose information is collected.
- Transparency in the collection and use of the information.
- Protection of the records being collected.

Federal organizations meet the requirements of this law by creating banners on sites collecting data to inform users and by issuing a "System of Records Notice (SORN)," which is a public notification that documents the purpose of a system of records. A system of records is a group of records controlled by an agency.

## Freedom of Information Act

The Freedom of Information Act (FOIA), inaugurated on July 5, 1967, stands as a testament to the United States' commitment to transparency and the empowerment of its citizenry. Envisioned as a tool to strengthen democratic engagement, it affirms every citizen's right to seek and access information held within the confines of the US federal government's various departments. A visit to FOIA.gov serves as the portal through which individuals can exercise this right, demystifying the operations and decisions of governmental entities. While FOIA is anchored in the ethos of openness, it is also pragmatic. Recognizing the need for security and privacy, the act includes specific exemptions, ensuring that information which could jeopardize national security, infringe on personal privacy, or hinder governmental functions remains protected. Thus, while promoting transparency, FOIA also respects the boundaries essential for effective governance and the safeguarding of the nation's interests.

## Cybersecurity Information Sharing Act (CISA)

### What is CISA?

In the cybersecurity profession, we often associate the acronym CISA with the Cybersecurity & Infrastructure Security Agency (CISA.gov). But in cybersecurity law, "CISA" stands for the Cybersecurity Information Sharing Act. The CISA act was made into law in December 2015. This law's main objective is to enhance cybersecurity in the U.S. through improved collaboration between private entities and the federal government. It provides two primary provisions for companies: First, it permits companies to implement specific monitoring and defensive measures to safeguard their data and information systems. Second, it offers incentives, like protection from liability and protection from Freedom of Information Act (FOIA) disclosure, to motivate companies to voluntarily share cyber threat indicators and defensive measures with the federal government, state and local governments, and even other private entities. To qualify for these protections, any shared data must have irrelevant personal information removed to ensure the privacy of individuals is upheld.

The Key provisions under this law are:

**Monitor and Defend Information Systems**

It allows companies and organizations to monitor their information systems and defend them against threats while protecting them from the liability of monitoring the said data and systems.

**Mutual sharing of threat indicators and Defensive measures**

Under this, a company can share and receive information about cyber threat indicators and defensive measures to federal, state, and local governments, other companies, and private entities.

**Scrubbing of Personal Information**

Any information about threat indicators or defense measures that will be shared should be scrubbed of all PII.

**Protections for Sharing Information (As Applicable)**

Protection from liability. There is no liability for sharing and receiving relevant information.

- Antitrust exemption. Companies aren't considered in

violation of trust if they share properly scrubbed relevant information or receive such information.

- Non-waiver of privilege. Companies are not considered in violation of privilege and legal protections when they share threat data or defensive measures.
- Information shared under CISA is exempt from disclosure under the FOIA.
- This information cannot be used to regulate or take action against lawful activities.

Other requirements and provisions include restrictions on the sharing and use of data, implementation of security controls, voluntary participation, and the proper use of data by the federal government.

## *Federal Guidance for the Private Sector*

The Department of Homeland Security (DHS) and the Department of Justice (DOJ) have released guidelines on what data can and cannot be shared under the act.

## *Information that may be shared*

Information about threat actors. For example, information on new phishing techniques, analysis of a new piece of malware, a vulnerability found in software, or an attack a company faces.

Information about the defensive measures a company is using. For example, a new computer program, a new malware signature, or an AI technique for malware detection etc.

*Information that may not be shared*

A company should not share procedures for removing personal information. They can do an internal assessment of how and what they are scrubbing.

Protected Health information, human resources information, consumer or transaction histories, and financial information are examples of information that must not be shared.

*Implications and Recommendations*

The broader idea behind CISA is to encourage information sharing between companies and the government. This provides everyone involved with a larger pool of information that can help them equip themselves to better defend against certain crimes overall.

Because of the legal protections provided under CISA, there is a greater motivation for all companies to share at least the baseline level of data and information.

In sharing such information, a company should consider the impact of a cyber threat and the cost and benefit of sharing such information. They should also make a realistic assessment of the strengths and limitations of the government protections. They should implement procedures to determine, collect, process, and share the information.

# Gramm-Leach-Bliley Act (GLBA)

## What is GLBA?

The Gramm-Leach-Bliley Act (GLBA), also known as the Financial Modernization Act of 1999, is a law that applies to financial institutions. According to this law, all financial institutions must explain how they share and protect their users' data. They must inform their customers about handling the collected personal data and grant them the right to opt-out of certain information sharing. As a documented security plan outlines, they must also implement specific protection measures for the collected customer data. This act comprises two rules and one provision.

### *Financial Privacy Rule:*

Financial institutions or companies that receive non-public personal information from such institutions must adhere to this rule. This encompasses most personal information, such as names, dates of birth, and Social Security numbers, as well as transactional data like card and bank account numbers. Furthermore, it includes any personal data acquired during a transaction.

### *Safeguards Rule:*

This rule mandates that companies protect private information under the GLBA. Firms must have both physical and technological means to securely collect, store, transmit, and process their customers' personal information. This involves having appropriate software, routinely testing vulnerabilities, and training employees to safeguard private data.

### *Pretexting Provisions:*

This provision dictates that financial institutions must put measures in place to prevent unauthorized access to data.

## Benefits of GLBA

For financial institutions, GLBA compliance results in fewer penalties and a reduced risk of reputational damage. Customers also benefit, as their personal information is better protected and safeguarded. No personal data can be collected without their knowledge and consent, and all user activity is monitored to prevent unauthorized or suspicious access or data leaks.

## Potential GLBA Penalties

According to De Groot (Digital Guardian, 2023), if case non-compliance is proven, it can have life-altering effects that include:

- Financial institutions found in violation face fines of $100,000 for each violation.
- Individuals in charge found in violation face fines of $10,000 for each violation.
- Individuals found in violation can be imprisoned for up to 5 years.

## Best Practices

To protect customer data, an institution must have an information security plan in place that is tailored to the kind of data they collect, the size of their organization, how they store and process data, and so forth. According to the Safeguards Rule, as mentioned by De Groot (2023), covered financial institutions must:

- Designate one or more employees to coordinate its information security program.
- Identify the risks to customer information in each area of the company's operation and evaluate the effectiveness of the current safeguards for controlling these risks.

- Chosen service providers must apply and maintain safeguards to the data; it should be part of the contract, and the institutions must ensure the safeguards are maintained.
- Evaluate and adjust the program in light of changing circumstances in business and the threat landscape.

## California Consumer Privacy Act (CCPA)

### *What is CCPA?*

The California Consumer Privacy Act (CCPA) is a law that provides personal information rights to all residents of California. Beyond consumers of household goods and services, this act also extends rights to individuals employed, engaged in independent contract-based employment, and other members of the workforce, as well as contacts from business customers or vendors based in California.

Under the CCPA, "personal information" is defined broadly as any data that directly or indirectly identifies relates to, or can be reasonably linked with a consumer or household.

You might think the CCPA applies to all entities in California collecting personally identifiable information, but it only applies to organizations that hit certain requirements. The CCPA's requirements apply to for-profit entities doing business in California that collect consumers' personal information and meet any of the following thresholds:

- Annual gross revenue exceeding $25 million (adjusted for inflation).
- Annually buying, receiving, sharing, or selling the personal information of over 50,000 consumers, households, or devices for commercial purposes.
- Deriving 50% or more of their annual revenues from selling

consumers' personal information.

## *Exceptions to CCPA*

The CCPA has specific exceptions, including:

- Business needs such as sharing information during mergers or acquisitions.
- Conflicts of law scenarios, like defending against legal claims, cooperating with law enforcement, or complying with other applicable regulations.
- Jurisdictional situations, for example, if all transactions and business operations occur entirely outside of California, or if another data privacy regulation, like Health Insurance Portability and Accountability Act, applies.

## *Consumer Rights under CCPA*

Under the CCPA, consumers have the right to:

- Know how a business collects, stores, uses, and shares personal information.
- Request the deletion of any personal information about them that a business holds, with some exceptions.
- For those aged 16 and older, opt-out of personal information sales.
- Those aged 15 or younger require an opt-in for personal information sales.
- Exercise their CCPA rights without facing discrimination.

## *Business Obligations*

To protect all consumer rights under the CCPA, compliant organizations are supposed to take several measures to meet the requirements. According to Thomson Reuters, to meet these requirements, businesses should:

- Protect personal information through appropriate security practices and procedures.
- Make all required CCPA notice disclosures, like notices when data is collected, when a privacy policy is updated, the right to opt-out of sales, etc.
- Establish processes to receive and respond to customer rights requests.
- Review all price or service of product quality differences based on collection or non-collection of information to ensure non-discriminations.
- Meet required employee training and documentation obligations.
- Review and monitor any contracts with service providers and third-party contracts to comply with the CCPA's requirements.

## *Enforcement*

The California Attorney General (AG) is the regulatory authority for the CCPA. When a business violates the CCPA, the AG must give the business or individual in question a notice and at least 30 days to fix the issues. If the violations are not fixed within this time frame, the AG can seek penalties of up to $2500 per violation or $7500 per intentional violation.

The CCPA extends California's data breach rules by including a private right of action to consumers to seek damages for unauthorized access, theft, privacy violation, or data breach on certain personal information.

# Children's Online Privacy Protection Act

# (COPPA)

## What is COPPA?

COPPA, the Children's Online Privacy Protection Act, is a law designed to protect the privacy of children online. As more young people turn to online devices and services for daily activities, ensuring the privacy of children under thirteen has become crucial. This law establishes stringent guidelines for collecting and processing children's personal data, granting parents and guardians greater control over their children's online privacy and security.

## Requirements under COPPA

COPPA sets forth several requirements to safeguard children's privacy and shield them from deceptive data collection, usage, and sharing practices. These requirements include:

- **Notification:** Websites must provide clear notifications and disclosures about the collection of information from children and the intended uses of that information.
- **Parental Consent:** Before collecting information from a child, explicit consent must be obtained from the child's parent or guardian.
- **Review Mechanisms:** Parents must be offered mechanisms and procedures to review any collected information about their child.
- **Minimal Data Collection:** Stipulations around collecting only the minimal necessary information from children.
- **Data Protection:** Establish and maintain procedures that ensure the ongoing privacy and security of the collected data.

## Applicability

This law does not apply to every platform, website, or service. COPPA applies to an individual or entity if:

- They run a website or web service targeted to children under thirteen years of age and collect personal information from them or allow other entities to collect it.
- They knowingly run a plug-in, ad network, or other services on a website targeted to children aged thirteen and under and collect personal information from them.
- Their service is directed towards a general population, but knows that children under thirteen years access it, and their personal information is collected.

# Electronic Communications Privacy Act (ECPA)

## What is ECPA?

The Electronic Communications Privacy Act (ECPA) is an evolution of the Federal Wiretap Act 1968. The Federal Wiretap Act originally focused on intercepting telephone conversations on traditional landlines and did not encompass online communications. ECPA was designed to bridge this gap, reflecting citizens' privacy expectations and law enforcement's legitimate needs. Today, the act covers various communications, including emails, telephone conversations, chats, and other data transmitted via the Internet.

The ECPA amalgamates three pivotal legal provisions under a single framework:

**The Wiretap Act:** Originating from regulations on landline telephone communications, this act makes it illegal to:

- Intentionally intercept wire, oral, or electronic communications while transmitting.
- Unlawfully use or disclose any intercepted communications.

**The Stored Communications Act:** safeguards both wire and electronic communications when they're not in transit (i.e. when they're "at rest"). Specifically, it's illegal to:

- Access any system used for transmitting wired or electronic communications without proper authorization.
- Alter, obtain, or prevent someone's lawful access to communications stored on such systems via unauthorized access.

**The Pen Register and Trap and Trace Devices Statute** regulates how the government can use "pen registers" and "trap and trace devices" to capture information about, but not the content of, wire or electronic communications.

While the laws highlighted above are among the most frequently cited in cybersecurity and privacy in the U.S., this is just an overview. Numerous other laws can apply or be exempted based on industry, geographical location, and specific circumstances. Regardless of the applicable laws, the most common way to start the compliance process is to enforce regulations, acts and standards in a local security policy approved and authorized by upper management. Leadership must implement the rules of the policy in the organization's process. This will also protect the information on critical assets.

# Chapter 3: Understanding the NIST 800 RMF Framework

One of the key U.S. Cybersecurity laws, FISMA, discussed in Chapter 2, spawned the creation of security guidance from the National Institute of Standards and Technology (NIST). The guidance is published in the NIST 800 special publications. They detail the US federal government's risk-management framework (RMF). Following the NIST 800 special publications aligns the organization with cyber laws that are required for federal systems.

## What is the NIST RMF Framework?

The NIST fully documents the guidance for properly managing security capabilities in the NIST 800 or NIST Risk Management Framework. To account for its wide applicability and to ensure multiple departments could benefit from the guidelines, this framework was designed in partnership with the Department of Defense (DoD), the Office of the Director of National Intelligence, and the Committee on National Security Systems. The framework emphasizes risk management by incorporating security and privacy capabilities throughout the software development life cycle (SDLC). The aim is to integrate security and privacy requirements and controls into every part of the organization, like enterprise architecture, SDLC, acquisition processes, and systems engineering processes. The framework is policy and technology-neutral and was designed with the ever-changing scope of the industry in mind. It provides a repeatable process that considers the available controls and encourages the use of automation for real-time risk management. An organization can also establish a feedback loop using precise metrics, which can help identify an efficient, cost-effective way to make decisions about the risk and best support the missions and business functions.

## *Purpose of the RMF*

NIST identifies a few main objectives behind establishing the RMF as follows:

- The biggest objective behind having a framework is to build a security and privacy management system that aligns with an organization's mission and business objectives.
- To implement privacy, security, and response strategies that can protect individuals, information, and information systems best.
- To support informed authorization decisions and to maintain transparency in the security and privacy controls.
- To integrate security and privacy requirements into the granular level of the organization so that it becomes a natural part of every aspect of the organization.
- To promote the implementation of the Framework for Improving Critical Infrastructure Cybersecurity within federal agencies.

## How to Manage Security and Privacy Risk

RMF provides guidelines on managing security and privacy risks so that organizations can mold these guidelines based on their business goals and needs. Before discussing the details of these guidelines, let's first look at some of the concepts from which these guidelines were born.

## Organization-Wide Risk Management

Risk management is not an isolated process but an organization-wide undertaking. As mentioned, risk management should be addressed at every level, from mission and business planning activities to the enterprise architecture, the SDLC processes, and the systems engineering activities. It is a multi-level approach where senior leaders provide the vision and top-level goals, mid-level leaders plan, execute, and

manage projects, and system-level engineers implement, operate, maintain, and iterate on projects supporting risk management within business objectives.

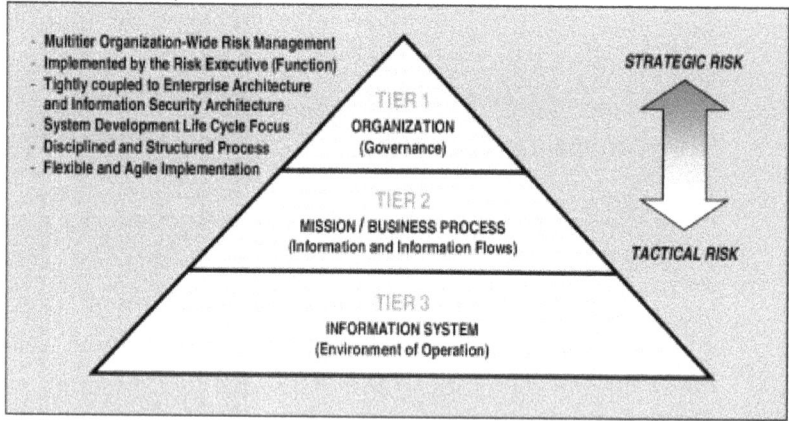

- Multitier Organization-Wide Risk Management
- Implemented by the Risk Executive (Function)
- Tightly coupled to Enterprise Architecture and Information Security Architecture
- System Development Life Cycle Focus
- Disciplined and Structured Process
- Flexible and Agile Implementation

TIER 1
ORGANIZATION
(Governance)

TIER 2
MISSION / BUSINESS PROCESS
(Information and Information Flows)

TIER 3
INFORMATION SYSTEM
(Environment of Operation)

STRATEGIC RISK

TACTICAL RISK

Organization-wide risk management can be divided into three main tiers: the organization level, the mission/business process tiers, and the information systems Tiers. An open feedback and reporting loop needs to exist in both directions to ensure that risk objectives are achieved and maintained throughout the organization.

Activities at Tiers 1 and 2 include not just managing the risk posture but understanding and planning for the integration of risk to the system level processes and must include considerations for:

- Modernization of the technologies and automation of tasks.

- The business goals and objectives.
- Optimization of the enterprise architecture.
- Resource management for maximum efficiency and cost-effectiveness.

To prepare for the proper implementation of a risk management framework within an organization, there are a few things we need to establish first:

- Risk tolerance within an organization.
- Business functions an information system is supporting.
- Key stakeholders within that information system.
- Identifying privacy and security requirements.
- Determining authorization boundaries and common access controls.

In tandem with this, organization and system-wide risk assessments should be conducted to make a risk management strategy. Based on that, threats to the systems, as well as threats to the people, need to be identified. Assets should also be identified and prioritized. Once all this information is gathered and established, we can devise a risk strategy for an information system.

Based on the decisions and strategies identified at Tier 1 and Tier 2, Tier 3 implements these decisions and controls at the ground level. Tier 3 handles the augmentation or integration of these controls, which can be common to multiple organizations/business functions or specific to the information system they are at.

The traceability of these security and privacy controls to the established requirements is also important in ensuring that identified risks are addressed at each level in the hierarchy.

## RMF Steps and Structure

The NIST RMF identifies seven basic steps that must be followed for a thorough and successful risk management implementation.

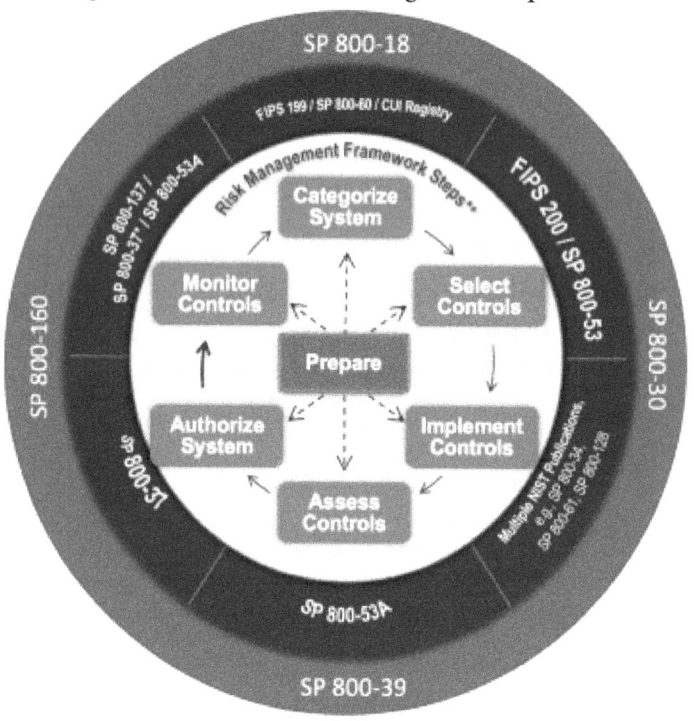

1. **Prepare.** This includes all the essential activities needed for the organization to manage risk.
2. **Categorize.** Based on impact analysis, identify and categorize the information and systems analyzed.
3. **Select.** Select the security and privacy controls you wish to implement based on risk assessments.
4. **Implement.** Implement, deploy, and document the selected controls.
5. **Assess.** Regularly assess if the controls are relevant and working as intended.

6. Authorize. Based on the risk, authorize the systems and controls to operate within the organization.
7. **Monitor.** Continuously monitor the controls and re-evaluate the risk within the system.

All steps after the preparation step can be executed in a non-sequential way based on the requirements and risk posture of the organization. These steps can also be iterated to ensure the organization's risk management is updated.

## *Information Security and Privacy in RMF*

RMF provides a framework for implementing both Information Security and privacy controls. While both seem to have the same objectives, they can differ. Security focuses on providing confidentiality, integrity, and availability for information and information systems. Therefore, the objective is to protect the collection, use, modification, destruction, and authorized access to data and information systems. Privacy deals with the risk of collecting, using, modifying, and deleting an individual's personally identifiable information (PII).

So whenever a system interacts with PII, it becomes key that the security and privacy controls collaborate to secure the data and protect it from unauthorized use, as well as protect the individual's privacy by disallowing access or use without the individual's consent. While these may sound extremely similar, the key here is that privacy violations can occur even with authorized system activities if the individual is not provided appropriate notice of data use and retention and the transparency of such use is not maintained.

Because of the nuanced differences in privacy and security operations, it's important to ensure collaboration of both types of controls from the very beginning to preserve both objectives during risk planning and implementation.

## System and System Elements

The system elements include all parts of an information system, like the technology, the hardware, funds, and personnel, which are machine elements, human elements, and physical or environmental elements. Each element included in a system corresponds to a specific system requirement.

The authorization boundary is an important aspect of the system definition as it is key in determining which components fall within the core of an information system. This is defined during the "prepare" phase of RMF execution. An authorization boundary needs to be identified with great care and precision. If it's too broad, it can make risk management difficult, and if it's too limited, it might introduce gaps. It should include all the people, processes, and information resources directly supporting the system's business function. The scope of an authorization boundary should be revisited periodically as part of the continuous monitoring of the risk management process.

For proper RMF execution and to ensure risk is managed well, we define certain components in the entire operating environment. The system is the primary resource that needs risk management; several other factors may not fall within direct protection or authorization boundaries but interact with the system.

One of these factors is the *enabling systems*. Enabling systems are any systems that support the primary resource; they may or may not fall within the authorization boundary. They provide secondary or supporting functionalities to the system, like network services, authentication, or monitoring capabilities.

*Other systems* include those with which the primary resource might interact but do not directly or indirectly affect the functionalities of the primary system.

When executing RMF strategies, it can be helpful to identify the different systems interacting within a business function to better manage similar security and privacy requirements.

## Requirements and Controls

Before doing any software implementation, we determine the requirements for the software. Similarly, we must know the security and privacy requirements before applying the risk management framework. These requirements include the legal and policy obligations a company must fulfill and the stakeholder requirements to protect data and systems.

When thinking about controls, we can view them as the capabilities available to fulfill a security or privacy objective or requirement. Controls interplay with requirements since they define the appropriate safeguards corresponding to the requirements.

## Security and Privacy Posture

The security and privacy posture of an organization or a business function is important in determining how to approach risk management. Similarly, ongoing assessment and monitoring activities must be present even after implementing the RMF to ensure the positioning of security and privacy risk management remains optimum.

## Supply-Chain Risk Management (SCRM)

Supply chain risk management comes into play because many organizations rely on external service providers for many products and services they use to fulfill their business functions. Because of interaction with entities external to the organization, managing the risk posed by such products and services becomes important. For this, companies apply an SCRM policy, which is guided and informed by applicable laws, executive orders, directives, policies, and regulations. This policy also determines the integration of risk management between the external service and the business.

## Executing the RMF

For proper execution of the NIST RMF, check out the NIST 800 Cybersecurity series by Bruce Brown and Convocourses. These books include:

- RMF ISSO: Foundations (Guide): NIST 800 Risk Management Framework for Cybersecurity Professionals (NIST 800 Cybersecurity Book 1)
- RMF ISSO: NIST 800-53 Controls: NIST 800 Control Families in Each RMF Step (NIST 800 Cybersecurity Book 2)
- RMF Security Control Assessor: NIST 800-53A Security Control Assessment Guide (NIST 800 Cybersecurity Book 3)

# Chapter 4: Global Cybersecurity Laws and Regulations

Looking at the laws present only in the US gives a good idea of how important legal protection can be in providing incentives for security and privacy measures and protecting both users and organizations. This chapter will look at cyber laws worldwide to get a better context for rules and regulations designed to protect information and information systems.

## Europe

### Cyber Resilience Act (CRA)

The Cyber Resilience Act was created when it was realized that the cost of vulnerable hardware and software components was getting too high and needed to be addressed fundamentally. They found that products suffered from two major flaws.

1. A low level of cybersecurity by design, as seen by the number of vulnerabilities and a lack of sufficient security updates for patching new issues.
2. A lack of understanding of cybersecurity among users, which prevented them from making choices with good security posture and/or using security measures available incorrectly or not at all

Because of this gap, the CRA was established because most of the hardware and software products were not covered by EU legislation. The aims behind this act were twofold.

The first was to encourage the manufacturers to take security and privacy seriously, creating conditions where secure products were a part of the design and development phase in a product life cycle.

The second was to create conditions for users to consider cybersecurity when choosing products with digital elements.

According to the Cyber Resilience Act - Shaping Europe's Digital Future (2022), to achieve these aims, the following four objectives were laid out as part of the CRA:

- Ensure that manufacturers improve the security of products with digital elements from the design and development phase and throughout the whole life cycle.
- Ensure a coherent cybersecurity framework, facilitating compliance for hardware and software producers.
- Enhance the transparency of security properties of products with digital elements.
- Enable businesses and consumers to use products with digital elements securely.

## *General Data Protection Regulation (GDPR)*

**What is GDPR?**

General Data Protection Regulation (GDPR) is an effort to unify the data protection and privacy rules across the European Union. It went into effect in 2018 and replaced the EU Data Protection Directive 1995. GDPR aims to protect the data and individuals whose data is collected by ensuring that the companies who are collecting and storing this data are doing so in a responsible manner. It also defines the reasons for which data can be collected from individuals. The regulation says the collected data should be "limited to what is necessary in relation to the purposes for which they are processed."

Under GDPR, a person's personal information can only be processed if it meets one of the following criteria:

- The company has expressed consent to the data subject.
- Processing is necessary to perform a contract with the data subject or to take steps to enter a contract.
- Processing is necessary for compliance with a legal obligation.
- Processing is necessary to protect a data subject's or another person's vital interests.
- Processing is necessary for the performance of a task carried out in the public interest.
- Processing is necessary for legitimate interests pursued by the controller or a third party, except where the interests, rights, or freedoms of the data subject override them.

Under GDPR, a person's name, biometric data, location, identification numbers, healthcare information, political opinions and beliefs, union memberships, or any other information that is a part of the physical, physiological, genetic, mental, economic, cultural or social identity of that person can be safeguarded.

## 7 Principles of GDPR

Rules of compliance of the GDPR are based on seven basic principles. These are:

1. Lawfulness, fairness, and transparency. A person collecting data must be clearly informed about how their data will be used.
2. Purpose limitation. Data can be collected only for specific

purposes.
3. Data minimization. The data collected is limited to what is necessary for that specific processing.
4. Organizations collecting data must ensure its accuracy and update it as necessary. Data must be deleted or changed when the person makes such a request.
5. Storage limitation. Collected data won't be retained longer than needed.
6. Integrity and confidentiality. Appropriate protection measures must be applied to personal data to ensure it's secure and protected against theft or unauthorized use.
7. Entities collecting personal data are responsible for ensuring compliance with the GDPR.

These seven principles are based on each individual's specific rights under GDPR.

- Right to be forgotten. All individuals can ask for their PII to be erased from an organization's database.
- Right of access. Individuals can always access and review the data they have provided to an organization.
- Right to object. An individual can always refuse permission to provide any personal data.
- Right to rectification. Individuals can ask for inaccurate personal information to be corrected.
- Right of portability. An individual may at all times view and transfer their personal information.

**Who Does It Apply To?**

All organizations collecting, storing, processing, or sharing any personal information of an EU member citizen are required to comply with GDPR. The organization may or may not reside within the EU but should be in compliance if they are collecting data from the citizens of a member nation.

In case of a breach, the organization is required to notify the supervisory authority within 72 hours of the breach. If this notification isn't made within 72 hours, the organization must provide a justifiable reason for the delay. The breach notification must include at least the nature of the breach, the number and types of data subjects' data that could be compromised, and the number of data records that could be involved. All breach victims must also be informed individually about the potential loss or data leak, not as a general announcement.

**Best Practices**

Some of the best practices to follow to ensure GDPR compliance are:

- Proper disclosure before collecting any information.
- Collecting only that which is required, since whether an organization uses some data or not, they will be responsible for all the collected data.
- All data, while stored and transmitted, must be encrypted to ensure confidentiality.
- Ensure that there are at least two backups of the data at two separate off-site locations, which are kept up-to-date.
- Provide individuals with the option to modify and erase the personal data they have provided.

# Japan

## Act on the Protection of Personal Information (APPI)

### What is APPI?

APPI, or the Act on the Protection of Personal Information, stands as a beacon of data protection in Japan, marking the nation's commitment to safeguarding personal information. This pioneering legislation was not only one of the first privacy laws to be established in Asia but also holds the distinction of being the first law to receive an adequacy decision from the EU post the inception of the GDPR.

Administered and upheld by the Personal Information Protection Committee (PPC), the APPI sets itself apart with a dedicated stipulation mandating reviews and updates every three years. This ensures its provisions remain relevant and robust in the ever-evolving data protection landscape.

The law casts a wide net, applying to all business operators—both within and outside of Japan—that handle personal data from individuals in Japan. However, government organizations and other administrative entities under distinct regulations enjoy exemption from the APPI.

The APPI categorizes personal data into two distinct types: "personal information" and "special care-required personal information." The former encompasses typical PII, such as names, addresses, dates of birth, email addresses, biometric data, and other unique identifiers like driver's license or passport numbers.

On the other hand, "special care-required" personal information covers data that has potential discriminatory implications. This includes, but is not limited to, medical histories, marital status, race, religious beliefs, and criminal records.

With its rigorous guidelines and stipulations, the APPI stands as a testament to Japan's dedication to safeguarding individual privacy rights, striking a balance between the increasing utility of personal information in advanced societies and the rights and interests of individuals.

**Rights and Responsibilities**

**Users' Rights:**
The Act on the Protection of Personal Information (APPI) empowers individuals with several rights regarding their data:

- **Disclosure Request:** Users can inquire how their data is stored, processed, and shared.
- **Complaint Mechanism:** They have a right to clear information on where to submit complaints related to data usage and handling.
- **Data Erasure or Limited Use:** Individuals can request either deleting their data or limiting its usage to specific operations.
- **Legal Recourse:** If business operators don't provide the requested information within two weeks, users can initiate legal action against them.
- **Data Retention Period:** The aforementioned rights are applicable irrespective of the data storage duration, whether short-term or long-term.

**Business Operators' Responsibilities:**
To comply with APPI, business operators are expected to:

- Privacy Policy: Establish a privacy policy clearly articulating the reasons for data collection.
- Data Security: Implement robust privacy and security

measures to safeguard the collected personal data.
- User Request Procedure: Set up and maintain procedures to handle user requests related to data disclosure and handling.
- Data Breach Notification: Post the 2020 amendment, in the event of a data breach, businesses are obligated to inform both the PPC and the affected users promptly.

**Data Transfers**

Before the 2020 amendments, APPI did not mandate businesses to notify users when sharing their data with third-party vendors unless the user had actively chosen to opt out after being informed. This oversight allowed for potentially unauthorized data sharing with other entities.

However, the 2020 amendment addressed and rectified this gap. Businesses must obtain clear and explicit user consent before transferring their data to third-party organizations. Exceptions exist for matters of public interest, such as legal proceedings or national security, where prior consent is deemed unnecessary.

For international data transfers, APPI stipulates that businesses should ensure that recipient countries or companies adhere to data protection standards that are on par with those upheld in Japan.

**Penalties Under the 2020 APPI Amendments:**

The amendments made to APPI in 2020 introduced stringent penalties for non-compliance:

Organizations: Businesses or entities found violating the provisions of APPI can now be levied with significant fines. The ceiling for these financial penalties has been set at ¥100 million, which translates to approximately USD 815,000.

Individuals: On a personal level, individuals involved in breaches of the APPI can face severe repercussions. They might be subjected to incarceration for durations extending up to a year. Alternatively, they can be slapped with monetary penalties, going as high as ¥1 million - approximately USD 8,150.

False Reporting: The amendments also emphasize the reporting process's integrity. Individuals or entities found guilty of submitting fabricated or misleading reports to the Personal Information Protection Committee (PPC) can incur fines up to ¥500,000, equivalent to around USD 4,000.

These revamped penalties underscore the seriousness with which Japan regards data protection, ensuring that businesses and individuals think twice before engaging in any malpractices related to personal data.

# China

## *Cyber Security Law*

The Cybersecurity Law, enacted in 2017 by the People's Republic of China, provides comprehensive measures to protect data, ensure data localization, and fortify national cybersecurity. As Wagner (2017) highlights, this law mandates certain network operators to store specific data domestically and permits Chinese authorities to conduct ad-hoc reviews of a company's network operations. While the exact stipulations of the law are often perceived as somewhat ambiguous, several key provisions warrant attention:

**Article 28:** This law section stipulates that "network operators" — a term broadly interpreted to encompass social media platforms, application developers, and other tech entities — must cooperate with public security agencies such as the Ministry of Public Security. They are obligated to provide requested information when called upon.

**Article 35:** This article primarily focuses on acquiring foreign software or hardware by government bodies or "critical information infrastructure operators." It mandates that any such purchased hardware or software be vetted by Chinese agencies, including entities like China's State Cryptography Administration.

**Article 37:** Central to the theme of data localization, this provision dictates that foreign tech companies functioning in the Chinese landscape must house data related to Chinese users within servers located on the Chinese mainland.

## Information Security Technology – Personal Information Security Specification

**What is the Specification?**

This data protection specification came into effect in 2018. Although not a mandatory regulation, it represents a significant advancement in the context of China's Cyber Security Law. Given the increasing global focus on privacy considerations, this specification merits individual discussion. Analogous to APPI, it categorizes personal information into two types:

**Sensitive Personal Information:** This category encompasses data whose disclosure could jeopardize a person's safety or lead to prejudice or discrimination. This type of data includes ID card numbers, biological identifiers, bank account details, religious beliefs, and sexual orientation, among others.

**General Personal Information:** This type typically covers data such as names, dates of birth, and the like.

**Data Collection Requirements:** The specification outlines requirements to ensure the justified collection and usage of individual data:

- **Minimization Principle:** This principle emphasizes that only information directly relevant to the business's objective should be collected and stored. Superfluous data collection should be strictly avoided.
- **Prior Consent:** Individuals must be informed

before collecting data, and their explicit consent should be secured.

**Exceptions to Mandatory Consent:** Certain circumstances may bypass the general consent rule. As delineated by Norton Rose Fulbright in January 2018, these exceptions come into play when:

- Collecting personal information pertains directly to national security, public interest, or judicial processes.
- Collecting personal information is essential to protect specific individuals' personal interests, property rights, or other crucial legal interests, especially when obtaining consent is impracticable.
- The data stems from publicly disclosed information by the individual or legitimate public news sources.
- Personal data collection serves the intent of forming and executing a contract per an individual's request.
- Collecting personal data is vital for maintaining a product or service, such as software bug resolution.
- Personal data collection serves the purpose of legitimate news reporting.
- Personal data collection aids academic research, provided the data is anonymized before publication.
- Any other scenarios defined by existing laws and regulations.

# Singapore

## *Cybersecurity Act*

The Cybersecurity Act stands as Singapore's primary legislation for cybersecurity matters. It is designed to establish a robust legislative framework for protecting Critical Information Infrastructure (CII) and to empower the Cybersecurity Agency of Singapore (CSA) with the authority to address cybersecurity incidents within Singapore.

A computer or system qualifies as a CII if:

- It provides essential services, the disruption of which could significantly impede the normal operation of these services.
- It exists either entirely or partially within Singapore.

The "Cybersecurity Code of Practice for Critical Information Infrastructure" (often referred to as the Cybersecurity Code) has been instituted to supplement this act. This code specifies the standard practices that CII owners are expected to adhere to. As stipulated by the Cybersecurity Code:

- CII owners are mandated to establish, implement, and continually uphold a cybersecurity risk management framework.
- They must also have a cybersecurity incident response plan in place, coupled with a crisis communication strategy.
- Moreover, developing a Business Continuity Plan (BCP) and a Disaster Recovery Plan (DRP) is essential for CII owners.

Singapore's Cybersecurity Act serves as the nation's primary cybersecurity legislation. The core purpose of this law is to establish a robust legislative framework for safeguarding Critical Information Infrastructure (CII) and bestowing upon the Cybersecurity Agency of Singapore (CSA) the mandate to manage cybersecurity incidents within the country. A system is designated as CII if:

It's a computer or information system that delivers essential services, where any disruption could critically affect the regular operation of these services.

This system is located either entirely or partially within Singapore.

The "Cybersecurity Code of Practice for Critical Information Infrastructure" (often called the Cybersecurity Code) was rolled out in tandem with this act. This code delineates the benchmark practices CII owners should adhere to. According to the Cybersecurity Code:

- CII owners must establish, implement, and persistently uphold a cybersecurity risk management framework.
- They must also maintain a cybersecurity incident response plan and a crisis communication strategy.
- Furthermore, CII owners must formulate a Business Continuity Plan (BCP) and a Disaster Recovery Plan (DRP).

## *Personal Data Protection Act (PDPA)*

The PDPA addresses the protection and privacy of personal data, not limited to online environments. It often complements other industry-specific laws by enhancing them. Under the PDPA, organizations are bound by specific obligations related to data collection and storage, and it also emphasizes an individual's rights over their data.

## CYBER LAW & FISMA COMPLIANCE

Obligations for Data Collection:

- Notification Obligation: Organizations must inform individuals about their data's intended collection and use.
- Consent Obligation: Organizations must obtain clear consent from individuals before collecting their data.
- Purpose Limitation Obligation: Organizations can only collect personal data that is necessary and relevant for a legitimate purpose.

Obligations for Data Storage and Maintenance:

- Accuracy Obligation: Organizations must ensure the accuracy of their personal data.
- Protection Obligation: Organizations must implement security measures to protect personal data from unauthorized access or leaks.
- Retention Limitation Obligation: Personal data should be deleted or anonymized once it's no longer needed for the purpose for which it was collected.
- Transfer Limitation Obligation: Personal data can only be transferred to a country or territory if it offers a comparable standard of data protection as the PDPA.

Individual's Rights Over Personal Data:

- Access and Correction: Individuals have the right to access and correct their data held by organizations.
- Breach Notification: In the event of a data breach, organizations must notify affected individuals about the breach and its potential impact.

- Data Portability Obligation: Upon request, organizations must transfer an individual's data to another organization of the individual's choosing, subject to certain conditions.

# India

## *Information Technology (IT) Act*

The IT Act is the foundational legislation addressing most privacy and security regulations for entities operating within India. This Act draws inspiration from the United Nations Model Law on Electronic Commerce 1996 (UNCITRAL Model). According to the IT Act, if the source of an offense, such as the computer or device utilized, is situated in India, then the perpetrator can be prosecuted under the provisions of this Act.

Objectives of the IT Act:

- To safeguard transactions conducted electronically.
- To offer legal validity to electronic communications and exchanges.
- To authenticate digital signatures used for legal purposes.
- To monitor and regulate the activities of digital intermediaries, ensuring they operate within legal bounds.
- To ensure the privacy of citizens' data.
- To govern and secure sensitive data on social media platforms and other electronic intermediaries.
- To officially recognize books of accounts maintained electronically per the standards set by the Reserve Bank of India Act, 1934.

Penalties under the IT Act:

# CYBER LAW & FISMA COMPLIANCE

An offender who, without the rightful owner's permission, causes damage to a computer or system is liable to compensate for the harm inflicted. Additionally, penalties can be imposed on individuals who:

- Unlawfully download, copy, or access data from a system.
- Introduce malicious software or viruses to a computer system.
- Cause disruptions in the functioning of the system.
- Deny system access to the rightful owner or authorized personnel.
- Tamper with, alter, or manipulate the system.
- Illegally delete, modify, or alter data stored in the system.
- Steal or unlawfully retrieve information from the system.

It's worth noting that while the discussed regulations provide a general framework, several other data privacy and security laws are operational in different nations, each with its unique stipulations. The laws mentioned here are among the most widely applicable and enforced. However, they possess intricacies not covered in this brief overview. To ensure complete compliance with any given law, it's crucial to undertake a comprehensive review of its provisions and conduct periodic assessments.

# Chapter 5: Industry-Specific Cybersecurity Laws and Regulations

In this chapter, we delve into industry-specific cyber laws and regulations. Each industry, with its unique set of challenges and vulnerabilities, has tailored cyber laws and regulations to mitigate risks and enhance security postures. The harmonization and enforcement of these laws across various sectors are paramount to fostering a safe, secure, and resilient cyberspace. In this chapter, we will explore the specific laws, their implementations, compliance challenges, and the ramifications for non-compliance, offering readers insights into the multifaceted world of industry-specific cyber regulations.

- **Health Care:** The health care industry has acts and laws to guard sensitive patient health records and ensure the privacy of medical data.
- **Retail:** Retail stores have protections for consumer details and transaction records to maintain the integrity of online commerce.
- **Financial:** Banks and financial institutions have laws that ensure the security of financial transactions, user banking details, and other proprietary financial information.
- **Government & Defense:** Federal and state governments are subject to laws that safeguard national data and citizen records and ensure the resilience of critical infrastructure.
- **Manufacturing:** For manufacturers, some regulations protect intellectual properties, ensure safe and secure automated systems, and guard trade secrets.
- **IT Services:** Information technology companies must adhere to laws and regulations safeguarding digital

infrastructure. These regulations protect data during the transit and storage of client data and ensure robustness against cyber threats.
- **Hospitality**: The hospitality industry consists of other sectors like tourism, theme parks, bars, hotels, and restaurants (just to name a few). Organizations in the hospitality industry need to protect the information of guests. They must also protect reservation systems and payment details while ensuring privacy and security in an increasingly digital hospitality sector.
- **Pharmaceuticals (Pharma)**: The pharma sector has special protections that overlap with other industries, such as health care. This sector has laws designed to protect drug research data and patient trial information and maintain the confidentiality of proprietary formulas.

There are countless sectors, industries, and niches shaped by cybersecurity law. We will spotlight a few to offer an understanding of how these regulations span various industries. This chapter will cover health care, retail, and finance. Government and Defense will be covered in the next chapter.

The necessity for such tailored laws arises from the unique nature of the data each industry manages. Beyond just personal identifiable information (PII), these sectors deal with data—ranging from health records to proprietary drug formulations—that could have significant implications if mishandled or breached. In the following sections, we'll provide an overview of some of the most influential cybersecurity laws in the U.S. While our discussion aims to be informative, it's essential to note that this is not an exhaustive catalog. Specific laws might vary in relevance depending on the industry under consideration and their location.

# HealthCare

Healthcare has emerged as one of the most important industries regarding data privacy and security. A patient's health data is important and can differentiate between life and death. For this, there need to be special requirements on how this data is collected and handled at all times.

## *Health Insurance Portability and Accountability Act (HIPAA)*

**What is HIPAA?**

HIPAA stands for the Health Insurance Portability and Accountability Act. It is a federal privacy and security regulation that applies to the healthcare industry in general. All healthcare corporations and organizations handling healthcare information are required to be compliant with HIPAA to be able to operate in the US. It has been designed to protect a patient's sensitive information and prevent its disclosure without their knowledge and consent. With the rising health insurance costs, it was developed with the idea that a patient may be able to carry forward their health insurance even after losing their jobs. To protect them from discrimination because of pre-existing health conditions and to guarantee coverage renewability with a new employer. To provide all this, the law was divided into two parts: the privacy rule and the security rule.

**The Privacy Rule**

The privacy rule primarily deals with maintaining the privacy of a patient's protected health information (PHI). The rule invokes duality because, for effective treatment, the PHI needs to be shared and transferred to the relevant healthcare providers. Still, at the same time, the patients have the right for their medical and PII to remain confidential.

For this, the Minimum Necessary Standard is applied, according to which the healthcare providers can access the information they need to do their job but nothing beyond that. Any other disclosures of a patient's information cannot happen without their consent except when it is required by law, to another covered entity, or if the disclosure is in the patient's or public's interest.

Another mandate is that the patient can always access and review their own data and request modifications and restrictions over their data.

**The Security Rule**

The security rule applies to healthcare corporations in that they must maintain the necessary safeguards over PHI to maintain the privacy and security of the data. This should include administrative, physical, and technical measures. According to Josh Fruhlinger (CSO Online, Jan 2021), the overall goals are:

- Ensure the confidentiality, integrity, and availability of all PHI handled or transmitted.
- Protect against reasonably anticipated threats to the security or integrity of the information.
- Protect against reasonably anticipated but impermissible uses or disclosures.
- Ensure workplace compliance.

That said, the rule does not mandate how these measures should be taken, and corporations can determine how best to implement these practices based on their unique needs.

## Covered Entities

According to the Centres for Disease Control and Prevention, The following entities are covered under HIPAA:

- Healthcare providers: Every healthcare provider, regardless of the practice size, electronically transmits health information in connection with certain transactions.
- Health plans: All health plans, including health, dental, vision, and prescription drug insurers; Health maintenance organizations (HMOs), Medicare, Medicaid, Medicare+Choice, and Medicare supplement insurers; long-term care insurers, employer-sponsored group health plans, government- and church-sponsored health plans.
- Healthcare clearinghouses: Service providers receive and process non-standard information to standard values and formats.
- Business associates: These people provide other services to covered entities that involve using PHI, like claims processing, billing, etc.

## Uses and Disclosures

The law permits the use or disclosure of PHI without a patient's authorization only under the following situations:

- Disclosure to the individual
- For treatment, operations, and payments
- Incident to an otherwise permitted use or disclosure
- Limited dataset for research, public health, or healthcare operations
- Public interest and benefit activities

## Health Information Trust (HITRUST) Common Security Framework (CSF)

Even though it's not a law, we will quickly mention HITRUST since it is a framework often used to help healthcare organizations comply with cyber law. The Health Information Trust (HITRUST) Alliance originally created the HITRUST Common Security Framework to encompass HIPAA and other healthcare laws. The HITRUST Alliance wanted a framework that, when implemented, would cover these laws, and a company then did not have to do a lot of extra work to maintain compliance with all the laws. Since then, It has expanded to include laws like PCI-DSS, GDPR, and others to create a unified framework. Under HITRUST, there are a set of policies and procedures to improve the cyber security strategies of an organization to bring them in compliance with the laws. Because it unifies so many laws, HITRUST would suggest different policies and procedures to different organizations based on the laws they must comply with.

**What is the certification?**

The HITRUST CSF certification is not government-mandated. In the case of external audits, showing a HITRUST certification does not directly imply compliance with a certain law; proof of all the different policy compliance must be provided. However, because the framework consists of policies for all the different laws, having a HITRUST certification means that no extra effort is needed to pass audits and meet compliance requirements for a law. Because of this, it has become standard industry practice to have this certification. It can be especially useful for service providers and third-party organizations who don't directly fall under a specific law but process some data or provide a service requiring compliance. A HITRUST certification can assure other organizations that all required practices are being followed. For this reason, many contracts now include a HITRUST certification requirement.

**HITRUST Requirements**

The specific means and ways for following a control defined within the objectives are called requirements. Based on an organization's size and business functions, these requirements and implementations can look very different from one organization to the other. For this, the requirement levels are defined. They are tailored based on different organizations' type, size, and capacities.

Josh Fruhlinger (CSO Online, May 2021) describes that the process of becoming HITRUST certified begins with a detailed institutional self-assessment. This questionnaire asks about your organization's size, risk exposure, and other factors. The answers to this questionnaire will determine which controls, requirements, and levels you'll need to implement.

# Retail

Companies like Walmart, Target, and TJMax rely heavily on consumers to buy retail products. They may have other services that dabble in health care or other sectors. Still, most of their business and infrastructure are dedicated to buying or creating bulk manufactured products and selling them at a marked-up retail price. These organizations are in the retail sector. Their supply chain, logistics, and technical infrastructure give them unique cybersecurity challenges that require specific solutions and laws.

The main way that these institutions collect money is point of sale (POS) devices. The old name for these systems is "cash registers." These POS systems have evolved to take digital transactions. Most transactions in the developed world are done with credit, debit, or phone transactions, which can be an easy target for criminal hackers. The response to the increase in digital transactions was laws to protect them.

## *Payment Card Industry Data Security Standard (PCI-DSS)*

### What is PCI-DSS?

This law is primarily designed to protect the payment card industry from fraud and improve data security within the industry. Any organization that accepts, stores, processes, or transfers payment card data, like debit or credit cards, must comply with PCI-DSS. It's not mandated by federal law but by the Payment Card Industry Security Standards Council, which comprises major credit card companies and has been included in many state laws.

### Who Needs to Comply?

PCI-DSS primarily applies to:

- Merchants. Even if all the PCI-DSS activities are outsourced, as a seller online, they are responsible for all contracted parties being compliant.
- Service providers. If they receive, store, process, or transmit cardholder information or can affect the security of cardholder data in any way, they are required to comply.

### The Twelve Requirements

There are twelve requirements that every compliant organization must meet:

1. Installing and maintaining a firewall. Since firewalls provide network monitoring and protection, they are useful to protect data during transmission.
2. Updating the vendor-supplied defaults for system passwords and security parameters. Defaults can be weak, exposed, or otherwise redundantly used.
3. Protecting stored data. Protecting cardholder data at rest by encrypting it, restricting access, using secure storage facilities, and destroying data timely.
4. Encrypting data during transmission. Especially when transferring over open or public networks, data should be encrypted.
5. Updating security software. Keep all anti-virus and other security software up to date and apply all security patches on time.
6. Developing and maintaining secure systems. Organizations can develop inherently secure systems and software by introducing security into their SDLC.
7. Restricting access. Access to cardholder data should be restricted to the employees on a need-to-know basis.
8. Uniquely identifying each person with access. Assigning them a unique ID so that their activities can be appropriately monitored.
9. Restricting physical access to data. All the devices storing or processing cardholder data should have restricted access.

1. Tracking and monitoring all network activities. To ensure sensitive cardholder information is not being accessed without authorization or requirement.
2. Putting a security policy in place for all employees and contractors.
3. Regularly Testing Security Systems and Processes:

Implement a robust testing schedule to regularly check security systems, including firewalls, antivirus, and encryption protocols, to ensure they are functioning optimally.

**Penalties**

The penalties for non-compliance can be monetary and non-monetary. Non-monetary losses can include loss of customer confidence, loss of business and jobs, diminishing sales, termination of the ability to accept payment cards, etc. Whereas monetary losses include legal costs, settlements, fines, penalties, cost of reissuing payment cards, higher subsequent cost of compliance, etc.

# Financial Sector

Because of the complexity of the stock market and trading, companies are more likely to skirt ethical practices. There are more chances for an individual's data to be lost, exposed, or misused when dealing with publicly traded companies. For this, the Sarbanes-Oxley Act was created.

## *Sarbanes-Oxley (SOX) Act*

**What is SOX?**

The SOX Act, drafted by congressmen Paul Sarbanes and Michael Oxley, was passed by the US Congress to protect individual investors from fraudulent and unethical practices by corporations. Tunggal (2022) states, "The legislation set new and expanded requirements for all U.S. public company boards, management, and public accounting firms to increase transparency in financial reporting and formalizing systems for internal controls."

This means that a public company must individually certify the accuracy of a financial statement. The legislation also increased the independence of the external reviewers of financial reporting and increased the responsibilities of the board of directors with respect to the correctness of reporting. There are mandates to limit access to this data as well, which, as a side benefit, also increases the security and privacy of the sensitive data.

**Five Pillars of Data Security**

SOX data security frameworks have five fundamentals to follow:

1. Ensuring the security of financial data.
2. Preventing unauthorized access and tampering with data.
3. Tracking breach attempts and documenting and implementing remediation measures.

1. Monitoring data access and other controls and having logs available for auditors.
2. Demonstrating compliance on an ongoing basis.

**Who Should Comply?**

The following types of organizations must comply with SOX:

- All publicly traded companies, wholly-owned subsidiaries, foreign companies that are publicly traded and do business in the United States, and even accounting firms that audit public companies.
- Private companies planning their Initial Public Offering (IPO) must comply with SOX before going public.

Private companies, charities, and non-profits generally do not need to comply, but they can have penalties imposed for knowingly destroying or falsifying financial information.

There are some more stipulations for the organizations which are required to comply. Firms that audit a company's books cannot be involved in any other business function for the said company, including business valuations, designing and implementing information systems, etc. Whistleblower protection is available where a company cannot retaliate against someone potentially reporting a federal offense. Payroll system controls must be established, and the company's workforce, salaries, benefits, incentives, paid time off, and training costs must be accounted for.

**Requirements for SOX**

To comply with SOX regulations, organizations must conduct yearly audits that account for the integrity of all data processes and financial statements and ensure adequate data security. Some of the most important requirements are discussed below:

- Section 302. Section 302 states that the Chief Executive Officer (CEO) and Chief Financial Officer (CFO) are responsible for the accuracy, documentation, and submission of all financial reports and the internal control structure to the SEC.
- Section 404. It requires that all annual financial reports include an Internal Control Report where the management takes responsibility for internal controls and an assessment of said controls to ensure they are adequate.
- Section 409. Accordingly, any material changes in the financial conditions or operations must be reported in real-time.

- Section 802. This imposes penalties of up to 20 years imprisonment for falsifying financial statements or tampering with legal investigations.
- Section 806. It protects against retaliation by whistleblowers against a company.

**Penalties**

Penalties for non-compliance with SOX include but are not limited to fines, removal and delisting from public stock exchanges, and invalidation of D&O insurance policies.

# Chapter 6: Cybersecurity Laws in Government and Defense

Similar to healthcare and payment card industries, the federal government has rules that pertain to it. Certain government organizations have to follow special regulations because of the kind of data they receive and work with. Any contractor, service provider, or third-party organization working with these government bodies must also adhere to the same or similar standards to maintain data security and privacy of citizens' data. The National Aeronautics and Space Administration (NASA) and the Department of Defense (DoD) are two such entities that require special data handling procedures and are discussed in this chapter.

## NASA Cyber Security Policies

NASA has its cybersecurity policy and procedures as defined by the office of the Chief Information Security Officer. The main policy is called the NASA Policy Directive (NPD) 2810.

### *What is NPD 2810?*

The NPD 2810 is a policy directive defining the policies protecting classified and unclassified information within NASA. Since the threat of cyber attacks on NASA systems and networks is higher, they must take additional protection measures.

According to the NPD 2810.1F - Main (2022), the following policies apply:

- Secure all NASA information and information systems, both classified and unclassified, in a manner commensurate with their national security classification level, sensitivity, value, and criticality.

- Fully implement the guidance in the NIST SP 800 series on computer security policies, procedures, and guidelines, and the NIST Federal Information Processing Standards (FIPS) as directed in Office of Management and Budget Circular A-130, "Managing Information as a Strategic Resource" and the Federal Information Security Modernization Act (FISMA) of 2014.
- Incorporate information security throughout the entire system life cycle to protect NASA information and information systems.
- Manage the cybersecurity of all classified and unclassified information systems acquired, developed, or used to support NASA missions, programs, projects, and institutional partnerships through the complete system life cycle.
- Establish and manage sound risk management and cybersecurity processes.
- Conduct continuous monitoring and reviews of NASA information systems to verify compliance with applicable Federal laws and NASA policies.
- Investigate information security incidents and develop after-action reports following significant incidents to address issues and improve future responses.
- Ensure information security policy requirements, audits, and forensic investigations are implemented and coordinated across Centers and contracts.
- Implement applicable cybersecurity policy best practices and guidance.
- Ensure that software developed to support NASA missions, programs, and projects and used on NASA information systems is secure.
- Ensure all information systems, classified and unclassified,

operating within the NASA environment operate under valid authorization from an Authorizing Official per the Assessment and Authorization process.

## *Applicability*

The NASA cybersecurity policy applies to:

- NASA Headquarters and NASA Centers, including Component Facilities and Technical and Service Support Centers.
- The Jet Propulsion Laboratory (JPL), a Federally Funded Research and Development Center, other contractors, grant recipients, or parties to agreements only to the extent specified or referenced in the contracts, grants, or agreements.
- All NASA users of information systems (e.g., civil servants and contractors) when supporting Agency projects, programs, and missions.

## *Responsibilities*

Primarily, the responsibility is shared between the Office of the Chief Information Officer (OCIO), responsible for protecting unclassified information, and the Office of Protective Services (OPS), responsible for protecting classified information. However, the NPD 2810 further expands on the other key stakeholder responsibilities with respect to the cybersecurity policy.

**The NASA Administrator**

An example of NASA roles and responsibilities is the NASA administrator. According to the NPD 2810, they do the following:

- Provides information security protections commensurate with the risk and magnitude of the harm resulting from unauthorized access, use, disclosure, disruption, modification, or destruction of information collected or maintained by or on behalf of NASA or within information systems used or operated by NASA, by a NASA contractor, or another organization on behalf of NASA.
- Ensures Agency information systems comply with FISMA and other Federal laws, related policies, procedures, standards, and guidelines on unclassified information security and national security systems (i.e., classified systems).
- Ensures that information security management processes are integrated with NASA's strategic and operational planning processes.
- Ensures that senior NASA officials provide information security for the information and information systems that support the operations and assets under their control with the help of proper risk assessments to determine the level of security controls, provide the required resources, and implement and monitor the procedures.

NASA and other federal organizations use internal policies such as NPD 2810 to comply with laws and regulations. The policy is implemented through procedures and processes for all employees and contractors working with federally controlled data.

## DoD Security Requirements

The Department of Defense (DoD) has to follow several security rules and regulations regarding the kind of data and information they have available to them. Contractors, service providers, and third-party organizations working with DoD must follow the same regulations. Previous chapters have discussed the NIST 800 risk management framework security standards. In this chapter, we will introduce others mandated by federal laws.

## Defense Federal Acquisition Regulation Supplement (DFARS)

### What is DFARS?

Defense Federal Acquisition Regulation Supplement (DFARS) was implemented in 2015 after the Executive Order (EO) 2010 was deemed incomplete to protect Controlled Unclassified Information (CUI). The primary purpose behind DFARS was for the DoD and allied organizations to be able to protect the confidentiality of that information, which is sensitive and in the interest of the US but not strictly regulated by the federal government. The NIST 800-171 is a big part of DFARS and is discussed separately in the next section.

### Who must Comply?

Anyone contracted by the DoD with access to CUI must comply with DFARS. Larger or smaller defense contractors or potential contractors looking to get defense contracts must all comply with DFARS to be eligible to work with the DoD.

### Requirements

The minimum requirement for DFARS is that any CUI that resides in or moves through an organization's information system must be protected by adequate security measures.

Contractors and non-federal organizations must conduct a readiness assessment and provide objective proof that addresses all these requirements before becoming DFARS compliant. The categories of DFARS requirements are as follows:

- Access Control
- Awareness and Training
- Audit and Accountability
- Configuration Management
- Identification and Authentication
- Incident Response
- Maintenance
- Media Protection
- Personnel Security
- Physical Protection
- Risk Assessment
- Security Assessment
- System and Communications Protection
- System and Information Integrity

## *NIST SP 800-171*

### What is NIST 800-171?

NIST 800-171 is a set of cybersecurity standards that must be adhered to by organizations that process or store Controlled Unclassified Information (CUI) on behalf of the US government. Such organizations might include Department of Defense contractors, universities and research institutions that receive federal grants, and entities offering services to government agencies. To ensure compliance with NIST 800-171, organizations handling CUI must perform self-assessments to ascertain and maintain this compliance.

This framework is distinct from NIST 800-37, a risk management framework. While NIST 800-37 primarily focuses on federally owned systems that process federal data, usually within federal facilities, and can range from unclassified to classified data, NIST 800-171 specifically addresses supporting organizations collaborating with the Department of Defense. All NIST 800 standards are based on FISMA.

**Requirements**

There are about 110 requirements under the NIST 800-171, divided into 14 families.

1. Access Control. This family of requirements deals with access to networks, systems, and information. These also determine the flow of information within the system and who can and cannot access certain information.
2. Awareness and Training. This includes ensuring system administrators and users know security risks and related cybersecurity procedures and that employees are trained to perform security-related roles.
3. Audit and Accountability. This focuses on auditing and analyzing system and event logs, the best practices for analyzing the logs, and reporting on data.
4. Configuration Management. This includes ensuring the proper configuration of hardware, software, and devices across the organization's system and network. It also provides restrictions for unauthorized software downloads and installs.
5. Identification and Authentication. This family of requirements ensures that only authenticated users can access the organization's network or systems.

6. Incident Response. This family is responsible for ensuring proper plans and procedures are in place to deal with possible security incidents.
7. Maintenance. This family provides insight into best practices for systems and network maintenance procedures.
8. Media Protection. These requirements cover best practices for storing and destroying sensitive information and media in physical and digital formats.
9. Personnel Security. This deals with ensuring that the personnel accessing the secure information are screened for security and also manages the cleaning up of data and access after the termination of personnel or contracts.
10. Physical Protection. This includes physically protecting all the hardware, devices, and equipment an information system uses.
11. Risk Assessment. Under this family, organizations are required to conduct regular assessments of their systems and devices, analyze them for vulnerabilities, and maintain their security posture.
12. Security Assessment. This is specifically to ensure the procedures and plans used for security are working as expected and achieving the security objectives they are designed for.
13. System and Communications Protection. This family mainly focuses on protecting data in transit, ensuring secure network communications, and only allowing authorized transfers.
14. System and Information Integrity. This deals with the ongoing protection and maintenance of all the systems in an organization.

## Who Should Comply?

Although 800-171 applies to all organizations dealing with CUI. In particular, some of the common types of organizations that need to comply are:

- Defense contractors
- Organizations providing financial services
- Web and communication service providers
- Healthcare data processors
- Systems Integrators
- Colleges and universities that utilize federal data or information
- Research institutes and labs receiving federal grants and information

## Best Practices

Because the NIST 800-171 compliance relies on self-assessments, some of the standard best practices to follow for executing a self-assessment are:

- Form an assessment team with input from senior information security stakeholders.
- Set an assessment plan, including a time frame and objectives.
- Begin an internal communication campaign to spread awareness of the project.
- Create a contact list of personnel with relevant responsibilities, such as system administrators and information security specialists.
- Collect relevant documents, including existing security

policies, system records and manuals, previous audit results and logs, admin guidance, and system architecture documents.
- Assess individual requirements in the NIST 800-171 document and record a statement for each.
- Create an action plan outlining how any unmet requirements will be achieved.
- Include all evidence for compliance in a System Security Plan (SSP) document.

## *Cybersecurity Maturity Model Certification (CMMC)*

**What is CMMC?**

Cybersecurity Maturity Model Certification (CMMC) is an amalgamation of the above DFARS and NIST 800-171 regulations and additional rules to create a unified national standard for cybersecurity. It was created by the Office of the Under Secretary of Defense (OUSD) for Acquisition & Sustainment. It seeks to respond to cyber threats by standardizing how DoD contractors secure critical information. The biggest difference between NIST 800-171 and CMMC is that while NIST 800-171 allows organizations to self-assess their cybersecurity compliance, CMMC requires third-party assessments to ensure that contractors meet certain cybersecurity standards before they can be awarded contracts.

This shift to third-party assessment aims to provide higher assurance that contractors are adequately protecting sensitive data, and it introduces five levels of certification, each with a set of supporting practices and processes. While NIST 800-171 has requirements that organizations must meet, CMMC expands upon those requirements and adds a certification element to verify that the practices and processes are not just implemented but also effective and sustainable. CMMC also integrates additional cybersecurity best practices from other standards, references, and sources.

CMMC provides a more structured and verifiable approach to cybersecurity, aiming to ensure a baseline of security measures across all contractors in the defense industrial base to protect sensitive defense information from cyber threats.

**Who Must Comply?**

The CMMC maturity model applies to every company within the DoD supply chain, including those in the defense industrial base and those in procurement, construction, or development. This includes prime contractors who interact directly with the DoD and subcontractors who work with contractors to execute DoD contracts. The size of an organization or the amount of involvement with DoD does not matter for compliance. Any organization which wishes to do any work with DoD needs to comply.

**What is Protected?**

Along with CUI protection, which has been discussed so far, under the CMMC, there is protection for Federal Contract Information (FCI) as well. FCI includes any information the government creates or provides under contract to an organization to provide them with a service or product that is not disclosed to the public.

**Certification Levels**

There are five levels of CMMC certification that an organization can receive.

1. Level 1: Basic cyber hygiene. This includes error-free data, proper access controls, obfuscation/encryption for PII, and data quality assurance.
2. Level 2: Intermediate cyber hygiene. At this stage, a company must protect FCI and CUI in a repeatable way. Auditing, media protection, backup and recovery, maintenance, and system integrity are important at this level.
3. Level 3: Good cyber hygiene. Companies at this level typically deal with controlled but unclassified information. It requires a strong plan to deal with cybersecurity threats and the means to carry them out through awareness, training, and incident response.
4. Level 4: Proactive cyber hygiene. This includes all the plans and procedures for protection against threats as described for level 3 and added responsibility for regular assessments and revisions to policies and procedures.
5. Level 5: Advanced cyber hygiene. This level is required for companies dealing with highly desirable information. It includes everything up to level 4 and more sophisticated tools such as anomaly detection and the ability to respond flexibly to threats.

The NIST 800-171 and the CMMC go through changes to keep up with additional laws, regulations, and best security practices in the industry. CMMC is moving away from Model 1.0, and NIST 800-171 will be moving from Revision 2.

# Chapter 7: How to Implement Cybersecurity Law Compliance in Your Organization

While many more laws and regulations may apply to an industry or organization based on the niche they operate in, the above chapters cover the most generally applicable laws to provide readers with an idea of the different regulations they might want to consider when going through compliance. But given the complexity and variety of the different laws, how they should be implemented can be an even bigger challenge. This chapter discusses some practical steps to consider when implementing organizational compliance.

## What Laws To Comply With?

One of the primary concerns an organization must deal with is knowing which laws to comply with. What laws apply to a specific organization? There is no catch-all answer to this very important question; unfortunately, because of each organization's unique needs and processes, different laws may or may not apply.

The applicability of different laws can be narrowed down based on certain criteria. Some of the questions to be considered when understanding this are:

- What kind of data is being collected and used? Whether PII is being collected or not, how sensitive is the data being collected, if it's payment data or other types of sensitive data, or if the information is personal and could be cause for discrimination if exposed? These are a few things to consider when answering this question.
- Is the organization using a product or service? Whether the organization is providing a product or a service, while

this may seem irrelevant on a bigger scale, the organization's approach towards security and privacy and operational policies differ based on whether a product is being sold vs. a service.
- Is there a contract involved and what industry is involved? Suppose the organization is working with government contracts. As discussed in various laws, federal contracts require many extra steps to be taken with respect to privacy and security, as their data and information systems tend to be more sensitive and prone to cyber threats.
- What is the location? Location of the users where the product or service is being offered. As seen in previous chapters, when operating internationally, there are many extra privacy and security regulations that an organization needs to comply with depending on which country the product or service is being offered. Similarly, many states in the US have their own compliance requirements that must be followed to operate in that state. Where a company is based becomes an important consideration when covering compliance.
- What products or services are an organization using for its processes and operations? This can seem odd, but every organization has certain products and services for smooth functioning. These products and services come with their own security and privacy restrictions, which they must comply with and require for the best functioning of their products and services.
- Are there any special needs for the data or internal security and privacy considerations? How an organization protects its data and information systems is often important when considering compliance. For example, many companies have proprietary software and/or hardware that needs to be

covered by IP laws. Similarly, there can be other security and privacy concerns that may require certain compliance.

While this is not an exhaustive list, these questions can form starting points to consider when understanding which laws to comply with. Irrespective of compliance, determining a baseline of security and privacy requirements that an organization must follow and implement is always a good practice.

There is a paper trail that will lead the organization directly to which laws and regulations are applicable. White papers in the industry or sector will often reference the applicable laws. Academic papers and even vendor data sheets in the industry will cite relevant laws.

Frameworks like the NIST RMF and NIST Cybersecurity framework can provide a sound all-around approach. Apart from compliance, having and following a baseline can protect an organization from monetary losses, reputational damages, and many other side effects of data breaches.

# Using the NIST CSF to Ensure Compliance with Laws and Regulations

Navigating the intricate landscape of cybersecurity laws can be daunting. With an array of requirements and benchmarks set by different laws across the globe, the challenge for organizations is to find a universally recognized framework that simplifies and unifies their compliance efforts. The NIST Cybersecurity Framework (NIST CSF) is an efficient tool to meet this need.

Before diving into the merits of the NIST CSF, it's essential to distinguish it from the NIST RMF 800 series. The Risk Management Framework (RMF) 800 series is an exhaustive set of processes tailored mainly for large government systems. While universal in its application, it includes over 1,000 security controls and a very results-based process that can take months or even years to fully implement.

In contrast, the NIST CSF is nimble, adaptable, and designed for entities of all sizes across various industries.

## *Origin and Purpose of NIST CSF*

The NIST Cybersecurity Framework (NIST CSF) was inspired by Executive Order 13636, "Improving Critical Infrastructure Cybersecurity," issued by President Barack Obama on February 12, 2013. This Executive Order directed the NIST to work with stakeholders to develop a voluntary framework to reduce cybersecurity risks to critical infrastructure. The result of this collaboration was the NIST Cybersecurity Framework. Its primary objective is to offer guidance that can thwart or, at the very least, mitigate the impact of cyber-attacks.

**Functional Areas of NIST CSF**

The framework operates on a business function model, concentrating on five pivotal areas:

- Identify: Recognize and manage cybersecurity risks to systems, assets, data, and capabilities.
- Protect: Implement necessary safeguards to ensure the delivery of critical infrastructure services.
- Detect: Identify potential cybersecurity events promptly.
- Respond: Take action regarding a detected cybersecurity event.
- Recover: Restore any capabilities or services impaired due to a cybersecurity incident.

For each of these functions, there are specific controls to reinforce the organization's privacy and security posture.

## *Implementation Tiers of NIST CSF*

Understanding that organizations have varied capabilities and resources, the NIST CSF outlines Implementation Tiers that assist entities in gauging their cybersecurity readiness:

- Tier 1 (Partial): Organizational cybersecurity is not formalized. Responses to threats are reactive.
- Tier 2 (Risk-Informed): Management is aware of the risks, but there's no organization-wide approach to addressing them.
- Tier 3 (Repeatable): The organization has a structured risk management process and routinely reviews and updates its cybersecurity practices.
- Tier 4 (Adaptive): The organization adapts its cybersecurity practices based on lessons learned and predictive indicators. It's in a continuous improvement state.

## *Aligning with Laws and Regulations*

The adaptability and thoroughness of the NIST CSF make it an excellent tool for ensuring compliance with myriad cybersecurity laws. By aligning an organization's security posture with the NIST CSF, entities can be assured that they adhere to best practices, which often meet or exceed regulatory requirements. This alignment aids organizations in reducing compliance gaps, streamlining audit processes, and establishing a solid foundation for expanding their cybersecurity maturity.

While the landscape of cybersecurity laws is vast and ever-evolving, the NIST CSF offers a consistent, structured, and holistic approach to compliance. Adopting and implementing this framework will enhance an organization's security and instill confidence in stakeholders that the organization is resilient against cyber threats.

For more on the NIST CSF, check out the Convocourses series, which dives much deeper into the controls and implementation:

- NIST Cybersecurity Framework for Information Systems Security
- Cyber Security Program and Policy Using NIST CSF

https://www.amazon.com/dp/B0C9376Y8N

## Education on Laws and Compliance

Education and training are other important aspects when preparing for and implementing security and privacy laws for compliance. IT professionals with knowledge of the various laws can make a good compliance plan into a great one. There are often details and nuances within the implementation and processes of the various information systems that non-technical people can miss. But these little details can count when aiming to comply with cyber law. IT professionals trained for compliance are key to filling these gaps and meeting an organization's compliance goals.

Compliance teams should focus on employee training and education as part of ongoing efforts to remain compliant. Often, employee training is part of compliance with many cyber laws, reinforcing the importance of having employee awareness about the different data processing and handling standards. There are several ways to go about employee training for compliance.

- Organizations can design education programs based on data and information system handling patterns and processes.

- Organizations can enlist external training organizations and/or online learning platforms to educate employees and meet the training standards.
- Based on the degree of education an employee may need, organizations can have options for professional certifications available for employees. Some teams may need a more extensive understanding of compliance by more intensive data and system handling. Several organizations provide professional certifications for specific and generic cyber law education.

After identifying the laws an organization needs to comply with, education can be vital for the implementation of cyber laws correctly.

## Risk Assessments

Before implementing a compliance or risk management framework, having an organization-wide risk assessment can be incredibly helpful in determining what to protect, where to allocate resources, and what needs to be improved, updated, or developed to meet compliance requirements. The first step to risk assessment is to assemble a cross-departmental team to cover all aspects within an organization's scope. As a minimum, a risk assessment team should consist of:

- Senior management to provide oversight.
- The chief information security officer to review network architecture.
- A privacy officer to locate personally identifiable information.
- The compliance officer to identify compliance issues.
- Technical experts from the system team.

Once an optimum team has been assembled, we can follow a five-step approach toward risk assessment.

## Step 1: Catalog Information Assets

This includes all of the business's information assets. Systems, processes, as well as the data it processes. This includes all the network assets, software as a service (SaaS), platform as a service (PaaS), infrastructure, third-party vendors, and contractors.

To understand the kind of data that your organization may be handling, it can be good to ponder over these questions:

- What kinds of information are departments collecting?
- Where are they storing that information?
- Where do they send that information?
- From where are they collecting it?
- Which vendors does each department use?
- What access do those vendors have?

Which authentication methods, such as multi-factor authentication, do you use for information access?

- Where, physically, does your company store information?
- Which devices do workforce members use?
- Do remote workers access information? How so?
- Which networks transmit information?
- Which databases store information?
- Which servers collect, transfer, and store data?

## Step 2: Categorize the Risk

After listing down all an organization's different assets, the next step is to categorize the risk associated with each asset. This is important because every asset, every vendor, and every piece of data and information can be secure or insecure to varying degrees. For example, some systems may be multiple layers deep into an organization's environment and, therefore, will have a lesser risk of exposure than other systems. Some vendors may already have many security features built into their systems. Because of these differences, categorizing the risk can be a very valuable exercise. When trying to categorize, some of the questions to consider are:

- Which systems, networks, and software are critical to business operations?
- What sensitive information or systems must maintain availability, confidentiality, and integrity?
- What personal information do you store, transmit, or collect that needs to be anonymized in case of an encryption failure?
- Which devices are most at risk of data loss?
- What is the potential for data corruption?
- Which IT systems, networks, and software might cybercriminals target for a data breach?
- What reputation harm might arise from a security incident?
- What financial risks are posed by a potential data breach or data leak?
- What business operation risks would stem from a cybersecurity event?
- Do you have a business continuity plan allowing you to rapidly return to business operations after an IT disruption?

## *Step 3: Analyze the Risk*

The next step should be to analyze the risks associated with each asset and to create a priority framework for them. This primarily depends on two factors: the likelihood or probability of a cybercrime or data breach affecting the asset and the impact damage or loss of said asset can have on the business and different business functions. Based on these two things, we can analyze an asset's actual risk and decide on each asset.

To calculate the risk, an organization can use the formula:

- Risk = (Likelihood of Breach x Impact)/Cost

Here, cost means the monetary losses or expenses incurred to repair or replace the asset. This can help determine, for example, if a resource marked high priority poses a significant risk to an organization's security. This can help to understand which assets or business functions may require more vs. less investment from a security and privacy perspective.

## *Step 4: Establish Risk Tolerance*

The classification of risk above makes it easy to determine risk tolerance. For each asset, based on the risk, it can be determined if the risk is to be accepted, avoided, transferred, or mitigated.

If a risk is accepted, then no action needs to be taken for risk management as, according to the above analysis, it is established that incurring the loss/impact of the risk is the most favorable outcome for the asset.

If a risk is to be avoided, then the actions taken would be to prevent that behavior from happening. This can be through coding safeguards, physical barriers, placing logical layers before the risky asset, asset isolation, or several other ways depending on the asset under consideration.

If a risk is to be transferred, there are several ways to go about it. You can either transfer the processing or handling of an asset to a third-party vendor or to a different business unit within the same organization, one that is better equipped to deal with the risk.

Letting somebody with the right resources and expertise handle the risk is more effective than trying to mitigate it.

If a risk is to be mitigated, an organization needs to develop a protection plan and set up policies to mitigate the risk as and when it appears.

## Choosing a Framework

Choosing a framework becomes much simpler with a good understanding of the risk profile. When deciding which framework to use, some of the questions to be considered are:

- **What will be the scope of coverage?** This includes all the different areas within an information system or the different information systems covered within the same framework. Within each pillar, the details that will be covered are also important factors for consideration.
- **What is the existing security culture within the organization? An** organization lacking an existing security perspective among its employees can struggle if many sudden restrictions and regulations are introduced. For this, it is important to ensure that the framework chosen is adaptable for most employees, increasing the likelihood that the regulations will be maintained over time.
- **What, if any, risk management strategies already exist within the organization?** This can help to identify if the framework in consideration will align with the existing policies and plans within the organization.
- **What are the compliance requirements?** As discussed, not all regulations will apply to all organizations, and knowing which requirements apply and which don't will be a big factor in deciding which framework should be chosen. Consider the industry that the organization is associated

with. For example, a company that sells medical equipment is aligned with the health care industry and might consider the HITRUST framework.

## Setting and Updating Policies and Controls

Based on the risk tolerance established previously, the policies and controls can be decided for different assets. For example, if the risk is to be mitigated, identify who it will be transferred to and which vendor or business unit will be responsible for mitigating it. Or if a risk is to be mitigated, what actions will be taken in the event of a cyber attack on the asset or before an attack as a preventative measure?

Some examples of controls for risk mitigation are incident response plans and actions and insurance on the risk asset. Whereas preventative measures can include data encryption, security products like firewalls, Virtual Private Networks (VPN), etc.

Keeping these policies and controls up to date should be an ongoing feature when implementing risk management. As risks and their impact continue to evolve, revisiting and updating the controls for better management can often be the difference between a failed and a successful data breach attempt. Regular updates should be built into a good risk management plan to easily adjust policies and controls.

## Monitor, Respond, and Iterate

Because threats are evolving almost daily, threat actors always look for new ways to enter an organization. For preventing and mitigating an attack, logging and monitoring can be imperative. Therefore, monitoring and logging should be part of a risk management plan. It also helps to view historical data and identify patterns for future attacks; monitoring and logging can be extremely useful in cybersecurity risk management.

An incident response plan is just as important when planning for risk. It becomes a guidebook for all the steps needed in case of an active incident to prevent further damage than what has already occurred and has proven extremely effective in practice.

Iterating periodically over the risk management plan can identify the existing plan's validity and help identify any gaps, new attack vectors, or new assets that need protection. Just like regular updates of controls and control software can help to keep a strong security posture, periodic iterations can validate the strength of the existing plan.

They should be an important part of the implementation plan.

These are just some things that can be done to implement a process that complies with cybersecurity laws.

# Chapter 8: Privacy Laws and Their Impact on Cybersecurity

In discussing the different cyber laws, privacy, and security are often put in the same group and thought of as a collective entity. Organizations often make the mistake of clumping these two together when planning and implementing for compliance. More often than not, the focus is on security, and privacy takes a back seat, or it is assumed that meeting security requirements should be enough to fulfill the privacy requirements as well. Although with the prevalence of GDPR and CCPA, the understanding and awareness around privacy as a distinct aspect within cyber security has increased. There are still significant issues that can come up when privacy goals and security goals conflict with each other.

## Privacy Is Not The Same as Security

In theory, it is pretty obvious that privacy and security are not the same thing. But in practice, this distinction can often be blurred. As discussed at the beginning of the book, privacy deals with keeping people's information and information systems private, away from the public eye, or unavailable for general viewing on the internet. Security involves protecting data and information systems, ensuring that it is safe and the integrity of the data and information systems is maintained.

When discussing security laws, the focus is on rules to bring certain data breaches within the law's scope to investigate, identify, and penalize attackers. Organizations and individuals can benefit from cybersecurity laws as they give them a way to address their losses caused by breaches or even an organization's negligence.

When discussing privacy laws, the focus is on individual people and their personal information. The rules are designed to protect individuals from organizational bad practices in data handling and sometimes even intentional data sharing by organizations in an unethical manner.

The perspective behind both types of laws is different. This is quite frequently why security and privacy laws have conflicting interests. For example, security requires that an organization retain information. The information is kept because it can be helpful during investigations to identify the attack source, victims, and other relevant information. However, privacy requires that all personal information, which includes system information and IP addresses, be scrubbed to remove PII. Both requirements become counterintuitive to each other. Maintaining a balance between privacy and security requirements and compliance with both laws can be challenging and intricate.

# Common Challenges

Privacy and security are deeply interconnected and face some common challenges.

## *The Complexity of the Environment*

With the fast evolution of technology, the cyber environment is becoming increasingly complex. Options like Single-Sign-On and OAuth credentials, etc., are making data, accounts, and user information interconnected between different apps and organizations. Not only that, with targeted ads and tracking of online activities, the boundaries of who has and uses a person's information are becoming increasingly blurry. With more and more "always on" devices like smart home devices, mobile devices, etc., the online environment has become very complex and difficult to protect both from a privacy and a security perspective.

## Sophisticated Threats

Threats and cyber attacks are also becoming more sophisticated. With things like ransomware-as-a-service, there has been a "professionalization" of cybercrime. Rootkits and Advanced Persistent Threats (APTs) are some common examples of extremely sophisticated cyber attacks. As threats evolve, the challenges of privacy and security become more intricate.

## The Shift of Threat Landscape to Mobile Devices

There has been an increased use of mobile devices within the past decade, and the capabilities available to these devices have made them an easy target for exploitation. With smart cars, smart TVs, smart refrigerators, and other "internet of things," everything is connected. These devices may seem simplistic, but when exploited, they can be used for sophisticated attacks. The Denial of Service on the Dyn DNS server, which leveraged the Mirai botnet primarily comprised of internet-connected security cameras, is a prime example of the threat mobile devices can pose to an organization.

## "Big Data" Paradox

Big data is a large collection of data, often rich in information, useful for organizations to improve customer experiences. Because of this, collected data's size, storage, manipulation, and processing pose new challenges, especially from a security and privacy perspective. This data is as valuable to attackers as it is to organizations. Many PII in this data type create major privacy and security risks.

## Compliance Vs. Risk Management

With the increased push for compliance with various laws, companies might take a mechanical approach toward security and privacy. But being compliant will not guarantee a secure environment automatically.

Compliance includes so many governance where tasks are document and management heavy that the actual cyber risks are sometimes sidelined. When done properly, deliberate risk management can imply that compliance obligations are fulfilled. Therefore, how a company approaches compliance and risk management can affect the security and privacy within an organization.

## Impact of Privacy Laws on Organizations

Because of mandatory compliance requirements for privacy laws, organizations must maintain certain practices concerning their data and information systems. This has impacted organizations incorporating many otherwise ignored or de-prioritized practices into their system development life-cycle. Before privacy laws, many ethically sound practices were put in the backseat for practical reasons and for keeping up with the market demands. With the introduction of privacy compliance, this problem has been reduced, and the safety of everyone on the internet has increased. Some of the practices which have come up because of this are:

- Regular updates to data privacy policies. Because of consent and notifications compliance requirements, most organizations have had to revise and update their data privacy policies as and when they update how they collect and use data.
- Review of privacy standards. Regularly review and assess their privacy standards to ensure they meet the standards and identify gaps in their risk management.
- Implement best practices. Organizations implement many recommended practices based on legal guidelines to meet

the requirements and remain compliant.
- Regular employee training. Often, employee training and education are a part of compliance requirements. This ensures organizations are training their employees and that all employees know the required privacy and security practices they should implement individually. Therefore, creating a more secure environment.

## Security and Privacy Together

It may seem like an easy task to enforce security and privacy together. But as discussed repeatedly, privacy and security can often be at odds. Or, the nuances of implementation can differ, making it difficult to implement both optimally. There has been a lot of work put into solving the challenge of security without violating privacy standards, and a lot of common ground has been found in the teams dealing with scrubbing data, analysis on aggregated data instead of individual data, decoupling PII from information essential for enhancing security, and so forth. However, it remains an ongoing effort to ensure that the best possible implementations of privacy and security can be made in tandem while remaining compliant with cyber and privacy laws.

# Chapter 9: Cybersecurity Laws and System Certifications

As proof of compliance and to ensure all the mandatory regulations are in place in an organization, several laws and standards require that the organization have a formal written approval from the head of the organization or a certification and accreditation process allowing a system to operate. This is also known as "authorization" and is where the head of the organization accepts the risks in writing. Based on assessment data, they decide their risk tolerance policies, i.e., which risks they will take or reject. National, state and local governments, as well as some industry regulations mandate certification, accreditation, and authorization.

By accrediting an information system, an agency official accepts responsibility for the system's security and is fully accountable for any adverse impacts to the agency if a breach of security occurs. Thus, responsibility and accountability are core principles that characterize security accreditation. Agency officials must have the most complete, accurate, and trustworthy information possible on the security status of their information systems to make timely, credible, risk-based decisions on whether to authorize the operation of those systems.

## Certifications In the Law

Here are some laws, regulations and standards that mention certifications and accreditations for compliance:

### *FISMA*

The FISMA law establishes the need for certification and accreditation. While there is no explicit mention of "certification" and "accreditation" in any specific section of the Act, the certification and accreditation process, as interpreted and applied based on the Act, involves reviewing and approving an information system's security controls. The NIST 800 is a guide for the US federal accreditation process in accordance with FISMA.

## *NIST SP 800-37 Authorization Process*

The certification and accreditation process is defined in NIST SP 800-37. Once the system documentation and risk assessment have been completed, the system's controls must be reviewed and certified to function appropriately. Based on the results of the review, the information system is accredited. The process used to be called "certification and accreditation," but now, in the most current NIST 800-37 revisions, it is known as "Assessment and authorization."

## *Office of Management and Budget (OMB) Circular A-130*

Security accreditation is the official management decision given by a senior agency official to authorize the operation of an information system and to explicitly accept the risk to agency operations, agency assets, or individuals based on the implementation of an agreed-upon set of security controls. OMB Circular A-130, Appendix III requires this process; it provides quality control and challenges managers and technical staff at all levels to implement the most effective security controls possible in an information system, given mission requirements, technical constraints, operational constraints, and cost/schedule constraints.

# ISO 27001

ISO 27001 is an international standard offering a systematic and structured framework to establish, implement, operate, monitor, review, maintain, and improve an Information Security Management System (ISMS). The standard delineates guidelines for effectively managing information security within a company.

Contrary to the accreditation process under FISMA, ISO 27001 does entail a rigorous certification process. The organization aspiring for certification is required to conduct a formal risk assessment and then implement security controls appropriate for managing the identified risks. These controls can be selected from the Annex A of the standard or elsewhere, tailored to the organization's specific needs.

The certification process for ISO 27001 involves several stages. Initially, an internal review is performed to comprehend the existing ISMS, followed by a gap analysis to pinpoint areas that need enhancement. The organization then works on the development and implementation of the ISMS, ensuring it is in line with ISO 27001 requirements. Comprehensive documentation is prepared to evidence the establishment and efficient operation of the ISMS.

An internal audit is then conducted to evaluate the ISMS's effectiveness, and any identified non-conformities are addressed through corrective actions. The management reviews the ISMS to ensure it aligns with the organization's objectives and is effective. Necessary adjustments and improvements are made accordingly.

The certification audit is a two-stage process: The first stage involves a documentation review by the certification body, and the second stage is an on-site audit to evaluate the implementation and effectiveness of the ISMS in a real-world scenario. If the organization satisfies the requirements, the ISO 27001 certificate is issued, typically valid for three years and subject to periodic surveillance audits.

The maintenance and continual improvement phase ensures that the ISMS is regularly monitored and updated to remain effective. The organization undergoes periodic surveillance audits to validate ongoing compliance with ISO 27001. A re-certification audit is required after three years to renew the certification.

Though ISO 27001 doesn't employ the exact terminology as used in NIST 800, its comprehensive process of risk assessment, implementation of controls, regular review, and external audit aligns with the core objective of ensuring the organization's information security measures are effective and fitting.

The distinct factor lies in the application scope - while FISMA is mandated for U.S. federal agencies, ISO 27001 is a voluntary standard adopted globally by any organization, though it can be a contractual or regulatory requisite in certain sectors or geographies.

## Certifications for PCI DSS

The PCI DSS has a form of certification and accreditation, but it operates differently than FISMA. Instead of being authorized to operate a system after a review by a senior official (as in FISMA), companies must validate their compliance with the PCI DSS annually. This can involve different processes depending on the volume of transactions the company processes and the specific rules of the individual card brands.

### *Certification Process*

A general idea of the process is discussed below.

- **Self-Assessment Questionnaire (SAQ).** Most small to medium businesses will complete an SAQ, a PCI Security Standards Council checklist. The SAQ includes questions related to the security controls that the company has in place.

- **External Vulnerability Scanning.** Companies that handle larger volumes of transactions must have their systems

scanned quarterly by a PCI-approved scanning vendor. The purpose of these scans is to identify vulnerabilities that attackers could exploit.
- **On-Site Audit.** The largest processors of credit card transactions and those that have suffered a breach must also have an on-site audit conducted by a Qualified Security Assessor (QSA) or Internal Security Assessor (ISA).
- **Attestation of Compliance (AOC).** Once the company has completed the appropriate validation process, it must submit an AOC to its acquiring bank and the card brands with which they do business.

So, while the specifics are different, the PCI DSS has a similar assessment and validation process (or "certification and accreditation") to ensure that companies follow the required security practices. However, unlike FISMA, which focuses on government information systems, PCI DSS is focused on the security of credit card data in the private sector.

## HIPAA Certification

According to Steve Alder (HIPAA journal, Feb 2023), HIPAA certification is defined as either a point in time accreditation demonstrating an organization has passed a HIPAA compliance audit or a recognition that members of the organization's workforce have achieved the level of HIPAA knowledge required to comply with the organization's policies and procedures. While not mandatory, both are useful accreditations to have. Also, having HIPAA certification does not automatically absolve organizations from negligent practices.

The biggest benefit of getting certified is that if a violation still occurs that results in an OCR investigation, a certificate of HIPAA compliance demonstrates "a reasonable amount of care to abide by the HIPAA Rules." This can be the difference between a HIPAA violation classified as a Tier 1 violation (minimum penalty per violation $120) and a Tier 2 violation (minimum penalty per violation $1.205).

For Business Associates and third-party vendors that deal with data classified under HIPAA, certification demonstrates an intention to operate compliantly, making an organization's services more attractive and reducing the amount of due diligence required before entering into a Business Associate Agreement.

Getting HIPAA certification for the workforce has a similar benefit in that a compliant workforce is less likely to violate HIPAA or make mistakes that could result in data breaches. Similarly, achieving workforce HIPAA certification demonstrates a reasonable amount of care to abide by the HIPAA Rules if an investigation or audit takes place. For compliant individuals, this can foster patient trust and boost their value in the job-competitive market.

Unintentional violations of HIPAA usually occur due to a lack of knowledge, shortcuts being taken "to get the job done," or because a cultural norm of noncompliance has been allowed to develop. Whatever the reason, violations of HIPAA can result in serious repercussions ranging from written warnings to loss of professional accreditation, all of which can be avoided by applying the concepts learned in a certification program.

Certification requirements for Covered Entities, Business Associates, and healthcare workers differ because each must follow the rules. The latest requirements can be found in the certifying authorities at the time of certification.

# COPPA Safe Harbor Program

COPPA has a Safe Harbor program, which organizations can submit to the COPPA commission self-regulatory guidelines that implement the rule's protections. The commission can then review the request for "safe harbor" treatment within 180 days of submission. After notice and comment, they can approve the request, making the organization a Safe Harbor organization.

The criteria for approval of self-regulatory guidelines, according to the Code of Federal Regulations, part 312.10, are:

1. Program requirements that ensure operators subject to the self-regulatory program guidelines ("subject operators") provide substantially the same or greater protections for children.
2. An effective, mandatory mechanism for independently assessing subject operators' compliance with the self-regulatory program guidelines. At a minimum, this mechanism must include a comprehensive review by the safe harbor program, to be conducted not less than annually, of each subject operator's information policies, practices, and representations. An independent enforcement program, such as a seal program, can provide

the assessment mechanism required under this paragraph.
3. Disciplinary actions for subject operators' non-compliance with self-regulatory program guidelines. This performance standard may be satisfied by:

   a. Mandatory public reporting of any action taken against subject operators by the industry group issuing the self-regulatory guidelines;
   b. Consumer redress;
   c. Voluntary payments to the United States Treasury in connection with an industry-directed program for violators of the self-regulatory guidelines;
   d. Referral to the Commission of operators who engage in a pattern or practice of violating the self-regulatory guidelines.

## GDPR Certification

The EU does not define a specific certification to be obtained for compliance with GDPR; rather, it defines rules and regulations for the certification companies to follow before providing a certification of GDPR compliance. These certifications are encouraged to be established at the union level for maximum uniformity in compliance.

According to Art. 42 GDPR - Certification - GDPR.eu (2018), the following guidelines are provided for certification organizations:

1. The Member States, the supervisory authorities, the Board, and the Commission shall encourage, in particular at the Union level, the establishment of data protection certification mechanisms and data protection seals and marks to demonstrate compliance with this regulation of processing operations by controllers and processors. The

needs of micro, small, and medium-sized enterprises shall be considered.
2. In addition to adherence by controllers or processors subject to this Regulation, data protection certification mechanisms, seals, or marks may be established to demonstrate the existence of appropriate safeguards provided by controllers or processors that are not subject to this Regulation. Such controllers or processors shall make binding and enforceable commitments, via contractual or other legally binding instruments, to apply those appropriate safeguards, including about the rights of data subjects.
3. The certification shall be voluntary and available via a transparent process.
4. According to this Article, a certification does not reduce the responsibility of the controller or the processor for compliance with this Regulation. It is without prejudice to the competent supervisory authorities' tasks and powers.
5. A certification shall be issued by the certification bodies or the competent supervisory authority based on criteria approved by that competent supervisory authority. Where the Board approves the criteria may result in a common certification, the European Data Protection Seal.
6. The controller or processor that submits its processing to the certification mechanism shall provide the certification body, or where applicable, the competent supervisory authority, with all information and access to its processing activities necessary to conduct the certification procedure.
7. Certification shall be issued to a controller or processor for three years. It may be renewed under the same conditions, provided the relevant criteria are met. Certification shall be withdrawn, as applicable, by the certification bodies or the

competent supervisory authority where the criteria for the certification are not or are no longer met.
8. The Board shall collate all certification mechanisms and data protection seals and marks in a register and make them publicly available by any appropriate means.

# Chapter 10: Future of Cybersecurity Laws

As technology evolves, cyber security and privacy requirements will continue to grow and change. New challenges are coming up daily as the world becomes increasingly interconnected and more and more activities happen online. Discussed next are some things predicted to change the landscape of cybersecurity and privacy in the next decade.

## Cybersecurity for the Internet of Things

According to Ahmed Banafa (OpenMind BBVA, April 2023), the rise of the Internet of Things (IoT) is also set to have a major impact on the future of cybersecurity. IoT devices are becoming increasingly common and are often used to control critical systems and infrastructure. However, many IoT devices have poor security features and can be easily compromised by cybercriminals. As a result, organizations will need to implement better security measures to protect against IoT-related cyber threats. As it is, many laws have started including amendments to add IoT security to their definitions.

- The EU recently added measures to include IoT privacy rules to GDPR. The EU Cybersecurity Act, effective June 27, 2019, became law in the European Union and the UK, which includes regulations for IoT devices. The NIS Directive (IoT infrastructure) became effective on May 24, 2018, in the EU and the UK.
- In the US, the IoT Cybersecurity Improvement Act of 2020 gives NIST the authority to manage cybersecurity risk arising from IoT devices and develop risk management frameworks.

- The California IoT cybersecurity law became effective in January 2020 and aims to manage cybersecurity risks.

Under the IoT Act of 2020, NIST has released guidelines called "Recommendations for IoT Device Manufacturers: Foundational Activities and Core Device Cybersecurity Capability Baseline," which aims to integrate secure development into IoT device SDLC. It defines six simple features that consumers should look for:

- A unique identifier (a serial number, for instance)
- The ability to change firmware configuration
- Data Protection
- Secure access to administrative control
- The ability to update firmware and software
- Cybersecurity event logging

## Child Privacy Laws

As children venture online more and more, this activity is often unsupervised. It is next to impossible to monitor every online activity a child does, given there is such a wide variety of information available, from education to entertainment, all aimed at children. COPPA is a great first step towards protecting the privacy of minors online. Still, as technology evolves, it may not be enough to protect the different forms of online interaction that are coming up.

Children's or minors' privacy is a bigger concern because they are more susceptible to suggestions and not psychologically equipped to deal with different stressors and influences. Cyberbullying, blackmailing, and fear tactics are some of the things that would affect minors more severely than adults. With newer avenues of online interactions appearing, there are many more avenues for threat actors to collect, steal, and sell minor's information online. With time, amendments will have to be made to COPPA, and new laws will be introduced to protect minors from the harmful effects of information oversharing.

## AI Laws

Governments and industries are adjusting to artificial intelligence capabilities. With the ability to mimic and remix creative works, copywrite is a concern. Since AI can be used as a tool in cyber attacks, the level of sophistication will need AI cyber defense backed by cyber law.

Governments and industry are drafting regulation to deal with AI.

As of 2023, the influx of Artificial Intelligence (AI) has triggered a global reevaluation and adaptation of legal frameworks and regulatory guidelines. AI's unprecedented growth and expanding capabilities necessitate this reassessment to manage potential ethical, privacy, and security challenges.

**Copyright Concerns:**

AI's ability to create, mimic, and remix creative works has ushered in new complexities in copyright laws. Traditional copyright frameworks are being challenged, as AI-generated content blurs the lines of authorship and originality. The legal systems are now grappling with questions like - Who owns the copyright of AI-generated content? Is it the creator of the AI, the user, or does it remain unowned? Legislators and policymakers are in the throes of establishing legal precedents and modifying existing copyright laws to address these concerns, ensuring that rights and royalties are fairly attributed and protected.

**AI in Cybersecurity:**

With AI becoming a potent tool in cyber-attacks, cybersecurity laws are also undergoing significant transformation. The sophistication of these attacks demands an equally advanced AI-backed defense system. Cyber laws are being updated to incorporate requirements for advanced security protocols, mandatory AI ethical standards, and accountability measures to counter AI-enabled cyber threats effectively. The role of AI in both cyber offenses and defenses is leading to a nuanced legal landscape where adaptability and anticipation of emerging threats are key.

**Regulatory Frameworks:**

Governments and industries worldwide are collaboratively drafting new regulations to address the multifaceted challenges posed by AI. These regulations aim to ensure that AI is developed and used in ways that are ethical, safe, and in the interest of the public. They are focusing on transparency, accountability, and fairness to mitigate biases and discrimination in AI applications. The establishment of international AI ethics standards is also on the agenda to foster global cooperation and ensure that AI benefits humanity as a whole.

**Privacy and Data Protection:**

AI's extensive reliance on data has also spotlighted privacy and data protection issues. Existing data protection laws like GDPR in Europe and CCPA in California are being revisited to incorporate specific provisions for AI. These include stricter consent requirements for data processing, transparency in automated decision-making processes, and the rights of individuals to opt out of AI-driven decisions.

**Ethical AI:**

Ethics in AI is another dominant theme. There's a growing consensus on the need for ethical guidelines that govern AI development and deployment. Ethical AI seeks to ensure that technology is used in a manner that is just, fair, and respects human rights. Initiatives to develop principles and guidelines for ethical AI are underway, with participation from a diverse range of stakeholders including governments, international organizations, civil society, and the private sector.

**AI Governance:**

AI governance is also emerging as a critical aspect, with frameworks being established to monitor and evaluate AI's impact on society continuously. These governance structures are designed to be dynamic, adapting to the rapid evolution of AI technologies and their applications.

The intersection of AI and law is evolving rapidly, shaped by ongoing technological advancements and the emerging challenges they present. Balancing innovation with ethical, security, and privacy concerns is central to the ongoing discourse, necessitating a multidimensional approach that encompasses legal, ethical, and technological perspectives. Adaptation and anticipation are the watchwords, with laws and regulations crafted to be as dynamic and innovative as AI itself.

# Conclusion

Cybersecurity and privacy laws have become imperative in today's landscape with increasing activities online. Practically anything of value that happens tends to happen online as well. With this hyper-connectivity, IT professionals are responsible for compliance and management of security and privacy. A comprehensive knowledge and understanding of the different cyber laws can go a long way when incorporating compliance into the SDLC. Increased connectivity also means national boundaries are blurred, and everyone is dealing with data worldwide. This makes compliance with international regulations of utmost importance. Given the amount of different laws and regulations, it can feel overwhelming to meet compliance requirements. However, a step-by-step approach with the support of the different risk management frameworks can be of immense value and simplify many requirements into bite-size implementable solutions.

With that said, how a risk management framework or a compliance requirement is implemented can make or break the security and privacy of an organization. More often than not, security measures are available but are not implemented or enabled in a manner that becomes useless for security. When using third-party tools, this can be even more relevant. Enabling and configuring certain features and rules can be a challenge in itself. Training and education on the various security tools and choosing those that fit the best with an organization's needs is an important exercise that should be done by any team looking to use tools like firewalls, IDS, IPS, and others from third-party vendors.

Education of non-IT professionals on the proper use of the various tools they interact with daily is also crucial. End users are often the most insecure aspect in the chain of command with security and privacy. Improper use of technology is a bigger risk than it seems when considering security and privacy. Users should be trained and made aware of the proper use of different technology and have explained the implications of careless actions over the internet to the organization. This can help with more responsible online conduct in a professional and personal environment, improving the security posture of the organization and the individual.

All stakeholders should be involved in risk management as an ongoing endeavor and participate in reviewing and updating security and privacy policies.

With the evolving threat landscape, it is difficult to anticipate what security and privacy will look like after a decade. IoT devices and smart home appliances have introduced a factor of risk that was previously unanticipated. The fact that devices with seemingly limited capabilities can still be exploited and used to launch larger attacks gives an idea of how sophisticated cyber attackers can be. With the involvement of nation-state-funded cybercrime groups, the threat is not just of monetary loss or data loss but also to national security. With the increased involvement of AI in business functions, new threats are being introduced every day as attackers try to fool or break the technology for their benefit. Keeping ahead of the curve is becoming more of a challenge as technology is evolving in multiple directions, and the competition to bring new technology to market is creating an artificial rush. Keeping security and privacy at the forefront during the SDLC is imperative as much as releasing patches for newly found vulnerabilities is. The perspective of IT professionals should be security first to make secure development a reality.

This shift begins with incorporating different risk management frameworks, compliance certifications, and employee training. Companies are prioritizing security and privacy and maintaining compliance. New laws and regulations to match up with emerging threats and amendments to old laws are helping organizations maintain the best possible security posture. White-hat hackers are uncovering different vulnerabilities and supporting organizations in maintaining the organization's security and privacy postures. Even as the threats evolve, organizations and governments vigilantly update themselves to match up.

# FISMA Compliance -
## Understanding US FEDERAL INFORMATION SECURITY LAW

## By Convocourses

© Copyright 2023 - All rights reserved.

The content contained within this book may not be reproduced, duplicated or transmitted without direct written permission from the author or the publisher.

Under no circumstances will any blame or legal responsibility be held against the publisher, or author, for any damages, reparation, or monetary loss due to the information contained within this book, either directly or indirectly.

Legal Notice:

This book is copyright protected. It is only for personal use. You cannot amend, distribute, sell, use, quote or paraphrase any part, or the content within this book, without the consent of the author or publisher.

Disclaimer Notice:

Please note the information contained within this document is for educational and entertainment purposes only. All effort has been executed to present accurate, up to date, reliable, complete information. No warranties of any kind are declared or implied. Readers acknowledge that the author is not engaged in the rendering of legal, financial, medical or professional advice. The content within this book has been derived from various sources. Please consult a licensed professional before attempting any techniques outlined in this book.

By reading this document, the reader agrees that under no circumstances is the author responsible for any losses, direct or indirect, that are incurred as a result of the use of the information contained within this document, including, but not limited to, errors, omissions, or inaccuracies.

# INTRODUCTION TO INFORMATION SECURITY IN THE FEDERAL CONTEXT

Unless you are working with governance, risk, compliance, legal, or upper management, you might only get to know the names of any cyber laws, and that's about it.

Regardless of your profession, developing a great understanding of these underlying laws can enhance your career because they are foundational to cyber security and information systems management in all industries, especially in the government sector.

The more you understand the laws and acts of governing bodies, the better you can understand the environment that shapes IT and cybersecurity.

In today's digital era, information security is critical to national security, economic stability, and public trust, particularly within the US government context. US Federal agencies are responsible for managing vast quantities of sensitive data, spanning from personal data of individual citizens to classified national security details. Ensuring information integrity, confidentiality, and availability can make or break national security and public trust.

The US government's information systems stand apart due to their immense scale, complexity, and the sensitive nature of the data they handle. These systems are frequent targets for various cyber threats, ranging from individual hackers to sophisticated state-sponsored attacks. These threats and the ever-evolving nature make federal information security challenging. It's not merely about data protection; it's about upholding the public's confidence in government institutions.

Protection of data assets of this scale and importance requires a robust federal information security framework. This framework must be dynamic, encompassing protection against unauthorized access and requirements for data integrity and system availability. It goes beyond technological solutions, involving comprehensive policies and procedures and emphasizing human aspects such as training and awareness.

Legislation plays a critical role in all federal information security. The Federal Information Security Management Act of 2002 and the amendment Federal Information Security Modernization Act of 2014 (FISMA) provide a legal structure for securing federal information systems. FISMA sets guidelines and assigns responsibilities while ensuring a standardized security approach across all government entities.

However, securing sensitive data in federal agencies isn't the only priority. This security must be balanced with the principles of transparency and accessibility, which are fundamental to the United States of America's principles of democratic institutions. Federal agencies must protect data while ensuring the public has access to non-sensitive information, upholding openness and accountability.

FISMA represents not just a legal mandate but a commitment to evolving and strengthening the security posture of federal information systems in the face of advancing technological landscapes and emerging cyber threats.

# CHAPTER 1

# FISMA BACKGROUND AND LEGISLATIVE HISTORY

The Federal Information Security Management Act of 2002 represented a significant step forward in standardizing security across all U.S. government systems processing, transmitting, and storing federal information. Before FISMA, federal agencies faced a fragmented landscape with no unified security framework. While guidelines like the Rainbow Series offered detailed security standards, these primarily targeted the Department of Defense and could not keep pace with rapid IT advancements, leading to disparate cybersecurity measures across different agencies.

The introduction of FISMA in 2002 sought to rectify this by bringing all federal systems under a common regulatory umbrella, promoting a standardized set of security controls, enforcing risk management guidelines, and encouraging continuous monitoring and adaptation to new threats. This legislative move was supported by the groundwork laid by the Government Information Security Reform Act (GISRA) and the pivotal role of the National Institute of Standards and Technology (NIST) in developing critical security standards and guidelines.

FISMA aimed at promoting a more secure, consistent, and repeatable approach for selecting and specifying security controls for information systems. The goal was to enhance the federal government's overall security posture. The shift from a decentralized approach to a more unified and standardized framework showed the U.S. federal government's focus on information security and its impact on the economy and the national security interests of the United States.

The updated FISMA of 2014 marks a pivotal moment in the evolution of cybersecurity legislation in the United States. Its genesis and development were driven by the increasing recognition that cybersecurity and the threats to sensitive data had undergone significant changes since the enactment of the original FISMA in 2002.

The 2002 Act, while groundbreaking at its inception, gradually revealed its limitations in addressing the sophistication and frequency of cyber threats that federal agencies faced in the digital age.

In the years leading up to 2014, a series of high-profile cyber incidents targeting federal information systems significantly exposed vulnerabilities within the United States' cybersecurity infrastructure. These incidents underscored the urgent need for a more comprehensive and adaptive legal framework to protect sensitive government data against increasingly sophisticated cyber threats.

Examples of such incidents include:

- The Office of Personnel Management (OPM) Data

Breach: Although this breach was disclosed in 2015, its roots are traced back to vulnerabilities exploited before 2014. Hackers accessed the personal information of over 21 million current and former federal employees. This incident highlighted the need for improved cybersecurity measures and continuous monitoring beyond the periodic assessments that were the norm under the original FISMA.
- **The 2013 Department of Energy (DOE) Hack:** In this breach, hackers accessed the personal information of over 100,000 individuals through a compromised Department of Energy database. The incident raised concerns about the ability of federal agencies to protect against unauthorized access and underscored the necessity for a more robust cybersecurity framework.
- **Operation Aurora:** Uncovered in 2010, this cyber-attack targeted several companies, including Google, and was attributed to Chinese hackers. While not solely focused on federal systems, Operation Aurora demonstrated the capability of state-sponsored actors to exploit vulnerabilities in highly secure systems, suggesting that similar tactics could be used against government systems.

These incidents showed that the strategies and measures outlined in FISMA 2002 were not keeping pace with the rapidly evolving cyber threat landscape. There was a growing consensus among policymakers, cybersecurity experts, and federal agencies that an overhaul of federal information security practices was necessary.

In the deliberations for FISMA 2014, lawmakers sought to craft a bill that addressed the shortcomings of the previous legislation while anticipating future cybersecurity challenges. The discussions focused on moving away from a compliance-based approach, which was often criticized for being too rigid and checklist-oriented, to a risk-based, dynamic approach that could adapt to ongoing changes in technology and cyber threats.

One of the fundamental driving forces behind the new legislation was recognizing the need for continuous monitoring and real-time assessments of federal information systems. FISMA 2014 was envisioned to provide a more flexible framework that allowed federal agencies to respond quickly and effectively to identified risks rather than merely complying with static requirements.

Developing FISMA 2014 involved a significant level of inter-agency collaboration. This collaboration aimed to ensure that the Act would set out a comprehensive set of requirements for federal information security while facilitating a coordinated approach across various federal agencies in responding to and managing cybersecurity threats.

## The Sections of FISMA

Federal organizations are governed by FISMA as amended in 2014, which includes both the principles of the 2002 legislation and the updates necessary to address changes to cybersecurity and threats. To get a better understanding of FISMA, let's take a look at the main topics of the 2002 law:

**Information Security**

Establishes a comprehensive framework for ensuring the effectiveness of information security controls across federal operations and assets, development of minimum controls, and a mechanism for improved oversight of federal agency information security programs.

**Management of Information Technology**

Amends Section 5131 of the Clinger-Cohen Act of 1996 to address responsibilities for federal information systems standards.

**National Institute of Standards and Technology**

Amends Section 20 of the National Institute of Standards and Technology Act to outline the Institute's mission in developing standards, guidelines, and methods for information systems, excluding national security systems.

**Information Security Advisory Board**

Amends Section 21 of the National Institute of Standards and Technology Act to rename the Computer System Security and Privacy Advisory Board to the Information Security Advisory Board, adjusting its responsibilities to focus more broadly on information security.

**Technical and Conforming Amendments**

Includes repeals and amendments to existing laws to align with the provisions of the Federal Information Security Management Act of 2002, such as repealing sections of the Computer Security Act of 1987 and making amendments to the Paperwork Reduction Act.

# Key Objectives and Scope of FISMA 2002

The primary objectives of the Federal Information Security Management Act of 2002 (FISMA 2002) aimed to:

- **Information Security Framework.** Establish comprehensive frameworks for ensuring the effectiveness of information security controls over information resources that support federal operations and assets.
- **Security Mandate for Federal Organizations.** Mandate federal agencies to develop, document, and implement an agency-wide program to provide security for the information and information systems that support their operations and assets, including those provided or managed by another agency, contractor, or other sources.
- **Risk Assessments.** Require periodic risk assessments to determine the adequacy of in-place security policies,

procedures, and practices.
- **Security Controls.** Promote the use of cost-effective security controls to achieve and maintain adequate security.
- **Continuous Monitoring.** Require agencies to continuously monitor their information security policies, procedures, and practices.
- **Improve Reporting.** Enhance the management and oversight of federal information security through director and agency reporting requirements.

In 2002, FISMA moved toward a systematic, structured approach to securing federal information systems, emphasizing risk management, continuous monitoring, and accountability within federal agencies.

Federal Information Security Modernization Act of 2014 builds and reforms the 2002 version. The main sections of this Act are as follows:

**Information Security**

The purposes of the new subchapter are outlined, including providing a comprehensive framework for federal information security and recognizing the need for effective governmentwide management and oversight of information security risks.

**Definitions**

Definitions relevant to the subchapter include terms such as "binding operational directive," "incident," and "information security."

**Authority and Functions of the Director and the Secretary**

Details the responsibilities of the Director of the Office of Management and Budget (OMB) and the Secretary of Homeland Security overseeing federal information security policies and practices.

**Federal Agency Responsibilities**

Outlines the responsibilities of federal agencies in ensuring information security, including the development, documentation, and implementation of an agency-wide information security program.

**Annual Independent Evaluation**

Each agency must annually evaluate its information security program and practices to determine their effectiveness.

**Federal Information Security Incident Center**

Mandates the operation of a central federal information security incident center by the Secretary of Homeland Security to assist in managing security incidents.

**National Security Systems**

Specifies responsibilities for agencies operating or controlling national security systems in ensuring information security protections.

**Effect on Existing Law**

Clarifies that the subchapter does not affect the authority of the President, OMB, the National Institute of Standards and Technology (NIST), or agency heads regarding the use or disclosure of information.

**Major Incident**

Directs the OMB Director to develop guidance on what constitutes a major incident for reporting purposes.

**Continuous Diagnostics**
Requires an assessment of the adoption of continuous diagnostics technologies by agencies in OMB's annual report.
**Breaches**
Updates requirements for data breach notifications and reporting, including specifying the timeline and content of notifications to Congress and affected individuals.
**Technical and Conforming Amendments**
Makes technical and conforming amendments to the table of sections for Chapter 35 of Title 44, U.S. Code, and other related acts and codes.
**Other Provisions**
Includes additional provisions, such as requiring the OMB Director to amend or revise Circular A-130 to eliminate inefficient or wasteful reporting and amending the role of the Information Security and Privacy Advisory Board.

# Key Objectives and Scope of FISMA 2014

The primary objectives of FISMA 2014 are to:

- **Update Federal Information Security Practices:** The Act keeps federal cybersecurity practices current with current technologies and methods. It emphasizes the importance of continuous monitoring and real-time assessments of federal information systems.
- **Enhance Risk Management Processes:** FISMA 2014 shifts the focus from a compliance-based approach to a more dynamic, risk-based approach. This change acknowledges that security is not a one-time checkbox but a continuous, evolving process.
- **Provide a Framework for Government-wide Coordination:** The Act establishes a framework for

collaboration and information sharing among federal agencies. This collaborative approach ensures a unified response to cybersecurity threats and incidents.
- **Increase Accountability:** Agency heads are accountable for implementing effective information security practices. The Act mandates regular reporting and evaluation of the security measures in place.
- **Improve Response to Cyber Incidents**: FISMA 2014 emphasizes the need for a coordinated response to cyber incidents, including timely information sharing and implementation of recovery plans.

The scope of FISMA 2014 extends to all federal agencies, including departments and independent agencies, with specific provisions applicable to national security systems. The Act does not cover state governments or private sector entities unless they are part of a federal information system or a contractor for a federal agency.

FISMA emphasizes a risk-based approach to information security, continuous monitoring, and the importance of cybersecurity as an element of national security and economic well-being.

# CHAPTER 2

# AUTHORITY AND FUNCTIONS UNDER FISMA 2014

FISMA 2014 delineates the critical roles and responsibilities of key federal entities, including the Office of Management and Budget (OMB), the Department of Homeland Security (DHS), and the Director of National Intelligence (DNI), in fortifying the United States' cybersecurity posture.

## The Role of the Office of Management and Budget (OMB)

Within the framework of FISMA 2014, the Office of Management and Budget (OMB) is vested with significant authority and responsibility. OMB's role includes policy development, budgetary oversight, and ensuring federal agencies' effective implementation and compliance with information security standards.

### *Policy Development and Implementation*

OMB is tasked with developing and issuing comprehensive policies, directives, and guidelines that govern the security of federal information systems. These policies are not static; they are regularly updated to address the dynamic nature of cyber threats and technological advancements. By setting government-wide standards, OMB ensures a unified approach to securing federal information assets, enhancing the overall posture of information security across all agencies. One of OMB's key policy development responsibilities is integrating cybersecurity considerations into the broader framework of federal information resources management. This approach ensures that information security is a fundamental component of the lifecycle management of federal information systems, from procurement to decommissioning.

## *Budgetary Oversight*

One of OMB's roles under FISMA 2014 is oversight of the budgetary allocations for cybersecurity across the federal government. OMB evaluates the sufficiency of budget requests related to information security and has the authority to recommend adjustments to ensure adequate resources are allocated for cybersecurity measures. This budgetary oversight function ensures that agencies have the necessary financial resources to implement robust information security programs without being overly wasteful.

OMB works closely with federal agencies to integrate information security expenditures into their budget planning and execution processes. This work includes reviewing and approving agency budgets for information security ensuring that investments in cybersecurity are prioritized and aligned with the strategic objectives of the federal government.

## *Compliance and Oversight*

OMB plays a key oversight role in monitoring and evaluating federal agencies' compliance with FISMA 2014 requirements. This oversight occurs through various mechanisms, including annual reviews, audits, and evaluations. OMB assesses the effectiveness of agency information security programs, identifies areas where agencies may fall short of federal information security standards, and mandates corrective actions.

In addition to evaluating compliance, OMB is responsible for coordinating the preparation and submission of an annual report to Congress on the state of federal information security. This report provides a government-wide overview of the effectiveness of information security policies and practices, highlighting achievements and identifying areas requiring improvement.

### *Facilitating Interagency Coordination*

OMB also plays a pivotal role in facilitating coordination and collaboration among federal agencies on cybersecurity matters. By fostering an environment of information sharing and joint initiatives, OMB enhances the collective ability of the federal government to address and mitigate cyber threats. This includes coordination with the National Security Council, the Department of Homeland Security, and other relevant entities on a cohesive approach to national cybersecurity.

## The Secretary of Homeland Security's Responsibilities

The Secretary of the Department of Homeland Security (DHS), the third-largest federal department in the United States, oversees an extensive team comprising 260,000 dedicated personnel across 22 distinct units. These units include the Transportation Security Administration (TSA), Customs and Border Protection (CBP), Immigration and Customs Enforcement (ICE), U.S. Citizenship and Immigration Services (USCIS), the Federal Emergency Management Agency (FEMA), the U.S. Coast Guard, the Secret Service, the Federal Law Enforcement Training Centers, the National Protection and Programs Directorate, and the Science and Technology Directorate.

Under the guidance of the Secretary, DHS is responsible for safeguarding the nation from terrorist threats, enhancing cybersecurity measures, securing aviation and maritime domains, ensuring border and port security, managing and enforcing immigration laws, safeguarding national leaders, protecting vital infrastructure, and responding effectively to natural and human-made disasters. Additionally, the Department is vigilant in detecting and defending against chemical, biological, and nuclear dangers to ensure the safety and security of the homeland.

FISMA charges the DNS with safeguarding federal information systems against cyber threats through a few different workstreams.

## *Enhanced Cybersecurity Framework and Collaboration*

DHS is responsible for developing and promoting a cybersecurity framework encompassing risk management practices, security protocols, and incident response strategies tailored to the federal domain.

## *Technical Assistance and Cybersecurity Services*

DHS must also provide technical assistance to federal agencies securing their information systems. This includes offering cybersecurity tools, conducting vulnerability assessments, and facilitating access to shared cybersecurity services. The goal is to equip agencies with the necessary resources and expertise to defend against cyberattacks, detect vulnerabilities, and respond effectively to security incidents.

## *Operational Security Measures and Incident Response*

DHS is also responsible for operational security measures. This includes overseeing the operation of the National Cybersecurity and Communications Integration Center (NCCIC), which plays a pivotal role in monitoring federal networks, sharing information on cyber threats, and coordinating incident response activities. The NCCIC is a central hub for cybersecurity information sharing, enabling timely and effective responses to cyber incidents.

## Coordination with Critical Infrastructure Sectors

Beyond federal agencies, DHS is also charged with helping protect critical infrastructure sectors from cyber threats. This involves working closely with critical infrastructure owners and operators to enhance their cybersecurity posture, share threat intelligence, and develop sector-specific security guidelines. This support of these sectors helps keep critical services such as energy, transportation, and finance secure and resilient against cyber disruptions.

## Advocacy for Cybersecurity Awareness and Education

To raise awareness about cyber threats, DHS also advocates for cybersecurity best practices, emphasizing the importance of cyber hygiene among government employees and the general public. Initiatives may include cybersecurity training programs, public awareness campaigns, and partnerships with educational institutions to develop the next generation of cybersecurity professionals.

## Policy Development and Legislative Engagement

DHS plays an instrumental role in shaping national cybersecurity policy and engaging with Congress on cybersecurity issues by providing policy recommendations, briefing lawmakers on cyber threats and security initiatives, and advocating for legislation that supports the nation's cybersecurity goals.

# Delegation of Authority to the Director of National Intelligence for Specific Systems

FISMA 2014 delegates authority to the Director of National Intelligence (DNI) for specific responsibilities regarding national security systems. National security systems are information systems used or operated by an agency or a contractor of an agency or other organization on behalf of an agency involving intelligence activities, national security missions, or classified activities of the Department of Defense. These systems require a level of security and confidentiality that goes beyond the standard measures applied to other federal information systems due to the sensitivity and importance of their content to national security.

## *Specific Responsibilities Entrusted to the DNI*

Tailoring Security Measures: The DNI is responsible for customizing federal information security policies, standards, and guidelines to meet the unique requirements of national security systems. This involves the development of specific security protocols that address the heightened threat these systems may face, including espionage, cyber-attacks, and other forms of intelligence activities aimed at compromising national security.

## *Risk Management and Security Oversight*

The DNI oversees the assessment of risks to national security systems, ensuring that risk management processes are integrated into the lifecycle of these systems. This includes authorizing security measures and monitoring their effectiveness in protecting against threats. The DNI also has the authority to mandate corrective actions when vulnerabilities are identified, ensuring that national security systems maintain the highest level of security.

## *Coordination with Federal Agencies*

The DNI works in close coordination with other federal agencies, including the Department of Defense (DoD) and DHS, to ensure a unified and comprehensive approach to national security across the federal government through activities like sharing intelligence about emerging threats, coordinating responses to security incidents, and aligning security practices across different sectors of the government.

## *Information Sharing and Cybersecurity Integration*

The DNI promotes sharing cybersecurity threat information and vulnerabilities within the intelligence community and other federal agencies. This effort is vital for anticipating and mitigating threats to national security systems. Furthermore, the DNI plays a key role in integrating cybersecurity intelligence into the broader national security strategy, ensuring that cyber threats are addressed in the United States' overall defense and intelligence posture.

## *Innovation and Technology Adoption*

Recognizing the rapid pace of technological advancements and the evolving nature of cyber threats, the DNI is also tasked with fostering innovation and constant iteration of cybersecurity measures for national security systems.

## *The Importance of the DNI's Role*

The delegation of authority to the DNI is FISMA 2014's way of guaranteeing specialized, high-level oversight to protect national security systems. By tailoring security measures to the specific needs of these systems and ensuring a coordinated effort across the intelligence and defense communities, the DNI plays a crucial role in safeguarding the nation's most sensitive information and maintaining the integrity of its national security operations.

# CHAPTER 3

# INFORMATION SECURITY POLICIES AND PRACTICES

FISMA 2014 mandates a departure from the conventional "one-size-fits-all" model, advocating for comprehensive policies that can evolve in tandem with the dynamic nature of cybersecurity threats. These policies are formulated based on a thorough risk assessment, enabling agencies to effectively tailor their security strategies to mitigate potential vulnerabilities and threats.

The National Institute of Standards and Technology (NIST) Risk Management Framework (RMF) and the security and privacy controls catalog are relied upon for guidance. FISMA also ensures a mechanism for compliance to enhance the security posture of federal information systems.

## Development and Implementation of Agency-specific Policies

FISMA 2014 mandates a significant transformation in how federal agencies approach the security of their information systems. Central to this transformation is developing and implementing agency-specific policies tailored to each agency's unique operational and risk environments while being flexible enough to adapt to the rapidly evolving landscape of cybersecurity threats. This approach moves away from a one-size-fits-all model, recognizing the diversity and complexity of the federal government's information infrastructure.

The process of developing these policies requires agencies to complete a comprehensive risk assessment to identify potential vulnerabilities and threats to their specific information systems. This assessment forms the foundation for a security strategy that addresses information security's physical and digital realms. Agencies are then tasked with crafting policies that cover a wide array of security measures, including but not limited to access control, user authentication, data encryption, and incident response protocols. These policies are expected to be holistic, covering every facet of information security from the ground up and ensuring that all information system layers are fortified against potential breaches.

Given the nature of cyber threats, agency-specific policies must be regularly reviewed and updated to incorporate new security technologies and countermeasures. Agencies are also encouraged to have a culture of security awareness among their personnel. This cultural shift will reinforce to every employee that they play a crucial role in maintaining the security and integrity of federal information systems.

The synergy between agency-specific policies and the guidelines provided by NIST further strengthens the federal government's security framework. While agency-specific policies may vary to suit operational needs, NIST guidelines keep the foundational level of security consistent and robust.

## Binding Operational Directives and Compliance

FISMA Binding Operational Directives (BODs) are a mechanism designed to strengthen compliance and enhance the overall security posture of federal information systems. These directives, issued by DHS, are authoritative mandates that require federal agencies to undertake specific actions within designated time frames to mitigate vulnerabilities, secure networks, and address emerging cybersecurity threats.

- **Purpose and Authority** -BODs aim to ensure a unified and swift response to known cybersecurity risks across the federal landscape. Given the dynamic nature of cyber threats, the ability of DHS to issue timely directives enables the government to respond proactively to vulnerabilities and incidents that could compromise federal information systems.

- **Compliance Mechanisms** -Compliance with BODs is a requirement. Federal agencies are mandated to report on compliance actions in response to a BOD, typically through mechanisms established by OMB and overseen by DHS. These reports allow DHS to monitor each agency's progress in addressing the directives, ensuring that vulnerabilities are mitigated and security postures are enhanced per the specified timelines. In collaboration with NIST and FISMA guidelines, DHS provides agencies with detailed instructions and methodologies for addressing the issues identified in a BOD to facilitate compliance. This collaborative approach ensures that agencies are equipped with the knowledge and resources to mitigate these issues effectively.
- **Enforcement and Accountability** - Enforcement of BOD compliance is a multi-layered process involving oversight by DHS, OMB, and Congress. Agencies failing to comply with directives may face various consequences, including but not limited to increased oversight, redirection of IT budgets, or public disclosure of non-compliance. Accountability is enforced through annual FISMA audits and evaluations, which assess an agency's information security program, including its adherence to BODs. These evaluations contribute to a broader understanding of the agency's compliance status and areas requiring improvement.

# Integration with National Institute of

# Standards and Technology (NIST) Guidelines

NIST's guidelines, particularly those outlined in the NIST Special Publication 800 series, provide a detailed and authoritative set of recommendations for information security. These publications cover risk management, cybersecurity, security and privacy controls, and incident response. NIST continuously updates these guidelines to reflect the latest cybersecurity research, threat intelligence, and technology advancements.

## *Key Aspects of NIST Integration*

One of the most significant contributions of NIST is the Risk Management Framework (RMF), detailed in NIST SP 800-37. The RMF provides a structured process for federal agencies to assess and manage risks to their information systems. It emphasizes the importance of selecting appropriate security controls, implementing them effectively, and continuously monitoring their performance. By integrating the RMF into their security policies, agencies can ensure a proactive and systematic approach to managing cybersecurity risks.

- **Security and Privacy Controls** - NIST SP 800-53 offers a comprehensive catalog of security and privacy controls for federal information systems and organizations. These controls are designed to address a wide range of security requirements and are customizable to support the diverse mission requirements of federal agencies. By adopting these controls, agencies can implement robust protective measures tailored to their specific operational and risk contexts.
- **Cybersecurity Framework** - Although primarily targeted at the private sector, the NIST Cybersecurity Framework

has also been widely adopted by federal agencies. This framework provides a flexible and adaptable approach to managing cybersecurity risk, organized around the core functions of Identifying, Protecting, Detecting, Responding, and Recovering. Integrating the Cybersecurity Framework into agency policies enhances the ability to manage cybersecurity risk in a dynamic threat environment.

- **Compliance and Continuous Monitoring** - Integration with NIST guidelines involves rigorous compliance efforts and continuous monitoring practices. Agencies must regularly assess their information systems against NIST standards to ensure ongoing compliance. This includes conducting security assessments, audits, and continuous monitoring activities to detect and promptly respond to security incidents and vulnerabilities.
- **Adaptation and Flexibility** - NIST encourages agencies to consider their unique mission needs, operational environments, and technological landscapes when implementing its guidelines to keep agencies compliant with federal standards but still effective in the specific context of each agency's operations.

# CHAPTER 4

# FEDERAL INFORMATION SECURITY INCIDENT CENTER (FISIC)

FISMA requires the operation of a Federal Information Security Incident Center (FISIC) within DHS to oversee and respond to information incidents.

## Role and Functions of FISIC

### Centralized Oversight for Cybersecurity

FISIC is the nerve center for the United States government's cybersecurity incident management. It provides centralized oversight and a unified response mechanism for information security incidents across all federal agencies, standardizing response efforts and creating a cohesive strategy.

### Proactive Threat Identification

One of FISIC's key roles is the proactive identification of cyber threats. Utilizing advanced cybersecurity tools and techniques, the Center analyzes vast amounts of data to detect potential security incidents before they can cause significant harm. This proactive approach allows the federal government to stay one step ahead of cyber adversaries.

## Expertise and Resource Hub

FISIC serves as a hub of expertise and resources for federal agencies, particularly those that might not have extensive cybersecurity capabilities. The Center offers technical guidance, best practices, and support for incident response activities, elevating the overall cybersecurity readiness of the federal government.

## Comprehensive Incident Management

The Center's incident management responsibilities extend beyond initial detection and reporting. FISIC coordinates the incident response lifecycle, from identification and analysis to containment, eradication, and post-incident recovery. This comprehensive management ensures that incidents are resolved efficiently and effectively, minimizing their impact on government operations.

## Collaborative Cybersecurity Ecosystem

FISIC fosters a collaborative cybersecurity ecosystem by facilitating communication and information sharing among federal agencies, private sector partners, and international allies. This collaboration addresses global cyber threats and leverages collective insights to enhance security measures.

## Cybersecurity Policy Development

In addition to its operational roles, FISIC is strategically developing federal cybersecurity policies and frameworks. By aggregating and analyzing data on cyber threats and incident responses, the Center identifies trends and vulnerabilities that inform the creation of robust cybersecurity policies.

## Training and Awareness Programs

FISIC implements training and awareness programs for federal employees. These programs are designed to develop the knowledge and skills of federal personnel, ensuring that they are equipped to identify, report, and respond to cyber threats effectively.

## Evaluation and Continuous Improvement

FISIC continuously evaluates the effectiveness of federal cybersecurity measures and incident response efforts. Through this evaluation, the Center identifies areas for improvement and innovation against an ever-changing threat environment.

# Incident Reporting and Response Coordination

Incident reporting and response coordination are central components of FISIC's operational mandate, essential for maintaining federal information systems' integrity, confidentiality, and availability. These processes ensure rapid, coordinated responses to cyber incidents, minimizing their impact on national security, economic stability, and public health and safety.

## Enhanced Incident Reporting

Incident reporting to FISIC is a procedural requirement and a critical early warning that activates the federal government's collective response capabilities. This reporting mechanism operates under several key principles:

- Timeliness: Agencies are mandated to report incidents within a specified timeframe from detection, ensuring that response measures can be activated promptly to contain

damage and mitigate threats.
- Standardization: Using standardized reporting formats and protocols facilitates the quick assimilation and analysis of incident data, allowing FISIC to assess the situation and prioritize actions rapidly.
- Comprehensive Detailing: Detailed reporting goes beyond notification. It documents and accounts for the nature of the incident, systems affected, and data compromised, and it also contains an initial impact assessment. This level of information is crucial for formulating an effective response strategy.

## *Strategic Response Coordination*

Once an incident is reported, FISIC's response coordination mechanism springs into action, typically comprised of several strategic phases:

- **Assessment and Classification:** FISIC evaluates the reported incident to classify its severity based on predefined criteria. This classification guides the level and nature of response efforts.
- **Incident Triage:** Following assessment, incidents undergo triage to determine the most appropriate response teams and resources. High-impact incidents may require the mobilization of specialized interagency cybersecurity teams.
- **Coordination and Mobilization:** FISIC coordinates the mobilization of federal resources and capabilities to address the incident. This includes facilitating interagency communication, deploying cybersecurity response teams, and engaging external partners if necessary.

- **Situational Awareness and Communication:** FISIC ensures that all stakeholders, including affected agencies, law enforcement, and, when appropriate, the public, are informed about the incident status and response actions to maintain situational awareness.
- **Recovery and Restoration:** FISIC coordinates efforts to recover affected systems and restore services, working closely with impacted agencies to implement recovery plans and mitigate the risk of future incidents.
- **Post-Incident Analysis and Feedback Loop:** After resolving an incident, a critical post-incident review is conducted to analyze the response's effectiveness, identify lessons learned, and integrate these insights into future security policies and response strategies. This feedback loop keeps federal cybersecurity preparedness in a state of continuous improvement.
- **The Role of Advanced Technologies:** FISIC leverages advanced technologies and cybersecurity tools to enhance incident reporting and response coordination. Automated systems facilitate real-time incident tracking and analysis, while artificial intelligence and machine learning algorithms help predict potential threats and vulnerabilities, enabling proactive defenses.

# CHAPTER 5

# REPORTING AND EVALUATION

Reporting and evaluation within the Federal Information Security Management Act of 2014 framework is critical. It keeps federal organizations honest and helps continuously improve federal cybersecurity efforts. Reporting and evaluation are not mere formalities but fundamental processes ensuring all federal organizations remain committed to maintaining security. Among these evaluations, the necessity for some to be conducted independently stands out as a testament to the seriousness of these measures.

## Annual Reports on the Effectiveness of Information Security Policies

FISMA 2014 mandates annual reporting to ensure transparency and accountability in the federal government's cybersecurity efforts. These reports are a critical tool for internal and external stakeholders to understand the effectiveness of information security policies across federal agencies.

### *Purpose and Importance of Reports & Evaluation*

The annual reports provide a structured mechanism for agencies to self-assess and document their cybersecurity readiness and the effectiveness of their information security policies. This process is important for several reasons:

- **Transparency:** It offers a transparent view into the agency's efforts to secure its information systems against potential cyber threats.
- **Accountability:** Agencies are held accountable for their cybersecurity measures, encouraging buy-in by agency

employees and continuous improvement in their security practices.
- **Policy Evaluation:** The reports allow for evaluating current information security policies, identifying areas where they succeed and need enhancement.
- **Strategic Planning:** Insights from these reports inform strategic planning and investment in cybersecurity infrastructure and capabilities.

## *Content of the Reports*

The report's content hits on some of the main features of a solid cybersecurity program. The content of the annual reports includes:

- **Security Program Overview:** A summary of the agency's information security program, including policies, procedures, and strategies in place.
- **Risk Management and Compliance:** Assessment of the agency's risk management processes and compliance with federal cybersecurity regulations and standards.
- **Incident Response and Management:** Evaluation of the agency's capability to detect, respond to, and recover from cybersecurity incidents.
- **Training and Awareness:** Overview of training programs and awareness initiatives available to educate employees about cybersecurity risks and best practices.
- **Security Controls Assessment:** Details on the effectiveness of implemented security controls and any deficiencies identified through security assessments.
- **Action Plans and Priorities:** Description of action plans and strategic priorities in place to address identified vulnerabilities.

## Process and Evaluation

The process of compiling the annual reports encourages a culture of continuous monitoring and evaluation within federal agencies. It involves:

- **Data Collection and Analysis:** Agencies collect and analyze data on various aspects of their information security programs, including incidents, response actions, and results of security control assessments.
- **Stakeholder Engagement:** Agencies gather insights and feedback from relevant stakeholders across the agency or department.
- **Benchmarking and Improvement Plans:** Agencies benchmark their progress against previous years and set goals for future measurable progress.

# Independent Evaluation of Agency Information Security Programs

FISMA also requires independent evaluation of agency information security programs. This requirement is designed to provide an unbiased assessment of the effectiveness and compliance of an agency's information security measures. The independent evaluation involves thoroughly reviewing the security policies, procedures, and controls agencies have implemented to protect their information systems and data from cyber threats.

## Purpose and Scope

The independent evaluation assesses compliance with FISMA 2014 requirements and other applicable federal information security laws, policies, and directives. The effectiveness of the information security policies, procedures, and practices are examined during the independent evaluation. This helps identify weaknesses and vulnerabilities within the agency's information security program. The information gathered helps the organization develop measures to mitigate these risks.

The scope of the evaluation covers all aspects of an agency's information security program, including:

- **Governance and Risk Management:** How well the agency manages information security risks and aligns its security practices with its mission and strategic objectives.
- **Policy and Procedure Implementation:** The adequacy and effectiveness of the agency's information security policies and procedures.
- **Security Control Effectiveness:** The effectiveness of physical, administrative, and technical controls in protecting information assets against threats and vulnerabilities.
- **Incident Response and Management:** The agency can detect, respond to, and recover from security incidents.

## Execution of the Evaluation

Independent evaluations are conducted by the agency's Inspector General (IG) or an independent external auditor. The choice between these two options depends on the agency's specific circumstances, resources, and the need to ensure that the evaluation is impartial and comprehensive.

The evaluation process typically involves:

- **Document Review:** The agency's information documented security policies, procedures, and guidelines.
- **System Assessments:** Testing the security controls implemented across the agency's information systems to verify their effectiveness.
- **Interviews and Surveys:** Engaging with key personnel to gain insights into the agency's information security program's practical implementation and day-to-day challenges.
- **Reporting:** Providing a detailed report outlining the evaluation findings, including identified weaknesses and vulnerabilities, and making recommendations for improvement.

## Outcome and Impact

The outcome of an independent evaluation is the previously mentioned detailed report. This report is a critical tool for:

- **Guiding Improvements:** Informing agency leadership and stakeholders about necessary updates to security policies, procedures, and controls.
- **Supporting Accountability and Transparency:** Holding agencies accountable for their cybersecurity posture and

ensuring transparency in addressing information security challenges.
- **Enhancing Federal Cybersecurity:** Contributing to strengthening the federal government's defense against cyber threats through shared insights and best practices.

# Major Incident Reporting Requirements

FISMA 2014 defines a major incident as one that significantly impacts information systems or data security, potentially leading to substantial harm to national security, economic stability, public health or safety, or any combination thereof. This definition is intentionally broad, capturing a range of incidents from large-scale data breaches involving sensitive personal information to targeted attacks on critical infrastructure.

## *Reporting Protocol*

The protocol for reporting major incidents is structured to ensure that relevant information reaches necessary stakeholders quickly and efficiently. The process is:

1. **Immediate Notification:** Upon detection of a major incident, the affected agency must immediately report the incident to the United States Computer Emergency Readiness Team (US-CERT) within the Department of Homeland Security, as well as OMB and, if national security systems are involved, the appropriate national security authorities.

1. **Preliminary Report:** Following the immediate notification, the agency must provide a preliminary report that includes an overview of the incident, the information or systems compromised, and the initial impact assessment. This report should be submitted within a defined timeframe, typically within 24 hours of the incident detection.
2. **In-Depth Analysis:** After the preliminary report, agencies must conduct and submit a detailed analysis of the incident. This analysis includes the nature of the data exposed, the suspected cause of the incident, the steps taken to mitigate the immediate impact, remediate longer-term impacts, and the measures being implemented to prevent a recurrence.
3. **Updates and Follow-Up:** Agencies must provide regular updates as more information becomes available or the situation evolves. Continuous communication ensures that all stakeholders are informed of the recovery process, the effectiveness of the response measures, and any changes in the incident's scope or impact.
4. **Post-Incident Analysis and Reporting:** A comprehensive post-incident analysis is conducted after the incident has been contained and resolved. This analysis focuses on the lessons learned, the adequacy of the response, and recommendations for future improvements to policies, procedures, and technologies.

## *Accountability and Transparency*

Major incident reporting requirements keep the federal government transparent and accountable to ensure that the wayside doesn't throw lessons learned and documentation during the emergency of a major incident response. By mandating the timely reporting of significant incidents, FISMA 2014 ensures that critical information is shared among relevant parties, including Congress, which can then take appropriate legislative or oversight actions. Furthermore, this process supports the development of a culture of continuous communication and improvement in cybersecurity practices across federal agencies.

# CHAPTER 6

# ENHANCED SECURITY MEASURES

FISMA 2014 brought a shift towards integrating cybersecurity readiness measures into the broader spectrum of budgetary and operational planning. The enhanced security measures mandated by FISMA 2014 highlight integrating security with fiscal and operational strategies, deploying automated tools for security assessments, and establishing special provisions for national security systems.

## Integration of Security with Budgetary and Operational Planning

FISMA 2014 intertwines information security with budgetary and operational planning. This integration signifies a departure from traditional practices where security measures were often considered in isolation or as an endpoint in the planning process. Instead, FISMA 2014 mandates that information security becomes an integral component of the initial planning stages for all federal operations and projects. Integration of security with the budget has the following key features:

- **Strategic Alignment**: The act advocates for strategic alignment between an agency's security posture and budgetary allocations. It necessitates that agencies develop a comprehensive understanding of their security needs and incorporate these requirements into their financial planning to allow for adequate resources to address security concerns at the outset of any project or operational activity.
- **Risk Management:** A critical aspect of integrating security with budgetary and operational planning is the emphasis

on risk management. Agencies must conduct thorough risk assessments, identifying potential vulnerabilities and the impact of security threats on their operations. This risk management approach enables agencies to prioritize their spending on security measures, directing funds toward mitigating the most significant risks. By doing so, agencies can optimize their budgets, ensuring that investments in security deliver maximum impact.

- **Operational Efficiency:** The integration also promotes operational efficiency by ensuring that security measures are seamlessly incorporated into daily operations. When security is considered alongside budgetary and operational planning, it becomes part of the agency's workflow, reducing the need for disruptive adjustments or implementing security measures as afterthoughts. This proactive approach contributes to the smooth execution of agency missions, minimizing the potential for security incidents that can derail operations or incur additional costs.
- **Fostering a Culture of Security Best Practice:** Beyond the practical benefits, integrating security with budgetary and operational planning fosters a security culture within federal agencies. It signals a shift towards recognizing information security as a fundamental aspect of all governmental functions and strategy, embedding a security mindset into the core of agency operations. This cultural shift encourages continuous vigilance.

## Automated Tools for Security Assessments

FISMA 2014's updated approach also provides guidance for automated tools for security assessments. These tools shift from traditional, manual security monitoring and evaluation processes to a more dynamic, efficient, and practical approach. By leveraging automated technology, agencies can continuously scan and evaluate their information systems for vulnerabilities, security gaps, and unauthorized activities, ensuring a proactive stance against potential threats.

### *Advantages of Automated Tools:*

- **Continuous Monitoring and Real-Time Alerts:** Automated tools enable continuous monitoring of information systems, providing real-time alerts when potential security threats are detected. This capability allows immediate action to mitigate risks long before they can escalate into serious breaches or have a noticeable impact. Continuous monitoring transcends the limitations of periodic assessments, offering a live picture of an agency's security posture at any given moment.
- **Comprehensive Coverage and Depth:** These tools can scan a wide range of systems and applications, covering more ground than manual assessments could feasibly manage. They can have immediate, scalable insight into the intricacies of each system, identifying vulnerabilities that human auditors might overlook. This thorough examination ensures that even the most subtle security weaknesses are detected and addressed.
- **Standardization and Consistency:** Automated security assessments provide a standardized approach to evaluating

cybersecurity risks. Unlike manual processes, which can vary significantly in thoroughness and accuracy, automated tools apply the same criteria and rigor across all systems, ensuring consistency in security assessments. This standardization is crucial for maintaining a uniformly high level of security across all federal information systems.
- **Efficiency and Resource Allocation:** By automating the routine tasks of security assessments, agencies can allocate their human (and more costly) resources to more complex and strategic security challenges. Automated tools can handle the labor-intensive work of scanning and monitoring, freeing cybersecurity personnel to focus on more in-depth analysis, response strategies, and preventive measures. This efficiency optimizes the use of budgetary resources dedicated to cybersecurity.

## *Challenges and Considerations*

While automated tools offer significant advantages, their implementation brings new challenges. Agencies must carefully select tools that align with their security needs and system configurations. Agencies must consider how these tools integrate with existing systems and stay compatible across diverse IT environments. Moreover, the reliance on automated tools necessitates ongoing updates and maintenance to keep pace with the latest cybersecurity threats and technologies.

In addition to technical considerations, these tools also require skilled personnel who can interpret the data generated by these tools, discern false positives from genuine threats, and implement appropriate response actions. These tools bring new needs for investment in training and development for cybersecurity teams to leverage their capabilities effectively.

# Special Provisions for National Security Systems

FISMA 2014 includes special provisions for national security systems, requiring a tailored approach to systems critical to the nation's defense and intelligence operations. These systems have unique vulnerabilities and higher stakes, requiring a specialized framework to ensure the utmost protection of national security information against cyber threats.

The term "national security system" refers to any network directly or indirectly involved in intelligence gathering, cryptologic operations of national security, military force command and control, weapon or weapons system components, or systems essential to the direct execution of intelligence or military missions. This description does not include payroll, finance, logistics, and personnel management systems because they are utilized for normal administrative and business tasks.

Given their criticality, national security systems are often targeted by sophisticated adversaries aiming to compromise national security through espionage, sabotage, or other malicious activities. To mitigate these threats, FISMA 2014 mandates several key measures:

- **Enhanced Security Requirements:** FISMA requires enhanced security requirements for national security systems, exceeding the standard protocols applied to general federal information systems. These enhanced requirements often involve advanced encryption standards, multi-factor authentication, and stringent access controls to ensure that only authorized personnel can access sensitive information.
- **Coordinated Defense Strategy:** FISMA requires a coordinated defense strategy among various government

agencies, including DoD, the Office of the Director of National Intelligence (ODNI), and DHS, to develop and implement a unified security framework. This collaborative effort ensures that the most effective defense mechanisms are employed across all national security systems, leveraging the expertise and resources of each agency.

- **Continuous Monitoring and Evaluation:** For national security systems, continuous monitoring and evaluation are vital to detect and respond to threats in real time. FISMA 2014 advocates deploying sophisticated monitoring technologies that can identify anomalous activities indicative of a cybersecurity threat. FISMA also mandates continuous evaluation of security controls and practices.
- **Specialized Training and Awareness:** Personnel involved in operating and managing national security systems must undergo specialized training, ensuring they have the knowledge and skills necessary to protect these critical assets. This training includes awareness of the latest cybersecurity threats, understanding advanced security technologies, and familiarity with incident response protocols.
- **Incident Response and Recovery:** FISMA 2014 strongly emphasizes developing robust incident response and recovery plans for national security systems. These plans are designed to ensure that any security breach can be quickly contained and mitigated, minimizing the impact on national security. FISMA also requires implementing rapid recovery processes to restore the integrity and functionality of compromised systems with minimal downtime.

# CHAPTER 7

# BREACH NOTIFICATION AND RESPONSE

In response to the escalating number of security breaches within federal organizations, FISMA has bolstered the government's approach to cybersecurity. This enhancement extends beyond mere procedural updates. It dives deep into the establishment of comprehensive policies, the delineation of clear roles, and the assignment of specific responsibilities related to the prevention, detection, and response to breaches.

## Policies for Data Breach Notifications

FISMA 2014 emphasizes a proactive and responsive approach to data breach notifications. Under FISMA, federal agencies must adopt comprehensive and strategic policies for notifying individuals and entities affected by data breaches. This shows the law's commitment to transparency, accountability, and privacy protection.

Effective data breach notification policies are a cornerstone of FISMA 2014, designed to mitigate the adverse effects of breaches on national security, public safety, and individual privacy. These policies provide clear guidelines on when, how, and what information must be communicated to impacted parties following a breach. The goal is to ensure that affected individuals are informed promptly and provided with actionable advice to safeguard themselves against potential harm, such as identity theft or financial fraud.

- **Notification Thresholds and Timelines:** FISMA establishes thresholds for determining the severity of a data breach and the subsequent necessity for notification. These thresholds are based on the sensitivity of the compromised

information and the potential impact on affected individuals. Breaches involving sensitive personal information, for example, social security numbers, financial data, or health records, require swift action. Notifications must be issued as soon as possible but no later than 30 days after the breach has been identified unless law enforcement needs or national security concerns justify a delay.
- **Content of Notification:** Notifications must be comprehensive, providing a clear description of the breach, including what happened, the types of personal information that were compromised, and when the breach occurred. They should also outline the steps the agency is taking to address the breach and prevent future incidents. Crucially, notifications must guide individuals in protecting themselves, including advice on monitoring credit reports, changing passwords, engaging with identity theft prevention services, and securing personal information.
- **Modes of Notification:** Agencies are required to select the most effective means of notification based on the breach's circumstances and the information available about affected parties. This may include direct notification methods such as email, postal mail, or phone calls, or, in cases where individual contact information is unavailable, broader methods such as public announcements or media releases may be used.
- **Role of Government Entities in Breach Response:** FISMA delineates roles for various government entities in breach response, emphasizing a coordinated approach to managing and mitigating breaches. OMB, DHS, and NIST each have defined responsibilities, from overseeing the implementation of policies to providing technical

assistance and setting standards for cybersecurity and breach response.
- **Reporting Requirements:** Agencies must report breaches to the appropriate authorities, including the DHS's US-CERT, on time. This immediate reporting facilitates a quick government-wide response to mitigate the breach's impact. Additionally, agencies must include breach information in their annual FISMA reports to Congress, providing transparency about their cybersecurity posture and efforts to manage breach risks.

## Roles of Different Government Entities in Breach Response

As mentioned above, FISMA 2014 assigns specific roles to different government entities to ensure a coordinated and effective response to data breaches. These roles mobilize resources, expertise, and authority to efficiently manage and mitigate the consequences of breaches. Below is an elaboration on the roles of key government entities involved in breach response:

- **Office of Management and Budget:** OMB is responsible for issuing guidelines and directives that align with FISMA 2014's objectives, ensuring that agencies have a consistent framework for responding to data breaches. OMB evaluates agency reports on data breaches to monitor compliance and effectiveness, making recommendations for improvements as needed. OMB also coordinates with DHS to ensure policies are effectively implemented across the federal landscape.
- **Department of Homeland Security (DHS):** DHS is tasked with a leading role in the federal government's operational response to cybersecurity incidents, including

data breaches. Through the National Cybersecurity and Communications Integration Center (NCCIC), DHS provides federal agencies with real-time monitoring, incident response, and technical assistance. It is a central hub for disseminating information on threats and vulnerabilities and coordinates the national response to significant cyber incidents. The DHS also works closely with the Federal Information Security Incident Center (FISIC) to enhance the nation's cybersecurity posture.

- **National Institute of Standards and Technology (NIST):** NIST plays a foundational role in shaping the standards and guidelines that underpin the security of federal information systems, including responses to data breaches. It develops comprehensive frameworks, such as the NIST Cybersecurity Framework, which agencies use to manage and mitigate cybersecurity risks. NIST's guidelines on incident response (e.g., NIST Special Publication 800-61) provide a structured approach to detecting, analyzing, containing, and eradicating cyber threats and recovering from incidents.
- **Individual Federal Agencies:** Each agency is directly responsible for preparing incident response plans, establishing communication protocols for breaches, conducting risk assessments, and executing response and recovery actions. Agencies are also tasked with reporting breaches to the appropriate authorities, including the DHS, OMB, and Congress, in line with established protocols.
- **United States Computer Emergency Readiness Team (US-CERT):** US-CERT plays a crucial role in providing timely and actionable information to federal agencies, state and local governments, and the public to address cybersecurity issues and incidents. It offers technical

expertise in analyzing cybersecurity threats, disseminating alerts and warnings, and coordinating the national response to significant cyber incidents.

# Reporting Requirements to Congress and Other Authorities

FISMA mandates reporting requirements regarding data breaches. These requirements not only mandate the timely sharing of information about breaches and cybersecurity incidents but also enforce a structured process for evaluating and improving federal information security practices. These include immediate and annual reporting:

## *Immediate Reporting*

Federal agencies must report the breach immediately to US-CERT upon detecting a data breach or cybersecurity incident. This immediate notification serves several purposes:

- **Rapid Response and Mitigation:** Facilitates a swift federal response to contain and mitigate the breach, leveraging DHS's resources and expertise in cybersecurity.
- **Information Sharing:** Ensures that relevant information about the breach is quickly disseminated across government entities, allowing for a coordinated response and helping other agencies to guard against similar threats.

The immediacy of this reporting is crucial for national security and the protection of sensitive information, emphasizing the need for agencies to have robust detection and notification protocols in place.

## *Annual Reporting*

FISMA 2014 requires that each federal agency submit an annual report to Congress, OMB, and DHS. This report must include:

- Summary of Incidents: A comprehensive summary of information security incidents, including data breaches, categorized by impact level, type of information compromised, and response actions taken.
- Effectiveness of Agency Information Security Practices: An evaluation of the agency's information security practices, highlighting successes and areas for improvement.
- Progress and Compliance: An assessment of the agency's progress towards compliance with FISMA requirements, including the implementation of information security policies, procedures, and standards.

This annual report provides a transparent overview of federal cybersecurity health, facilitating oversight and driving improvements in information security policies and practices.

# CHAPTER 8

# CONTINUOUS DIAGNOSTICS AND MITIGATION

The Continuous Diagnostics and Mitigation (CDM) program, under the auspices of the Cybersecurity and Infrastructure Security Agency (CISA), is a vital component of the broader cybersecurity framework established by FISMA. This integration underscores FISMA's role in fortifying government cybersecurity efforts by advancing and implementing security tools and practices. The CDM program is designed to equip federal agencies with the capabilities to continuously monitor and secure their digital environments against an evolving cyber threat landscape. By aligning with FISMA's principles for continuous monitoring and risk management, the CDM program ensures that agencies can identify vulnerabilities, mitigate risks promptly, and enhance the resilience of government information systems. This proactive approach is instrumental in safeguarding the nation's critical infrastructure and sensitive data from emerging cyber threats, emphasizing the importance of adaptability and vigilance in federal cybersecurity initiatives.

## Implementation of Advanced Security Tools

The Continuous Diagnostics and Mitigation program of CISA implements advanced security tools. This initiative aims to provide federal agencies with the capabilities to continuously monitor and secure their digital environments against evolving cyber threats.

## Key Components of Advanced Security Tools

- **Automated Vulnerability Management:** These tools scan systems and networks for vulnerabilities, using databases of known issues to identify potential security weaknesses. By automating this process, agencies can quickly identify and remediate vulnerabilities before attackers exploit them.
- **Intrusion Detection and Prevention Systems (IDPS):** IDPS tools monitor network and system traffic for suspicious activities that may indicate a cyberattack. These systems use a combination of signature-based detection (to catch known threats) and anomaly-based detection (to identify new or unusual patterns of behavior to alert security personnel to potential breaches.
- **Identity and Access Management (IAM):** IAM tools ensure that only authorized individuals can access sensitive information, enforcing policies for user authentication, authorization, and audit. This includes multi-factor authentication, role-based access control, and monitoring user activities within federal systems.
- **Data Encryption:** Encryption tools protect data at rest and in transit, ensuring that sensitive information remains confidential and is only accessible to authorized users. Strong encryption prevents data breaches and ensures the integrity of government communications and records.
- **Security Information and Event Management (SIEM):** SIEM tools aggregate and analyze log and event data from across an organization's IT environment to identify patterns that may indicate a cybersecurity threat. This centralized view allows quicker detection, investigation, and response to potential security incidents.

## Challenges and Considerations

Implementing these advanced security tools across diverse and complex federal IT environments presents several challenges, for example, ensuring the interoperability and compatibility of these tools with existing systems and technologies. Agencies must carefully integrate new security solutions with their current infrastructure to avoid creating new vulnerabilities or operational inefficiencies.

Agencies must also prepare to manage the sheer volume of data generated by these tools by organizing expertise and resources to analyze this data effectively and distinguish between false positives and genuine security threats.

## Strategic Implementation for Enhanced Security

The strategic implementation of these advanced security tools requires a comprehensive approach that includes policy development, workforce training, and establishing processes for ongoing monitoring and response. Agencies must develop clear policies for using these tools, ensuring that they align with federal guidelines and contribute to the overarching goals of the CDM program.

Personnel must be trained to leverage these tools effectively, both on the operation of the tools themselves and on broader cybersecurity best practices and incident response protocols.

Implementation of advanced security tools is an ongoing process that requires continuous evaluation and adaptation. As cyber threats evolve, so must the tools and strategies used to combat them. Agencies must remain vigilant, regularly assessing the effectiveness of their security tools and adapting their cybersecurity strategies to address emerging threats and vulnerabilities.

# OMB's Role in Assessing Agency Adoption of

# Security Technologies

OMB also plays a role in assessing agency adoption of security technologies and ensuring their effective utilization.

## Enhanced Oversight and Policy Guidance

OMB's role includes enhanced oversight and the provision of comprehensive policy guidance. By dictating specific cybersecurity practices and benchmarks, OMB ensures that all federal agencies align with a unified standard of security measures.

## Strategic Resource Allocation

OMB also oversees the strategic allocation of resources toward cybersecurity initiatives. This includes ensuring federal agencies can access and appropriately invest in the most effective and advanced security technologies. OMB reviews agency budget proposals, advocating for sufficient funding for cybersecurity measures and technologies that facilitate the CDM program's goals.

## Evaluation and Compliance

OMB is responsible for evaluating how federal agencies adopt and integrate advanced security technologies by reviewing agencies' cybersecurity policies, practices, and architectures to ensure they effectively incorporate the CDM program's tools and methodologies. OMB assesses compliance through various mechanisms, including but not limited to audits, reviews, and reporting systems that agencies must adhere to.

## Feedback and Continuous Improvement

OMB also provides agency feedback based on assessments, audits, and performance metrics. This feedback aims to drive continuous improvement in cybersecurity practices. OMB identifies gaps in agencies' cybersecurity defenses and recommends enhancements or adjustments to align with federal cybersecurity standards and objectives.

## Collaboration with DHS and Other Stakeholders

OMB collaborates closely with DHS, which administers the CDM program. This collaboration involves coordinating policy development, sharing best practices, and synchronizing efforts to address common challenges. OMB also engages with other stakeholders, including cybersecurity experts and industry leaders, to incorporate innovative practices and technologies into federal cybersecurity strategies.

# CHAPTER 9

# LEGAL AND REGULATORY IMPLICATIONS

This chapter outlines FISMA 2014's broad impact on enhancing risk management, reinforcing agency accountability, introducing continuous monitoring, fostering collaboration, and revising compliance mechanisms. It shifted the cybersecurity framework from a checklist mentality to a dynamic, continuous assessment model, placing direct accountability on agency heads for the security of their systems. By emphasizing real-time monitoring and information sharing within and beyond federal agencies, FISMA 2014 significantly improved the government's responsiveness to cyber threats. Additionally, it led to key amendments in related legislation and policies, including updates to NIST guidelines and the integration with acts like the Cybersecurity Enhancement Act of 2014, ensuring a cohesive approach to federal cybersecurity. This chapter provides a concise overview of how FISMA 2014 has reshaped federal information security practices and policies, setting a new standard for a flexible, effective cybersecurity posture.

## Impact on Existing Laws and Information Security Practices

### Enhanced Risk Management Focus

Before the enactment of FISMA 2014, federal information security was primarily driven by compliance with FISMA 2002, with a set of prescribed standards and procedures. This approach, while structured, often resulted in a checkbox mentality, where agencies were more focused on meeting specific compliance requirements rather than addressing the underlying cybersecurity risks or having a broader, holistic view of security. FISMA 2014 shifted this mentality to a risk management approach, emphasizing continuous assessment and mitigation.

## Strengthening Agency Accountability

FISMA 2014 placed a renewed emphasis on the accountability of agency heads in ensuring the security of their information systems. This marked a departure from previous practices, where responsibility could be more diffused. FISMA 2014 made it clear that agency leaders are directly responsible for implementing effective information security practices, conducting annual reviews, and reporting on the security status of their information systems.

## Integration of Continuous Monitoring

One of the most significant impacts of FISMA 2014 on information security practices was the introduction and emphasis on continuous monitoring of information systems. Instead of periodic assessments, agencies must implement real-time or near-real-time monitoring to detect, report, and respond to security incidents. This approach allows for a more agile response to threats and vulnerabilities, ensuring that security postures are adaptable to the rapidly changing cyber landscape.

## Collaboration and Information Sharing

FISMA 2014 also underscored the importance of collaboration and information sharing between federal agencies and other stakeholders, including the private sector. By fostering an environment where threats, vulnerabilities, and strategies are openly shared, FISMA 2014 has led to the development of stronger, better resources and tools.

## Revising Compliance and Reporting Mechanisms

Under FISMA 2014, the mechanisms for compliance and reporting were also revised to reflect the risk management approach more. This introduced more flexible, performance-based metrics for evaluating the effectiveness of information security programs. This allowed for a more nuanced assessment of an agency's security posture and encouraged adopting best practices tailored to specific risk profiles.

# Amendments to Other Related Acts and Policies

The enactment of FISMA 2014 brought additional legislative and policy modifications to ensure that federal cybersecurity policies were comprehensive and cohesive with FISMA 2014.

The amendments made in the wake of FISMA 2014 spanned several related acts and policies, reinforcing the act's objectives and ensuring a unified approach to federal cybersecurity:

## National Institute of Standards and Technology (NIST) Guidelines:

- Comprehensive NIST Update: Following FISMA 2014, NIST undertook a comprehensive review and update of its cybersecurity guidelines and standards. This aimed to align its publications with the new risk management and continuous monitoring paradigms introduced by FISMA 2014. For example, NIST Special Publication 800-37, Guide for Applying the Risk Management Framework to Federal Information Systems, was updated to incorporate the latest risk management strategies, emphasizing flexibility, effectiveness, and efficiency in cybersecurity efforts.

- Enhanced Cybersecurity Framework: NIST refined its Cybersecurity Framework to provide a more actionable guide for federal agencies. This included clearer guidance on implementing the framework's core functions – Identify, Protect, Detect, Respond, and Recover – within the context of FISMA 2014's requirements.

## *Integration with the Cybersecurity Enhancement Act of 2014:*

The Cybersecurity Enhancement Act of 2014, passed in the same legislative session as FISMA 2014, aimed to improve cybersecurity across the federal government through public-private partnerships and improved cybersecurity research and development. Amendments ensured that the goals of both acts were aligned, particularly in areas such as cybersecurity R&D, workforce development, and information sharing.

## *Revisions to the Clinger-Cohen Act:*

The Clinger-Cohen Act 1996 established a framework for managing information technology within the federal government. FISMA 2014 amendments to this act emphasized the need to incorporate information security as a critical component of IT management, ensuring that cybersecurity considerations are integrated into the lifecycle of federal information systems.

## *Updates to the Privacy Act of 1974:*

Recognizing the intertwined nature of privacy and information security, FISMA 2014 led to revisions in the Privacy Act of 1974 to ensure that privacy impact assessments are conducted with security risk assessments. This ensures that agencies consider their information systems' security and privacy implications, fostering a more holistic approach to protecting sensitive federal information.

## *Alignment with the Homeland Security Act of 2002:*

The Homeland Security Act established DHS in 2002 with a broad mandate, including cybersecurity. FISMA 2014 amendments further clarified and strengthened the role of DHS in overseeing the implementation of federal cybersecurity practices, emphasizing the department's central role in coordinating federal cybersecurity initiatives and responses.

# ORIGINAL TEXT OF THE ACT

An act is a statute or law passed by a legislative body. Both FISMA 2002 and its amendment were passed by the United States Congress. These Acts are structured in a hierarchical manner to organize their provisions clearly and logically. Here's a breakdown of its components:

## Title

A "Title" in legislative documents serves as a major division of the act, grouping together a set of related sections that deal with a broad area of the law. Titles are usually numbered (e.g., TITLE I, TITLE II) and given a descriptive name that summarizes the theme or focus of the sections within it. For example, in FISMA 2002, TITLE I is named "OFFICE OF MANAGEMENT AND BUDGET ELECTRONIC GOVERNMENT SERVICES" and focuses on the management and promotion of electronic government services under the oversight of the Office of Management and Budget.

## SECTION

A "SECTION" (often stylized as "Sec." in legislative texts) refers to a specific provision within the act. Each section is numbered (e.g., Sec. 101, Sec. 102) and contains a particular piece of legislation detailing specific actions, requirements, definitions, or regulations. Sections are used to break down the law into digestible, focused components that address individual aspects of the law's overall intent. For instance, Sec. 101 under TITLE I discusses "Management and promotion of electronic government services."

## *SEC*

"SEC" is simply another way to reference a section within the act. There is no difference between "SEC" and "SECTION" in terms of their function or purpose in the document; both denote individual provisions or clauses of the legislation. The use of "SEC" versus "SECTION" might vary due to drafting style, typographical preferences, or historical convention, but their meaning and use in the context of legislative documents are identical.

The act starts with a preamble that outlines its purpose, followed by the short title and table of contents. Then, it is divided into titles that broadly categorize the law's different areas of focus. Within each title, sections (Sec.) detail specific requirements, definitions, or regulations related to the title's overarching theme. This structure allows the act to cover a wide range of topics in an organized manner, making it easier for readers to find specific information within the legislation.

## *Open Quotes, Notes, and Annotations*

The open quotes and annotations you see in the text of an act, such as in the section you provided from legislation related to the establishment of the Office of Electronic Government, are part of the legal drafting and publication style used for federal statutes. Here's a breakdown of why they are used and what they signify:

Open Quotes: The use of `` (double open quotes) at the beginning of a section or subsection indicates that the text following it is being added to an existing body of law or is a new insertion into the legal code. This convention helps readers and legal professionals identify new statutory language that has been enacted or amended.

Annotations: Annotations like `<<NOTE: Establishment. Government organization.>>` serve as editorial or explanatory notes. These are not part of the law itself but provide context, additional information, or guidance about the intent and implementation of the statute. They can denote the purpose of a section, clarify terms, or point out the statutory authority behind certain provisions.

`<<NOTE: Establishment. Government organization.>>`: This annotation clarifies that the section establishes a government organization.

`<<NOTE: President.>>`: This note indicates that the following provision involves an action or responsibility of the President, such as appointing an Administrator.

Legislative Purpose and Clarity: The use of such formatting and notes helps make the legal text more navigable and understandable, indicating where new laws begin, highlighting important structural elements, and providing quick references about the content and purpose of specific provisions.

**Legal Drafting Tradition:** These conventions are part of the broader tradition of legal drafting, which aims to ensure that laws are written clearly, systematically, and in a manner that can be effectively integrated into the existing legal framework. The precise formatting can vary depending on the jurisdiction and the specific publication, but similar practices are observed in legislative documents worldwide to enhance readability and interpretability.

# Public Law 107-347- FISMA 2002

**An Act**

To enhance the management and promotion of electronic Government services and processes by establishing a Federal Chief Information Officer within the Office of Management and Budget, and by establishing a broad framework of measures that require using Internet-based information technology to enhance citizen access to Government information and services, and for other purposes.

<<NOTE: Dec.17, 2002 - [H.R. 2458]>>

<<NOTE: E-Government Act of 2002.>>

*Be it enacted by the Senate and House of Representatives of the United States of America in Congress assembled,*

## SECTION 1. SHORT TITLE; TABLE OF CONTENTS.

(a) Short Title.—This Act may be cited as the
(b) Table of Contents.—The table of contents for this Act is as follows:

``E-Government Act of 2002''.

Sec. 1. Short title; table of contents.

Sec. 2. Findings and purposes.

**TITLE I—OFFICE OF MANAGEMENT AND BUDGET ELECTRONIC GOVERNMENT SERVICES**

Sec. 101. Management and promotion of electronic government services.

Sec. 102. Conforming amendments.

<<NOTE: 44 USC 101 note.>>

**TITLE II—FEDERAL MANAGEMENT AND PROMOTION OF ELECTRONIC GOVERNMENT SERVICES**

Sec. 201. Definitions.

Sec. 202. Federal agency responsibilities.

Sec. 203. Compatibility of executive agency methods for use and acceptance of electronic signatures.

Sec. 204. Federal Internet portal.

Sec. 205. Federal courts.

Sec. 206. Regulatory agencies.

Sec. 207. Accessibility, usability, and preservation of government information.

Sec. 208. Privacy provisions.

Sec. 209. Federal information technology workforce development.

Sec. 210. Share-in-savings initiatives.

Sec. 211. Authorization for acquisition of information technology by State and local governments through Federal supply schedules.

Sec. 212. Integrated reporting study and pilot projects.

Sec. 213. Community technology centers.

Sec. 214. Enhancing crisis management through advanced information technology.

Sec. 215. Disparities in access to the Internet.

Sec. 216. Common protocols for geographic information systems.

## TITLE III—INFORMATION SECURITY

Sec. 301. Information security.
Sec. 302. Management of information technology.
Sec. 303. National Institute of Standards and Technology.
Sec. 304. Information Security and Privacy Advisory Board.
Sec. 305. Technical and conforming amendments.

## TITLE IV—AUTHORIZATION OF APPROPRIATIONS AND EFFECTIVE DATES

Sec. 401. Authorization of appropriations.
Sec. 402. Effective dates.

# TITLE V—CONFIDENTIAL INFORMATION PROTECTION AND STATISTICAL EFFICIENCY

Sec. 501. Short title.
Sec. 502. Definitions.
Sec. 503. Coordination and oversight of policies.
Sec. 504. Effect on other laws.

**Subtitle A—Confidential Information Protection**

Sec. 511. Findings and purposes.
Sec. 512. Limitations on use and disclosure of data and information.
Sec. 513. Fines and penalties.

**Subtitle B—Statistical Efficiency**

Sec. 521. Findings and purposes.

Sec. 522. Designation of statistical agencies.

Sec. 523. Responsibilities of designated statistical agencies.

Sec. 524. Sharing of business data among designated statistical agencies.

Sec. 525. Limitations on use of business data provided by designated statistical agencies.

Sec. 526. Conforming amendments.

## SEC. 2 FINDINGS AND PURPOSES.

*(a) Findings.—Congress finds the following:*

1. The use of computers and the Internet is rapidly transforming societal interactions and the relationships among citizens, private businesses, and the Government.
2. The Federal Government has had uneven success in applying advances in information technology to enhance governmental

functions and services, achieve more efficient performance, increase access to Government information, and increase citizen participation in Government.

3. Most Internet-based services of the Federal Government are developed and presented separately, according to the jurisdictional boundaries of an individual department or agency, rather than being integrated cooperatively according to function or topic.
4. Internet-based Government services involving interagency cooperation are especially difficult to develop and promote, in part because of a lack of sufficient funding mechanisms to support such interagency cooperation.
5. Electronic Government has its impact through improved Government performance and outcomes within and across agencies.
6. Electronic Government is a critical element in the management of Government, to be implemented as part of a management framework that also addresses finance, procurement, human capital, and other challenges to improve the performance of Government.
7. To take full advantage of the improved Government performance that can be achieved through the use of Internet- based technology requires strong leadership, better organization, improved interagency collaboration, and more focused oversight of agency compliance with statutes related to information resource management.

*(b) Purposes.—The purposes of this Act are the following:*

1. *To provide effective leadership of Federal Government efforts to develop and promote electronic Government services and processes by establishing an Administrator of a new Office of Electronic Government within the Office of Management and Budget.*
2. *To promote use of the Internet and other information technologies*

to provide increased opportunities for citizen participation in Government.
3. To promote interagency collaboration in providing electronic Government services, where this collaboration would improve the service to citizens by integrating related functions, and in the use of internal electronic Government processes, where this collaboration would improve the efficiency and effectiveness of the processes.
4. To improve the ability of the Government to achieve agency missions and program performance goals.
5. To promote the use of the Internet and emerging technologies within and across Government agencies to provide citizen-centric Government information and services.
6. To reduce costs and burdens for businesses and other Government entities.
7. To promote better informed decision-making by policy makers.
8. To promote access to high-quality Government information and services across multiple channels.
9. To make the Federal Government more transparent and accountable.

1. To transform agency operations by utilizing, where appropriate, best practices from public and private sector
2. organizations.
3. To provide enhanced access to Government information and services in a manner consistent with laws regarding protection of personal privacy, national security, records retention, access for persons with disabilities, and other relevant laws.

**TITLE I—OFFICE OF MANAGEMENT AND BUDGET ELECTRONIC GOVERNMENT SERVICES**
**SEC. 101. MANAGEMENT AND PROMOTION OF ELECTRONIC**

## GOVERNMENT SERVICES.

(a) In General.—Title 44, United States Code, is amended by inserting after chapter 35 the following:

## ``CHAPTER 36—MANAGEMENT AND PROMOTION OF ELECTRONIC GOVERNMENT SERVICES
``Sec.

``3601. Definitions.

``3602. Office of Electronic Government.

``3603. Chief Information Officers Council.

``3604. E-Government Fund.

``3605. Program to encourage innovative solutions to enhance electronic Government services and processes.

``3606. E-Government report.

**``Sec. 3601. Definitions**

`` In this chapter, the definitions under section 3502 shall apply, and the term—

`` (1) `Administrator' means the Administrator of the Office of Electronic Government established under section 3602;

`` (2) `Council' means the Chief Information Officers Council established under section 3603;

`` (3) `electronic Government' means the use by the Government of web-based Internet applications and other information technologies, combined with processes that implement these technologies, to—

``(A) enhance the access to and delivery of Government information and services to the public, other agencies, and other Government entities; or

``(B) bring about improvements in Government operations that may include effectiveness, efficiency, service quality, or transformation;

`` (4) `enterprise architecture'—

`` (A) means—

`` (i) a strategic information asset base, which defines the mission;

`` (ii) the information necessary to perform the mission;

`` (iii) the technologies necessary to perform the mission; and

`` (iv) the transitional processes for implementing new technologies in response to changing mission needs; and

`` (B) includes—

`` (i) a baseline architecture;

`` (ii) a target architecture; and

`` (iii) a sequencing plan;

`` (5) `Fund' means the E-Government Fund established under section 3604;

`` (6) `interoperability' means the ability of different operating and software systems, applications, and services to communicate and exchange data in an accurate, effective, and consistent manner;

`` (7) `integrated service delivery' means the provision of Internet-based Federal Government information or services integrated according to function or topic rather than separated according to the boundaries of agency jurisdiction; and

`` (8) `tribal government' means—

`` (A) the governing body of any Indian tribe, band, nation, or other organized group or community located in the continental United States (excluding the State of Alaska) that is recognized as eligible for the special programs and services provided by the United States to Indians because of their status as Indians, and

``(B) any Alaska Native regional or village corporation established pursuant to the Alaska Native Claims Settlement Act (43 U.S.C. 1601 et seq.).

``**Sec. 3602. Office of Electronic Government**

``(a) <<NOTE: Establishment. Government organization.>> There is established in the Office of Management and Budget an Office of Electronic Government.

``(b) <<NOTE: President.>> There shall be at the head of the Office an Administrator who shall be appointed by the President.

``(c) The Administrator shall assist the Director in carrying out—

`` (1) all functions under this chapter;

`` (2) all of the functions assigned to the Director under title II of the E-Government Act of 2002; and

`` (3) other electronic government initiatives, consistent with other statutes.

``(d) The Administrator shall assist the Director and the Deputy Director for Management and work with the Administrator of the Office of Information and Regulatory Affairs in setting strategic direction for implementing electronic Government, under relevant statutes, including—

`` (1) chapter 35;
`` (2) subtitle III of title 40, United States Code;
`` (3) section 552a of title 5 (commonly referred to as the` Privacy Act');
`` (4) the Government Paperwork Elimination Act (44 U.S.C. 3504 note); and
`` (5) the Federal Information Security Management Act of 2002.

``(e) The Administrator shall work with the Administrator of the Office of Information and Regulatory Affairs and with other offices within the Office of Management and Budget to oversee implementation of electronic Government under this chapter, chapter 35, the E-Government Act of 2002, and other relevant statutes, in a manner consistent with law, relating to—

``(1) capital planning and investment control for information technology;

``(2) the development of enterprise architectures;

``(3) information security;

``(4) privacy;

``(5) access to, dissemination of, and preservation of Government information;

``(6) accessibility of information technology for persons with disabilities; and

``(7) other areas of electronic Government.

``(f) Subject to requirements of this chapter, the Administrator shall assist the Director by performing electronic Government functions as follows:

``(1) Advise the Director on the resources required to develop and effectively administer electronic Government initiatives.

``(2) Recommend to the Director changes relating to Governmentwide strategies and priorities for electronic Government.

``(3) Provide overall leadership and direction to the executive branch on electronic Government.

``(4) Promote innovative uses of information technology by agencies, particularly initiatives involving multiagency collaboration, through support of pilot projects, research, experimentation, and the use of innovative technologies.

``(5) Oversee the distribution of funds from, and ensure appropriate administration and coordination of, the E-Government Fund established under section 3604.

``(6) Coordinate with the Administrator of General Services regarding programs undertaken by the General Services Administration to promote electronic government and the efficient use of information technologies by agencies.

``(7) Lead the activities of the Chief Information Officers Council established under section 3603 on behalf of the Deputy Director for Management, who shall chair the council.

``(8) Assist the Director in establishing policies which shall set the framework for information technology standards for the Federal Government developed by the National Institute of Standards and Technology and promulgated by the Secretary of Commerce under section 11331 of title 40, taking into account, if appropriate, recommendations of the Chief Information Officers Council, experts, and interested parties from the private and nonprofit sectors and State, local, and tribal governments, and maximizing the use of commercial standards as appropriate, including the following:

``(A) Standards and guidelines for interconnectivity and interoperability as described under section 3504.

``(B) Consistent with the process under section 207(d) of the E-Government Act of 2002, standards and guidelines for categorizing Federal Government electronic information to enable efficient use of technologies, such as through the use of extensible markup language.

``(C) Standards and guidelines for Federal Government computer system efficiency and security.

``(9) Sponsor ongoing dialogue that—

``(A) shall be conducted among Federal, State, local, and tribal government leaders on electronic Government in the executive, legislative, and judicial branches, as well as leaders in the private and nonprofit sectors, to encourage collaboration and enhance understanding of best practices and innovative approaches in acquiring, using, and managing information resources;

``(B) is intended to improve the performance of governments in collaborating on the use of information technology to improve the delivery of Government information and services; and

``(C) may include—

``(i) development of innovative models—

``(I) for electronic Government management and Government information technology contracts; and

``(II) that may be developed through focused discussions or using separately sponsored research;

``(ii) identification of opportunities for public-private collaboration in using Internet- based technology to increase the efficiency of Government-to-business transactions;

``(iii) identification of mechanisms for providing incentives to program managers and other Government employees to develop and implement innovative uses of information technologies; and

``(iv) identification of opportunities for public, private, and intergovernmental collaboration in addressing the disparities in access to the Internet and information technology.

`` (10) Sponsor activities to engage the general public in the development and implementation of policies and programs, particularly activities aimed at fulfilling the goal of using the most effective citizen-centered strategies and those activities which engage multiple agencies providing similar or related information and services.

`` (11) Oversee the work of the General Services Administration and other agencies in developing the integrated Internet-based system under section 204 of the E-Government Act of 2002.

`` (12) Coordinate with the Administrator for Federal Procurement Policy to ensure effective implementation of electronic procurement initiatives.

`` (13) Assist Federal agencies, including the General Services Administration, the Department of Justice, and the United States Access Board in—

``(A) implementing accessibility standards under section 508 of the Rehabilitation Act of 1973 (29 U.S.C. 794d); and

``(B) ensuring compliance with those standards through the budget review process and other means.

`` (14) Oversee the development of enterprise architectures within and across agencies.

`` (15) Assist the Director and the Deputy Director for Management in overseeing agency efforts to ensure that electronic Government activities incorporate adequate, risk- based, and cost-effective security compatible with business processes.

`` (16) Administer the Office of Electronic Government established under this section.

`` (17) Assist the Director in preparing the E-Government report established under section 3606.

``(g) The Director shall ensure that the Office of Management and Budget, including the Office of Electronic Government, the Office of Information and Regulatory Affairs, and other relevant offices, have adequate staff and resources to properly fulfill all functions under the E-Government Act of 2002.

``Sec. 3603. Chief Information Officers Council

``(a) <<NOTE: Establishment.>> There is established in the executive branch a Chief Information Officers Council.

``(b) The members of the Council shall be as follows:

`` (1) The Deputy Director for Management of the Office of Management and Budget, who shall act as chairperson of the Council.

`` (2) The Administrator of the Office of Electronic Government.

`` (3) The Administrator of the Office of Information and Regulatory Affairs.

`` (4) The chief information officer of each agency described under section 901(b) of title 31.

``(5) The chief information officer of the Central Intelligence Agency.

``(6) The chief information officer of the Department of the Army, the Department of the Navy, and the Department of the Air

Force, if chief information officers have been designated for such departments under section 3506(a)(2)(B).

``(7) Any other officer or employee of the United States designated by the chairperson.

``(c)(1) The Administrator of the Office of Electronic Government shall lead the activities of the Council on behalf of the Deputy Director for Management.

``(2)(A) The Vice Chairman of the Council shall be selected by the Council from among its members.

``(B) The Vice Chairman shall serve a 1-year term, and may serve multiple terms.

``(3) The Administrator of General Services shall provide administrative and other support for the Council.

``(d) The Council is designated the principal interagency forum for improving agency practices related to the design, acquisition, development, modernization, use, operation, sharing, and performance of Federal Government information resources.

``(e) In performing its duties, the Council shall consult regularly with representatives of State, local, and tribal governments.

``(f) The Council shall perform functions that include the following:

``(1) Develop recommendations for the Director on Government information resources management policies and requirements.

``(2) Share experiences, ideas, best practices, and innovative approaches related to information resources management.

''(3) Assist the Administrator in the identification, development, and coordination of multiagency projects and other innovative initiatives to improve Government performance through the use of information technology.

''(4) Promote the development and use of common performance measures for agency information resources management under this chapter and title II of the E-Government Act of 2002.

''(5) Work as appropriate with the National Institute of Standards and Technology and the Administrator to develop recommendations on information technology standards developed under section 20 of the National Institute of Standards and Technology Act (15 U.S.C. 278g-3) and promulgated under section 11331 of title 40, and maximize the use of commercial standards as appropriate, including the following:

''(A) Standards and guidelines for interconnectivity and interoperability as described under section 3504.

''(B) Consistent with the process under section 207(d) of the E-Government Act of 2002, standards and guidelines for categorizing Federal Government electronic information to enable efficient use of technologies, such as through the use of extensible markup language.

''(C) Standards and guidelines for Federal Government computer system efficiency and security.

''(6) Work with the Office of Personnel Management to assess and address the hiring, training, classification, and professional development needs of the Government related to information resources management.

''(7) Work with the Archivist of the United States to assess how the Federal Records Act can be addressed effectively by Federal information resources management activities.

''Sec. 3604. E-Government Fund

''(a)(1) There is established in the Treasury of the United States the E-Government Fund.

``(2) The Fund shall be administered by the Administrator of the General Services Administration to support projects approved by the Director, assisted by the Administrator of the Office of Electronic Government, that enable the Federal Government to expand its ability, through the development and implementation of innovative uses of the Internet or other electronic methods, to conduct activities electronically.

``(3) Projects under this subsection may include efforts to—

``(A) make Federal Government information and services more readily available to members of the public (including individuals, businesses, grantees, and State and local governments);

``(B) make it easier for the public to apply for benefits, receive services, pursue business opportunities, submit information, and otherwise conduct transactions with the Federal Government; and

``(C) enable Federal agencies to take advantage of information technology in sharing information and conducting transactions with each other and with State and local governments.

``(b)(1) The Administrator shall—

``(A) <<NOTE: Procedures.>> establish procedures for accepting and reviewing proposals for funding;

``(B) consult with interagency councils, including the Chief Information Officers Council, the Chief Financial Officers Council, and other interagency management councils, in establishing procedures and reviewing proposals; and

``(C) assist the Director in coordinating resources that agencies receive from the Fund with other resources available to agencies for similar purposes.

``(2) **When reviewing proposals and managing the Fund, the** Administrator shall observe and incorporate the following procedures:

``(A) A project requiring substantial involvement or funding from an agency shall be approved by a senior official with agency wide authority on behalf of the head of the agency, who shall report directly to the head of the agency.

``(B) Projects shall adhere to fundamental capital planning and investment control processes.

``(C) Agencies shall identify in their proposals resource commitments from the agencies involved and how these resources would be coordinated with support from the Fund, and include plans for potential continuation of projects after all funds made available from the Fund are expended.

``(D) After considering the recommendations of the interagency councils, the Director, assisted by the Administrator, shall have final authority to determine which of the candidate projects shall be funded from the Fund.

``(E) Agencies shall assess the results of funded projects.

``(c) **In determining which proposals to recommend for funding, the Administrator—**

``(1) shall consider criteria that include whether a proposal—

``(A) identifies the group to be served, including citizens, businesses, the Federal Government, or other governments;

``(B) indicates what service or information the project will provide that meets needs of groups identified under subparagraph (A);

``(C) ensures proper security and protects privacy;

``(D) is interagency in scope, including projects implemented by a primary or single agency that—

``(i) could confer benefits on multiple agencies; and

``(ii) have the support of other agencies; and

``(E) has performance objectives that tie to agency missions and strategic goals, and interim results that relate to the objectives; and

``(2) may also rank proposals based on criteria that include whether a proposal—

``(A) has Governmentwide application or implications;

``(B) has demonstrated support by the public to be served;

``(C) integrates Federal with State, local, or tribal approaches to service delivery;

``(D) identifies resource commitments from nongovernmental sectors;

``(E) identifies resource commitments from the agencies involved;

``(F) uses web-based technologies to achieve objectives;

``(G) identifies records management and records access strategies;

``(H) supports more effective citizen participation in and interaction with agency activities that further progress toward a more citizen-centered Government;

``(I) directly delivers Government information and services to the public or provides the infrastructure for delivery;

``(J) supports integrated service delivery;

``(K) describes how business processes across agencies will reflect appropriate transformation simultaneous to technology implementation; and

``(L) is new or innovative and does not supplant existing funding streams within agencies.

``(d) The Fund may be used to fund the integrated Internet-based system under section 204 of the E-Government Act of 2002.**

``(e) <<NOTE: Notification.>> None of the funds provided from the Fund may be transferred to any agency until 15 days after the Administrator of the General Services Administration has submitted to the Committees on Appropriations of the Senate and the House of Representatives, the Committee on Governmental Affairs of the

Senate, the Committee on Government Reform of the House of Representatives, and the appropriate authorizing committees of the Senate and the House of Representatives, a notification and description of how the funds are to be allocated and how the expenditure will further the purposes of this chapter.

``(f)(1) <<NOTE: Reports.>> The Director shall report annually to Congress on the operation of the Fund, through the report established under section 3606.

``(2) The report under paragraph (1) shall describe—

``(A) all projects which the Director has approved for funding from the Fund; and

``(B) the results that have been achieved to date for these funded projects.

``(g)(1) **There are authorized to be appropriated to the Fund—**

``(A) $45,000,000 for fiscal year 2003;
``(B) $50,000,000 for fiscal year 2004;
``(C) $100,000,000 for fiscal year 2005;
``(D) $150,000,000 for fiscal year 2006; and
``(E) such sums as are necessary for fiscal year 2007.

``(2) Funds appropriated under this subsection shall remain available until expended.

``Sec. 3605. Program to encourage innovative solutions to enhance electronic Government services and processes

``(a) Establishment of Program.—The Administrator shall establish and promote a Governmentwide program to encourage contractor innovation and excellence in facilitating the development and enhancement of electronic Government services and processes.

``(b) Issuance of Announcements Seeking Innovative Solutions.—Under the program, the Administrator, in consultation with the Council and the Administrator for Federal Procurement Policy, shall issue announcements seeking unique and innovative solutions to facilitate the development and enhancement of electronic Government services and processes.

``(c) Multiagency Technical Assistance Team.—(1) The Administrator, in consultation with the Council and the Administrator for Federal Procurement Policy, shall convene a multiagency technical assistance team to assist in screening proposals submitted to the Administrator to provide unique and innovative solutions to facilitate the development and enhancement of electronic Government services and processes. The team shall be composed of employees of the agencies represented on the Council who have expertise in scientific and technical disciplines that would facilitate the assessment of the feasibility of the proposals.

``(2) The technical assistance team shall—

''(A) assess the feasibility, scientific and technical merits, and estimated cost of each proposal; and

''(B) submit each proposal, and the assessment of the proposal, to the Administrator.

''(3) The technical assistance team shall not consider or evaluate proposals submitted in response to a solicitation for offers for a pending procurement or for a specific agency requirement.

''(4) After receiving proposals and assessments from the technical assistance team, the Administrator shall consider recommending appropriate proposals for funding under the E-Government Fund established under section 3604 or, if appropriate, forward the proposal and the assessment of it to the executive agency whose mission most coincides with the subject matter of the proposal.

''**Sec. 3606. E-Government report**

''(a) <<NOTE: Deadline.>> Not later than March 1 of each year, the Director shall submit an E-Government status report to the Committee on Governmental Affairs of the Senate and the Committee on Government Reform of the House of Representatives.

''(b) The report under subsection (a) shall contain—

''(1) a summary of the information reported by agencies under section 202(f) of the E-Government Act of 2002;

''(2) the information required to be reported by section 3604(f); and

''(3) a description of compliance by the Federal Government with other goals and provisions of the E-Government Act of 2002.''.

(b) Technical and Conforming Amendment.—The table of chapters for title 44, United States Code, is amended by inserting after the item relating to chapter 35 the following:

''**36. Management and Promotion of Electronic Government Services.3601''.**

**SEC. 102. CONFORMING AMENDMENTS.**

(a) **Electronic Government and Information** Technologies.—

(1) In general.—Chapter 3 of title 40, United States Code, is amended by inserting after section 304 the following new section:

``Sec. 305. Electronic Government and information technologies ``The Administrator of General Services shall consult with the Administrator of the Office of Electronic Government on programs undertaken by the General Services Administration to promote electronic Government and the efficient use of information technologies by Federal agencies.''.

(2) Technical and conforming amendment.—The table of sections for chapter 3 of such title is amended by inserting after the item relating to section 304 the following:

``305. Electronic Government and information technologies.''.

**(b) Modification of Deputy Director for Management Functions.** –
Section 503(b) of title 31, United States Code, is amended—

1. by redesignating paragraphs (5), (6), (7), (8), and (9), as paragraphs (6), (7), (8), (9), and (10), respectively; and

(2) by inserting after paragraph (4) the following:

``(5) Chair the Chief Information Officers Council established under section 3603 of title 44.''.

**(c) Office of Electronic Government.—**

(1) In general.—Chapter 5 of title 31, United States Code, is amended by inserting after section 506 the following:

``Sec. 507. Office of Electronic Government ``The Office of Electronic Government, established under section 3602 of title 44, is an office in the Office of Management and Budget.''.

(2) Technical and conforming amendment.—The table of sections for chapter 5 of title 31, United States Code, is amended by inserting after the item relating to section 506 the following:

``507. Office of Electronic Government.''.

# CYBER LAW & FISMA COMPLIANCE

**TITLE II—FEDERAL MANAGEMENT AND PROMOTION OF ELECTRONIC GOVERNMENT SERVICES**

**SEC. 201. <<NOTE: 44 USC 3501 note.>> DEFINITIONS.**

Except as otherwise provided, in this title the definitions under sections 3502 and 3601 of title 44, United States Code, shall apply.

**SEC. 202. <<NOTE: 44 USC 3501 note.>> FEDERAL AGENCY RESPONSIBILITIES.**

(a) In General.—The head of each agency shall be responsible for—

(1) complying with the requirements of this Act (including the amendments made by this Act), the related information resource management policies and guidance established by the Director of the Office of Management and Budget, and the related information technology standards promulgated by the Secretary of Commerce;

(2) ensuring that the information resource management policies and guidance established under this Act by the Director, and the related information technology standards promulgated by the Secretary of Commerce are communicated promptly and effectively to all relevant officials within their agency; and

(3) supporting the efforts of the Director and the Administrator of the General Services Administration to develop, maintain, and promote an integrated Internet-based system of delivering Federal Government information and services to the public under section 204.

(b) Performance Integration.—

(1) Agencies shall develop performance measures that demonstrate how electronic government enables progress toward agency objectives, strategic goals, and statutory mandates.

(2) In measuring performance under this section, agencies shall rely on existing data collections to the extent practicable.

(3) Areas of performance measurement that agencies should consider include—

(A) customer service;

(B) agency productivity; and

(C) adoption of innovative information technology, including the appropriate use of commercial best practices.

(4) Agencies shall link their performance goals, as appropriate, to key groups, including citizens, businesses, and other governments, and to internal Federal Government operations.

(5) As appropriate, agencies shall work collectively in linking their performance goals to groups identified under paragraph (4) and shall use information technology in delivering Government information and services to those groups.

(c) Avoiding Diminished Access.—When promulgating policies and implementing programs regarding the provision of Government information and services over the Internet, agency heads shall consider the impact on persons without access to the Internet, and shall, to the extent practicable—

(1) ensure that the availability of Government information and services has not been diminished for individuals who lack access to the Internet; and

(2) pursue alternate modes of delivery that make Government information and services more accessible to individuals who do not own computers or lack access to the Internet.

(d) Accessibility to People with Disabilities.—All actions taken by Federal departments and agencies under this Act shall be in compliance with section 508 of the Rehabilitation Act of 1973 (29 U.S.C. 794d).

(e) Sponsored Activities.—Agencies shall sponsor activities that use information technology to engage the public in the development and implementation of policies and programs.

(f) Chief Information Officers.—The Chief Information Officer of each of the agencies designated under chapter 36 of title 44, United States Code (as added by this Act) shall be responsible for—

(1) participating in the functions of the Chief Information Officers Council; and

(2) monitoring the implementation, within their respective agencies, of information technology standards promulgated by the Secretary of Commerce, including common standards for interconnectivity and interoperability, categorization of Federal Government electronic information, and computer system efficiency and security.

(g) E-Government Status Report.—

(1) In general.—Each agency shall compile and submit to the Director an annual E-Government Status Report on—

(A) the status of the implementation by the agency of electronic government initiatives;

(B) compliance by the agency with this Act; and

(C) how electronic Government initiatives of the agency improve performance in delivering programs to constituencies.

(2) Submission.—Each agency shall submit an annual report under this subsection—

(A) to the Director at such time and in such manner as the Director requires;

(B) consistent with related reporting requirements; and

(C) which addresses any section in this title relevant to that agency.

(h) Use of Technology.—Nothing in this Act supersedes the responsibility of an agency to use or manage information technology to deliver Government information and services that fulfill the statutory mission and programs of the agency.

(i) **National Security Systems.**—

(1) Inapplicability.—Except as provided under paragraph (2), this title does not apply to national security systems as defined in section 11103 of title 40, United States Code. (2) Applicability.—This section, section 203, and section 214 do apply to national security systems to the extent practicable and consistent with law.

## SEC. 203. <<NOTE: 44 USC 3501 note.>> COMPATIBILITY OF EXECUTIVE AGENCY METHODS FOR USE AND ACCEPTANCE OF ELECTRONIC SIGNATURES.

(a) Purpose.—The purpose of this section is to achieve interoperable implementation of electronic signatures for appropriately secure electronic transactions with Government.

(b) Electronic Signatures.—In order to fulfill the objectives of the Government Paperwork Elimination Act (Public Law 105-277; 112 Stat. 2681-749 through 2681-751), each Executive agency (as defined under section 105 of title 5, nited States Code) shall ensure that its methods for use and acceptance of electronic signatures are compatible with the relevant policies and procedures issued by the Director.

(c) Authority for Electronic Signatures.—The Administrator of General Services shall support the Director by establishing a framework to allow efficient interoperability among Executive agencies when using electronic signatures, including processing of digital signatures.

(d) Authorization of Appropriations.—There are authorized to be appropriated to the General Services Administration, to ensure the development and operation of a Federal bridge certification authority for digital signature compatibility, and for other activities consistent with this section, $8,000,000 or such sums as are necessary in fiscal year 2003, and such sums as are necessary for each fiscal year thereafter.

## SEC. 204. <<NOTE: 44 USC 3501 note.>> FEDERAL INTERNET PORTAL.

(a) In General.—

   (1) Public access.—The Director shall work with the Administrator of the General Services Administration and other agencies to maintain and promote an integrated Internet-based system of providing the public with access to Government information and services.

   (2) Criteria.—To the extent practicable, the integrated system shall be designed and operated according to the following criteria:

   (A) The provision of Internet-based Government information and services directed to key groups, including citizens, business, and other governments, and integrated according to function or topic rather than separated according to the boundaries of agency jurisdiction.

(B) An ongoing effort to ensure that Internet-based Government services relevant to a given citizen activity are available from a single point.

(C) Access to Federal Government information and services consolidated, as appropriate, with Internet- based information and services provided by State, local, and tribal governments.

(D) Access to Federal Government information held by 1 or more agencies shall be made available in a manner that protects privacy, consistent with law.

(b) Authorization of Appropriations.—There are authorized to be appropriated to the General Services Administration $15,000,000 for the maintenance, improvement, and promotion of the integrated Internet-based system for fiscal year 2003, and such sums as are necessary for fiscal years 2004 through 2007.

SEC. 205. <<NOTE: 44 USC 3501 note.>> FEDERAL COURTS.

(a) Individual Court Websites.—The Chief Justice of the United States, the chief judge of each circuit and district and of the Court of Federal Claims, and the chief bankruptcy judge of each district shall cause to be established and maintained, for the court of which the judge is chief justice or judge, a website that contains the following information or links to websites with the following information:

(1) Location and contact information for the courthouse, including the telephone numbers and contact names for the clerk's office and justices' or judges' chambers.

(2) Local rules and standing or general orders of the court.

(3) Individual rules, if in existence, of each justice or judge in that court.

(4) Access to docket information for each case.

(5) Access to the substance of all written opinions issued by the court, regardless of whether such opinions are to be published in the official court reporter, in a text searchable format.

(6) Access to documents filed with the courthouse in electronic form, to the extent provided under subsection (c).

(7) Any other information (including forms in a format that can be downloaded) that the court determines useful to the public.

(b) Maintenance of Data Online.—

(1) Update of information.—The information and rules on each website shall be updated regularly and kept reasonably current.

(2) Closed cases.—Electronic files and docket information for cases closed for more than 1 year are not required to be made available online, except all written opinions with a date of issuance after the effective date of this section shall remain available online.

(c) Electronic Filings.—

(1) In <<NOTE: Public information.>> general.—Except as provided under paragraph (2) or in the rules prescribed under paragraph (3), each court shall make any document that is filed electronically publicly available online. A court may convert any document that is filed in paper form to electronic form. To the extent such conversions are made, all such electronic versions of the document shall be made available online.

(2) Exceptions.—Documents that are filed that are not otherwise available to the public, such as documents filed under seal, shall not be made available online.

(3) Privacy <<NOTE: Regulations.>> and security concerns.—

(A)(i) The Supreme Court shall prescribe rules, in accordance with sections 2072 and 2075 of title 28, United States Code, to protect privacy and security concerns relating to electronic filing of documents and the public availability under this subsection of documents filed electronically.

(ii) Such rules shall provide to the extent practicable for uniform treatment of privacy and security issues throughout the Federal courts.

(iii) Such rules shall take into consideration best practices in Federal and State courts to protect private information or otherwise maintain necessary information security.

(iv) To the extent that such rules provide for the redaction of certain categories of information in order to protect privacy and security concerns, such rules shall provide that a party that wishes to file an otherwise proper document containing such information may file an unredacted document under seal, which shall be retained by the court as part of the record, and which, at the discretion of the court and subject to any applicable rules issued in accordance with chapter 131 of title 28, United States Code, shall be either in lieu of, or in addition, to, a redacted copy in the public file.

(B)(i) Subject to clause (ii), the Judicial Conference of the United States may issue interim rules, and interpretive statements relating to the application of such rules, which conform to the requirements of this paragraph and which shall cease to have effect upon the effective date of the rules required under subparagraph (A).

(ii) Pending issuance of the rules required under subparagraph (A), any rule or order of any court, or of the Judicial Conference, providing for the redaction of certain categories of information in order to protect privacy and security concerns arising from electronic filing shall comply with, and be construed in conformity with, subparagraph (A)(iv).

(C) <<NOTE: Deadlines. Reports.>> Not later than 1 year after the rules prescribed under subparagraph (A) take effect, and every 2 years thereafter, the Judicial Conference shall submit to Congress a report on the adequacy of those rules to protect privacy and security.

(d) Dockets With Links to Documents.—The Judicial Conference of the United States shall explore the feasibility of technology to post online dockets with links allowing all filings, decisions, and rulings in each case to be obtained from the docket sheet of that case.

(e) Cost of Providing Electronic Docketing Information. —Section 303(a) of the Judiciary Appropriations Act, 1992 (28 U.S.C. 1913 note) is amended in the first sentence by striking ``shall hereafter'' and inserting ``may, only to the extent necessary,''.

(f) Time <<NOTE: Deadlines.>> Requirements.—Not later than 2 years after the effective date of this title, the websites under subsection(a) shall be established, except that access to documents filed in electronic form shall be established not later than 4 years after that effective date.

(g) Deferral.—

(1) In general.—

(A) Election.—

(i) Notification.—The Chief Justice of the United States, a chief judge, or chief bankruptcy judge may submit a notification to the Administrative Office of the United States Courts to defer compliance with any requirement of this section with respect to the Supreme Court, a court of appeals, district, or the bankruptcy court of a district.

(ii) Contents.—A notification submitted under this subparagraph shall state—

(I) the reasons for the deferral; and

(II) the online methods, if any, or any alternative methods, such court or district is using to provide greater public access to information.

(B) Exception.—To the extent that the Supreme Court, a court of appeals, district, or bankruptcy court of a district maintains a website under subsection (a), the Supreme Court or that court of appeals or district shall comply with subsection (b)(1).

(2) Report.—Not <<NOTE: Deadline.>> later than 1 year after the effective date of this title, and every year thereafter, the Judicial Conference of the United States shall submit a report to the Committees on Governmental Affairs and the Judiciary of the Senate and the Committees on Government Reform and the Judiciary of the House of Representatives that—

(A) contains all notifications submitted to the Administrative Office of the United States Courts under this subsection; and

(B) summarizes and evaluates all notifications.

## SEC. 206. <<NOTE: 44 USC 3501 note.>> REGULATORY AGENCIES.

(a) Purposes.—The purposes of this section are to—

(1) improve performance in the development and issuance of agency regulations by using information technology to increase access, accountability, and transparency; and

(2) enhance public participation in Government by electronic means, consistent with requirements under subchapter II of chapter 5 of title 5, United States Code, (commonly referred to as the ``Administrative Procedures Act'').

(b) Information Provided by Agencies Online.—To the extent practicable as determined by the agency in consultation with the Director, each agency (as defined under section 551 of title 5, United States Code) shall ensure that a publicly accessible Federal Government website includes all information about that agency required to be published in the Federal Register under paragraphs (1) and (2) of section 552(a) of title 5, United States Code.

(c) Submissions by Electronic Means.—To the extent practicable, agencies shall accept submissions under section 553(c) of title 5, United States Code, by electronic means.

(d) Electronic Docketing. –

(1) In general.—To the extent practicable, as determined by the agency in consultation with the Director, agencies shall ensure that a publicly accessible Federal Government website contains electronic dockets for rulemakings under section 553 of title 5, United States Code.

(2) Information available.—Agency electronic dockets shall make publicly available online to the extent practicable, as determined by the agency in consultation with the Director—

(A) all submissions under section 553(c) of title 5, United States Code; and

(B) other materials that by agency rule or practice are included in the rulemaking docket under section 553(c) of title 5, United States Code, whether or not submitted electronically.

(e) Time Limitation.—Agencies shall implement the requirements of this section consistent with a timetable established by the Director and reported to Congress in the first annual report under section 3606 of title 44 (as added by this Act).

**SEC. 207. <<NOTE: 44 USC 3501 note.>> ACCESSIBILITY, USABILITY, AND PRESERVATION OF GOVERNMENT INFORMATION.**

a. Purpose.—The purpose of this section is to improve the methods by which

Government information, including information on the Internet, is organized, preserved, and made accessible to the public.

b. Definitions.—In this section, the term—

1. ``Committee'' means the Interagency Committee on Government Information established under subsection (c); and
2. ``directory'' means a taxonomy of subjects linked to websites that—

   A. organizes Government information on the Internet according to subject matter; and
   B. may be created with the participation of human editors.
   C. Interagency Committee. –

(1) Establishment.—Not <<NOTE: Deadline.>> later than 180 days after the date of enactment of this title, the Director shall establish the Interagency Committee on Government Information.

(2) Membership.—The Committee shall be chaired by the Director or the designee of the Director and—

(A) shall include representatives from—

   i. the National Archives and Records Administration;
   ii. the offices of the Chief Information Officers from Federal agencies; and
   iii. other relevant officers from the executive branch; and

(B) may include representatives from the Federal legislative and judicial branches.

(3) Functions.—The Committee shall—

(A) engage in public consultation to the maximum extent feasible, including consultation with interested communities such as public advocacy organizations;

(B) conduct studies and submit recommendations, as provided under this section, to the Director and Congress; and

(C) share effective practices for access to, dissemination of, and retention of Federal information.

(4) Termination.—The Committee may be terminated on a date determined by the Director, except the Committee may not terminate before the Committee submits all recommendations required under this section.

(d) Categorizing of Information. –

1. Committee <<NOTE: Deadline.>> functions.—Not later than 2 years after the date of enactment of this Act, the Committee shall submit recommendations to the Director on—

(A) the adoption of standards, which are open to the maximum extent feasible, to enable the organization and categorization of Government information—

(i) in a way that is searchable electronically, including by searchable identifiers; and (ii) in ways that are interoperable across agencies;

(B) the definition of categories of Government information which should be classified under the standards; and

(C) determining priorities and developing schedules for the initial implementation of the standards by agencies.

1. Functions <<NOTE: Deadline. Policies.>> of the director.—Not later than 1 year after the submission of recommendations under paragraph (1), the Director shall issue policies—

(A) requiring that agencies use standards, which are open to the maximum extent feasible, to enable the organization and categorization of Government information—

(i) in a way that is searchable electronically, including by searchable identifiers;

(ii) in ways that are interoperable across agencies; and

(iii) that are, as appropriate, consistent with the provisions under section 3602(f)(8) of title 44, United States Code;

(B) defining categories of Government information which shall be required to be classified under the standards; and

(C) determining priorities and developing schedules for the initial implementation of the standards by agencies.

(3) Modification of policies.—After the submission of agency reports under paragraph (4), the Director shall modify the policies, as needed, in consultation with the Committee and interested parties.

(4) Agency <<NOTE: Reports.>> functions.—Each agency shall report annually to the Director, in the report established under section 202(g), on compliance of that agency with the policies issued under paragraph (2)(A).

(e) Public Access to Electronic Information. –

1. Committee <<NOTE: Deadline.>> functions.—Not later than 2 years after the date of enactment of this Act, the Committee shall submit recommendations to the Director and the Archivist of the United States on—

(A) the adoption by agencies of policies and procedures to ensure that chapters 21, 25, 27, 29, and 31 of title 44, United States Code, are applied effectively and comprehensively to Government information on the Internet and to other electronic records; and

(B) the imposition of timetables for the implementation of the policies and procedures by agencies.

(2) Functions <<NOTE: Deadline. Policies.>> of the archivist.—Not later than 1 year after the submission of recommendations by the Committee under paragraph (1), the Archivist of the United States shall issue policies—

(A) requiring the adoption by agencies of policies and procedures to ensure that chapters 21, 25, 27, 29, and 31 of title 44, United States Code, are applied effectively and comprehensively to Government information on the Internet and to other electronic records; and

(B) imposing timetables for the implementation of the policies, procedures, and technologies by agencies.

1. Modification of policies.—After the submission of agency reports under paragraph (4), the Archivist of the United States shall modify the policies, as needed, in consultation with the Committee and interested parties.

(4) Agency <<NOTE: Reports.>> functions.—Each agency shall report annually to the Director, in the report established under section 202(g), on compliance of that agency with the policies issued under paragraph (2)(A).

(f) Agency Websites.—

(1) Standards <<NOTE: Deadline. Guidelines.>> for agency websites.—Not later than 2 years after the effective date of this title, the Director shall promulgate guidance for agency websites that includes—

(A) requirements that websites include direct links to—

  i. descriptions of the mission and statutory authority of the agency;
  ii. information made available to the public under subsections (a)(1) and (b) of section 552 of title 5, United States Code (commonly referred to as the ``Freedom of Information Act");
  iii. information about the organizational structure of the agency; and
  iv. the strategic plan of the agency developed under section 306 of title 5, United States Code; and

(B) minimum agency goals to assist public users to navigate agency websites, including—

  i. speed of retrieval of search results;
  ii. the relevance of the results;
  iii. tools to aggregate and disaggregate
  iv. data; and

v. Security protocols to protect information.

(2) Agency <<NOTE: Deadline.>> requirements.—(A) Not later than 2 years after the date of enactment of this Act, each agency shall—

  i. consult with the Committee and solicit public comment;
  ii. establish a process for determining which Government information the agency intends to make available and accessible to the public on the Internet and by other means;
  iii. develop priorities and schedules for making Government information available and accessible;
  iv. make such final determinations, priorities, and schedules available for public comment;
  v. post such final determinations, priorities, and schedules on the Internet; and
  vi. Submit such final determinations, priorities, and schedules to the Director, in the report established under section 202(g).

(B) Each agency shall update determinations, priorities, and schedules of the agency, as needed, after consulting with the Committee and soliciting public comment, if appropriate.

  1. Public domain directory of public federal government websites. –

(A) Establishment.—Not <<NOTE: Deadline.>> later than 2 years after the effective date of this title, the Director and each agency shall—

(i) develop and establish a public domain directory of public Federal Government websites; and

(ii) Post the directory on the Internet with a link to the integrated Internet-based system established under section 204.

(B) Development.—With the assistance of each agency, the Director shall—

(i) direct the development of the directory through a collaborative effort, including input from—

(I) agency librarians;

(II) information technology managers;

(III) program managers;

(IV) records managers;

(V) Federal depository librarians; and

(VI) other interested parties; and

(ii) Develop a public domain taxonomy of subjects used to review and categorize public Federal Government websites.

(C) Update.—With the assistance of each agency, the Administrator of the Office of Electronic Government shall—

(i) <<NOTE: Deadline.>> update the directory as necessary, but not less than every 6 months; and

(ii) Solicit interested persons for improvements to the directory.

(g) Access to Federally Funded Research and Development. –

1. Development and maintenance of government wide repository and website. –

(A) Repository and website.—The Director of the Office of Management and Budget (or the Director's delegate), in consultation with the Director of the Office of Science and Technology Policy and other relevant agencies, shall ensure the development and maintenance of—

(i) a repository that fully integrates, to the maximum extent feasible, information about research and development funded by the Federal Government, and the repository shall—

(I) include information about research and development funded by the Federal Government, consistent with any relevant protections for the information under section 552 of title 5, United States Code, and performed by—

(aa) institutions not a part of the Federal Government, including State, local, and foreign governments; industrial firms; educational institutions; not-for-profit organizations; federally funded research and development centers; and private individuals; and

(bb) entities of the Federal Government, including research and development laboratories, centers, and offices; and

(II) integrate information about each separate research and development task or award, including—

(aa) the dates upon which the task or award is expected to start and end;

(bb) a brief summary describing the objective and the scientific and technical focus of the task or award;

(cc) the entity or institution performing the task or award and its contact information;

(dd) the total amount of Federal funds expected to be provided to the task or award over its lifetime and the amount of funds expected to be provided in each fiscal year in which the work of the task or award is ongoing;

(ee) any restrictions attached to the task or award that would prevent the sharing with the general public of any or all of the information required by this subsection, and the reasons for such restrictions; and

(ff) such other information as may be determined to be appropriate; and

(ii) <<NOTE: Public information.>> 1 or more websites upon which all or part of the repository of Federal research and development shall be made available to and searchable by Federal agencies and non-Federal entities, including the general public, to facilitate—

(I) the coordination of Federal research and development activities;

(II) collaboration among those conducting Federal research and development;

(III) the transfer of technology among Federal agencies and between Federal agencies and non-Federal entities; and

(IV) Access by policymakers and the public to information concerning Federal research and development activities.

(B) Oversight.—The <<NOTE: Guidelines. >> Director of the Office of Management and Budget shall issue any guidance determined necessary to ensure that agencies provide all information requested under this subsection.

(2) Agency functions.—Any agency that funds Federal research and development under this subsection shall provide the information required to populate the repository in the manner prescribed by the Director of the Office of Management and Budget.

(3) Committee <<NOTE: Deadline.>> functions.—Not later than 18 months after the date of enactment of this Act, working with the Director of the Office of Science and Technology Policy, and after consultation with interested parties, the Committee shall submit recommendations to the Director on—

(A) policies to improve agency reporting of information for the repository established under this subsection; and

(B) policies to improve dissemination of the results of research performed by Federal agencies and federally funded research and development centers.

(4) Functions <<NOTE: Reports.>> of the director. —After submission of recommendations by the Committee under paragraph

1. the Director shall report on the recommendations of the Committee and Director to Congress, in the E-Government report under section 3606 of title 44 (as added by this Act).
2. Authorization of appropriations.—There are authorized to be appropriated for the development, maintenance, and operation of the Governmentwide repository and website under this subsection—

(A) $2,000,000 in each of the fiscal years 2003 through 2005; and
(B) such sums as are necessary in each of the fiscal years 2006 and 2007.

## SEC. 208. <<NOTE: 44 USC 3501 note.>> PRIVACY PROVISIONS.

(a) Purpose.—The purpose of this section is to ensure sufficient protections for the privacy of personal information as agencies implement citizen-centered electronic Government.

(b) Privacy Impact Assessments.—

(1) Responsibilities of agencies.—

(A) In general.—An agency shall take actions described under subparagraph (B) before—

> (i) developing or procuring information technology that collects, maintains, or disseminates information that is in an identifiable form; or
>
> (ii) initiating a new collection of information that—
>
> (I) will be collected, maintained, or disseminated using information technology; and
>
> (II) includes any information in an identifiable form permitting the physical or online contacting of a specific individual, if identical questions have been posed to, or identical reporting requirements imposed on, 10 or more persons, other than agencies, instrumentalities, or employees of the Federal Government.

(B) Agency activities.—To the extent required under subparagraph (A), each agency shall—

> (i) conduct a privacy impact assessment;
>
> (ii) ensure the review of the privacy impact assessment by the Chief Information Officer, or equivalent official, as determined by the head of the agency; and
>
> (iii) <<NOTE: Public information. Federal Register, publication.>> if practicable, after completion of the review under clause (ii), make the privacy impact assessment publicly available through the website of the agency, publication in the Federal Register, or other means.

(C) Sensitive information. —Subparagraph (B) (iii) may be modified or waived for security reasons, or to protect classified, sensitive, or private information contained in an assessment.

(D) Copy to director.—Agencies shall provide the Director with a copy of the privacy impact assessment for each system for which funding is requested.

# CYBER LAW & FISMA COMPLIANCE

(2) Contents of a privacy impact assessment.—

(A) In general.—The Director shall issue guidance to agencies specifying the required contents of a privacy impact assessment.

(B) Guidance.—The guidance shall—

> (i) ensure that a privacy impact assessment is commensurate with the size of the information system being assessed, the sensitivity of information that is in an identifiable form in that system, and the risk of harm from unauthorized release of that information; and
>
> (ii) require that a privacy impact assessment address—
>
> (I) what information is to be collected;
>
> (II) why the information is being collected;
>
> (III) the intended use of the agency of the information;
>
> (IV) with whom the information will be shared;
>
> (V) what notice or opportunities for consent would be provided to individuals regarding what information is collected and how that information is shared;
>
> (VI) how the information will be secured; and
>
> (VII) whether a system of records is being created under section 552a of title 5, United States Code, (commonly referred to as the ``Privacy Act'').

(3) Responsibilities of the director.—The Director shall—

> (A) <<NOTE: Guidelines.>> develop policies and guidelines for agencies on the conduct of privacy impact assessments;
>
> (B) oversee the implementation of the privacy impact assessment process throughout the Government; and
>
> (C) require agencies to conduct privacy impact assessments of existing information systems or ongoing collections of information that is in an identifiable form as the Director determines appropriate.

(c) Privacy Protections on Agency Websites.—

(1) Privacy policies on websites.—

(A) Guidelines for notices.—The Director shall develop guidance for privacy notices on agency websites used by the public.

(B) Contents.—The guidance shall require that a privacy notice address, consistent with section 552a of title 5, United States Code—

(i) what information is to be collected;

(ii) why the information is being collected;

(iii) the intended use of the agency of the information;

(iv) with whom the information will be shared;

(v) what notice or opportunities for consent would be provided to individuals regarding what information is collected and how that information is shared;

(vi) how the information will be secured; and

(vii) the rights of the individual under section 552a of title 5, United States Code (commonly referred to as the ``Privacy Act''), and other laws relevant to the protection of the privacy of an individual.

1. Privacy <<NOTE: Guidelines. >> policies in machine- readable formats.—The Director shall issue guidance requiring agencies to translate privacy policies into a standardized machine-readable format.

    a. Definition.—In this section, the term ``identifiable form'' means any representation of information that permits the identity of an individual to whom the information applies to be reasonably inferred by either direct or indirect means.

SEC. 209. <<NOTE: 44 USC 3501 note. >> FEDERAL INFORMATION TECHNOLOGY WORKFORCE DEVELOPMENT.

(a) Purpose.—The purpose of this section is to improve the skills of the Federal workforce in using information technology to deliver Government information and services.

(b) Workforce Development.—

(1) In general.—In consultation with the Director of the Office of Management and

Budget, the Chief Information Officers Council, and the Administrator of General Services, the Director of the Office of Personnel Management shall—

(A) analyze, on an ongoing basis, the personnel needs of the Federal Government related to information technology and information resource management;

(B) identify where current information technology and information resource management training do not satisfy the personnel needs described in subparagraph (A);

(C) oversee the development of curricula, training methods, and training priorities that correspond to the projected personnel needs of the Federal Government related to information technology and information resource management; and

(D) assess the training of Federal employees in information technology disciplines in order to ensure that the information resource management needs of the Federal Government are addressed.

(2) Information technology training programs.—The head of each Executive agency, after consultation with the Director of the Office of Personnel Management, the Chief Information Officers Council, and the Administrator of General Services, shall establish and operate information technology training programs consistent with the requirements of this subsection. Such programs shall—

(A) have curricula covering a broad range of information technology disciplines corresponding to the specific information technology and information resource management needs of the agency involved;

(B) be developed and applied according to rigorous standards; and

(C) be designed to maximize efficiency, through the use of self-paced courses, online courses, on-the-job training, and the use of remote instructors, wherever such features can be applied without reducing the effectiveness of the training or negatively impacting academic standards.

(3) Governmentwide policies and evaluation.—The Director of the Office of Personnel Management, in coordination with the Director of the Office of Management and Budget, shall issue policies to promote the development of performance standards for training

and uniform implementation of this subsection by Executive agencies, with due regard for differences in program requirements among agencies that may be appropriate and warranted in view of the agency mission. The Director of the Office of Personnel Management shall evaluate the implementation of the provisions of this subsection by Executive agencies.

(4) Chief information officer authorities and responsibilities.—Subject to the authority, direction, and control of the head of an Executive agency, the chief information officer of such agency shall carry out all powers, functions, and duties of the head of the agency with respect to implementation of this subsection. The chief information officer shall ensure that the policies of the agency head established in accordance with this subsection are implemented throughout the agency.

(5) Information <<NOTE: Records.>> technology training reporting.—The Director of the Office of Management and Budget shall ensure that the heads of Executive agencies collect and maintain standardized information on the information technology and information resources management workforce related to the implementation of this subsection.

(6) Authority to detail employees to non-Federal employers.—In carrying out the preceding provisions of this subsection, the Director of the Office of Personnel Management may provide for a program under which a Federal employee may be detailed to a non-Federal employer. <<NOTE: Regulations. >> The Director of the Office of Personnel Management shall prescribe regulations for such program, including the conditions for service and duties as the Director considers necessary.

(7) Coordination provision.—An assignment described in section 3703 of title 5, United States Code, may not be made unless a program under paragraph (6) is established, and the assignment is made in accordance with the requirements of such program.

(8) Employee participation.—Subject to information resource management needs and the limitations imposed by resource needs in other occupational areas, and consistent with their overall workforce development strategies, agencies shall encourage employees to participate in occupational information technology training.

(9) Authorization of Appropriations.—There are authorized to be appropriated to the

Office of Personnel Management for the implementation of this subsection, $15,000,000 in fiscal year 2003, and such sums as are necessary for each fiscal year thereafter.

(10) Executive agency defined.—For purposes of this subsection, the term ``Executive agency'' has the meaning given the term ``agency'' under section 3701 of title 5, United States Code (as added by subsection (c)).

(c) Information Technology Exchange Program.—

(1) In general.—Subpart B of part III of title 5, United States Code, is amended by adding at the end the following:

``CHAPTER 37—INFORMATION TECHNOLOGY EXCHANGE PROGRAM

``Sec.

``3701. Definitions.

``3702. General provisions.

``3703. Assignment of employees to private sector organizations.

``3704. Assignment of employees from private sector organizations.

``3705. Application to Office of the Chief Technology Officer of the District of Columbia.

``3706. Reporting requirement.

``3707. Regulations.

``Sec. 3701. Definitions

``For purposes of this chapter—

``(1) the term `agency' means an Executive agency, but does not include the General Accounting Office; and

``(2) the term `detail' means—

``(A) the assignment or loan of an employee of an agency to a private sector organization without a change of position from the agency that employs the individual, or

``(B) the assignment or loan of an employee of a private sector organization to an agency without a change of position from the private sector organization that employs the individual, whichever is appropriate in the context in which such term is used.

``Sec. 3702. General provisions

``(a) Assignment Authority.—On request from or with the agreement of a private sector organization, and with the consent of the employee concerned, the head of an agency may arrange for the assignment of an employee of the agency to a private sector organization or an employee of a private sector organization to the agency. An eligible employee is an individual who—

``(1) works in the field of information technology management;

``(2) is considered an exceptional performer by the individual's current employer; and

``(3) is expected to assume increased information technology management responsibilities in the future.

An <<NOTE: Eligibility.>> employee of an agency shall be eligible to participate in this program only if the employee is employed at the GS- 11 level or above (or equivalent) and is serving under a career or career- conditional appointment or an appointment of equivalent tenure in the excepted service, and applicable requirements of section 209(b) of the E-Government Act of 2002 are met with respect to the proposed assignment of such employee.

``(b) Agreements.—Each agency that exercises its authority under this chapter shall provide for a written agreement between the agency and the employee concerned regarding the terms and conditions of the employee's assignment. In the case of an employee of the agency, the agreement shall—

``(1) require the employee to serve in the civil service, upon completion of the assignment, for a period equal to the length of the assignment; and

``(2) provide that, in the event the employee fails to carry out the agreement (except for good and sufficient reason, as determined by the head of the agency from which assigned) the employee shall be liable to the United States for payment of all expenses of the assignment.

An amount under paragraph (2) shall be treated as a debt due the United States.

``(c) Termination.—Assignments may be terminated by the agency or private sector organization concerned for any reason at any time.

``(d) Duration.—Assignments under this chapter shall be for a period of between 3 months and 1 year, and may be extended in 3-month increments for a total of not more than 1 additional year, except that no assignment under this chapter may commence after the end of the 5- year period beginning on the date of the enactment of this chapter.

``(e) Assistance.—The Chief Information Officers Council, by agreement with the Office of Personnel Management, may assist in the administration of this chapter, including by maintaining lists of potential candidates for assignment under this chapter, establishing mentoring relationships for the benefit of individuals who are given assignments under this chapter, and publicizing the program.

``(f) Considerations.—In exercising any authority under this chapter, an agency shall take into consideration—

``(1) the need to ensure that small business concerns are appropriately represented with respect to the assignments described in sections 3703 and 3704, respectively; and

``(2) how assignments described in section 3703 might best be used to help meet the needs of the agency for the training of employees in information technology management.

``Sec. 3703. Assignment of employees to private sector organizations

``(a) In General.—An employee of an agency assigned to a private sector organization under this chapter is deemed, during the period of the assignment, to be on detail to a regular work assignment in his agency.

``(b) Coordination With Chapter 81.—Notwithstanding any other provision of law, an employee of an agency assigned to a private sector organization under this chapter is entitled to retain coverage, rights, and benefits under subchapter I of chapter 81, and employment during the assignment is deemed employment by the United States, except that, if the employee or the employee's dependents receive from the private sector organization any payment under an insurance policy for which the premium is wholly paid by the private sector organization, or other benefit of any kind on account of the same injury or death, then, the amount of such payment or benefit shall be credited against any compensation otherwise payable under subchapter I of chapter 81.

``(c) Reimbursements.—The assignment of an employee to a private sector organization under this chapter may be made with or without reimbursement by the private sector organization for the travel and transportation expenses to or from the place of assignment, subject to the same terms and conditions as apply with respect to an employee of a Federal agency or a State or local government under section 3375, and for the pay, or a part thereof, of the employee during assignment. Any reimbursements shall be credited to the appropriation of the agency used for paying the travel and transportation expenses or pay.

``(d) Tort Liability; Supervision.—The Federal Tort Claims Act and any other Federal tort liability statute apply to an employee of an agency assigned to a private sector organization under this chapter. The supervision of the duties of an employee of an agency so assigned to a private sector organization may be governed by an agreement between the agency and the organization.

``(e) Small Business Concerns.—

``(1) In general.—The head of each agency shall take such actions as may be necessary to ensure that, of the assignments made under this chapter from such agency to private sector organizations in each year, at least 20 percent are to small business concerns.

``(2) Definitions.—For purposes of this subsection—

> ``(A) the term `small business concern' means a business concern that satisfies the definitions and standards specified by the Administrator of the Small Business Administration under section 3(a)(2) of the Small Business Act (as from time to time amended by the Administrator);
>
> ``(B) the term `year' refers to the 12-month period beginning on the date of the enactment of this chapter, and each succeeding 12-month period in which any assignments under this chapter may be made; and
>
> ``(C) the assignments `made' in a year are those commencing in such year.

``(3) Reporting <<NOTE: Deadline.>> requirement.—An agency which fails to comply with paragraph (1) in a year shall, within 90 days after the end of such year, submit a report to the Committees on Government Reform and Small Business of the House of Representatives and the Committees on Governmental Affairs and Small Business of the Senate. The report shall include—

``(A) the total number of assignments made under this chapter from such agency to private sector organizations in the year;

``(B) of that total number, the number (and percentage) made to small business concerns; and

``(C) the reasons for the agency's noncompliance with paragraph (1).

``(4) Exclusion.—This subsection shall not apply to an agency in any year in which it makes fewer than 5 assignments under this chapter to private sector organizations.

``Sec. 3704. Assignment of employees from private sector organizations

``(a) In General.—An employee of a private sector organization assigned to an agency under this chapter is deemed, during the period of the assignment, to be on detail to such agency.

``(b) Terms and Conditions.—An employee of a private sector organization assigned to an agency under this chapter—

``(1) may continue to receive pay and benefits from the private sector organization from which he is assigned;

``(2) is deemed, notwithstanding subsection (a), to be an employee of the agency for the purposes of—

``(A) chapter 73;

``(B) sections 201, 203, 205, 207, 208, 209, 603, 606, 607, 643, 654, 1905, and 1913 of title 18;

``(C) sections 1343, 1344, and 1349(b) of title 31;

``(D) the Federal Tort Claims Act and any other Federal tort liability statute;

``(E) the Ethics in Government Act of 1978;

``(F) section 1043 of the Internal Revenue Code of 1986; and

``(G) section 27 of the Office of Federal Procurement Policy Act;

``(3) may not have access to any trade secrets or to any other nonpublic information which is of commercial value to the private sector organization from which he is assigned; and

``(4) is subject to such regulations as the President may prescribe.

The supervision of an employee of a private sector organization assigned to an agency under this chapter may be governed by agreement between the agency and the private sector organization concerned. Such an assignment may be made with or without reimbursement by the agency for the pay, or a part thereof, of the employee during the period of assignment, or for any contribution of the private sector organization to employee benefit systems.

``(c) Coordination With Chapter 81.—An employee of a private sector organization assigned to an agency under this chapter who suffers disability or dies as a result of personal injury sustained while performing duties during the assignment shall be treated, for the purpose of subchapter I of chapter 81, as an employee as defined by section 8101 who had sustained the injury in the performance of duty, except that, if the employee or the employee's dependents receive from the private sector organization any payment under an insurance policy for which the premium is wholly paid by the private sector organization, or other benefit of any kind on account of the same injury or death, then, the amount of such payment or benefit shall be credited against any compensation otherwise payable under subchapter I of chapter 81.

``(d) Prohibition Against Charging Certain Costs to the Federal Government.—A private sector organization may not charge the Federal Government, as direct or indirect costs under a Federal contract, the costs of pay or benefits paid by the organization to an employee assigned to an agency under this chapter for the period of the assignment.

``Sec. 3705. Application to Office of the Chief Technology Officer of the District of Columbia

``(a) In General.—The Chief Technology Officer of the District of Columbia may arrange for the assignment of an employee of the Office of the Chief Technology Officer to a private sector organization, or an employee of a private sector organization to such Office, in the same manner as the head of an agency under this chapter.

``(b) Terms and Conditions.—An assignment made pursuant to subsection (a) shall be subject to the same terms and conditions as an assignment made by the head of an agency under this chapter, except that in applying such terms and conditions to an assignment made pursuant to subsection (a), any reference in this chapter to a provision of law or regulation of the United States shall be deemed to be a reference to the applicable provision of law or regulation of the District of Columbia, including the applicable provisions of the District of Columbia Government Comprehensive Merit Personnel Act of 1978 (sec. 1-601.01 et seq., D.C. Official Code) and section 601 of the District of Columbia Campaign Finance Reform and Conflict of Interest Act (sec. 1-1106.01, D.C. Official Code).

``(c) Definition.—For purposes of this section, the term `Office of the Chief Technology Officer' means the office established in the executive branch of the government of the District of Columbia under the Office of the Chief Technology Officer Establishment Act of 1998 (sec. 1-1401 et seq., D.C. Official Code).

``**Sec. 3706. Reporting requirement**

``(a) In <<NOTE: Deadline.>> General.—The Office of Personnel Management shall, not later than April 30 and October 31 of each year, prepare and submit to the Committee on Government Reform of the House of Representatives and the Committee on Governmental Affairs of the Senate a semiannual report summarizing the operation of this chapter during the immediately preceding 6-month period ending on March 31 and September 30, respectively.

``(b) Content.—Each report shall include, with respect to the 6- month period to which such report relates—

``(1) the total number of individuals assigned to, and the total number of individuals assigned from, each agency during such period;

``(2) a brief description of each assignment included under paragraph (1), including—

``(A) the name of the assigned individual, as well as the private sector organization and the agency (including the specific bureau or other agency component) to or from which such individual was assigned;

``(B) the respective positions to and from which the individual was assigned, including the duties and responsibilities and the pay grade or level associated with each; and

``(C) the duration and objectives of the individual's assignment; and

``(3) such other information as the Office considers appropriate.

``(c) Publication.—A copy of each report submitted under subsection (a)—

``(1) <<NOTE: Federal Register, publication.>> shall be published in the Federal Register; and

``(2) <<NOTE: Public information.>> shall be made publicly available on the Internet.

``(d) Agency Cooperation.—On request of the Office, agencies shall furnish such information and reports as the Office may require in order to carry out this section.

``Sec. 3707. Regulations

``The Director of the Office of Personnel Management shall prescribe regulations for the administration of this chapter.''.

(2) Report.—Not <<NOTE: Deadline.>> later than 4 years after the date of the enactment of this Act, the General Accounting Office shall prepare and submit to the Committee on Government Reform of the House of Representatives and the Committee on Governmental Affairs of the Senate a report on the operation of chapter 37 of title 5, United States Code (as added by this subsection). Such report shall include—

(A) an evaluation of the effectiveness of the program established by such chapter; and

(B) a recommendation as to whether such program should be continued (with or without modification) or allowed to lapse.

(3) Clerical Amendment.—The analysis for part III of title 5, United States Code, is amended by inserting after the item relating to chapter 35 the following:

``37. Information Technology Exchange Program....................3701''.

(d) Ethics Provisions.—

(1) One-year restriction on certain communications. —Section 207(c)(2)(A) of title 18,

# CYBER LAW & FISMA COMPLIANCE 261

United States Code, is amended—

(A) by striking ``or" at the end of clause (iii);

(B) by striking the period at the end of clause (iv) and inserting ``; or"; and

(C) by adding at the end the following:

``(v) assigned from a private sector organization to an agency under chapter 37 of title 5.''.

(2) Disclosure of confidential information.—Section 1905 of title 18, United States Code, is amended by inserting ``or being an employee of a private sector organization who is or was assigned to an agency under chapter 37 of title 5,'' after ``(15 U.S.C. 1311-1314),''.

(3) Contract advice.—Section 207 of title 18, United States Code, is amended by adding at the end the following:

> ``(l) Contract Advice by Former Details.—Whoever, being an employee of a private sector organization assigned to an agency under chapter 37 of title 5, within one year after the end of that assignment, knowingly represents or aids, counsels, or assists in representing any other person (except the United States) in connection with any contract with that agency shall be punished as provided in section 216 of this title.''.

(4) Restriction on disclosure of procurement information.—Section 27 of the Office of Federal Procurement Policy Act (41 U.S.C. 423) is amended in subsection (a)(1) by adding at the end the following new sentence: ``In the case of an employee of a private sector organization assigned to an agency under chapter 37 of title 5, United States Code, in addition to the restriction in the preceding sentence, such employee shall not, other than as provided by law, knowingly disclose contractor bid or proposal information or source selection information during the three-year period after the end of the assignment of such employee.''.

(e) Report on Existing Exchange Programs.—

> (1) Exchange program defined.—For purposes of this subsection, the term ``exchange program" means an executive exchange program, the program under subchapter VI of chapter 33 of title 5, United States Code, and any other program which allows for—

(A) the assignment of employees of the Federal Government to non-Federal employers;

(B) the assignment of employees of non-Federal employers to the Federal Government; or

(C) both.

> (2) Reporting <<NOTE: Deadline.>> requirement.—Not later than 1 year after the date of the enactment of this Act, the Office of Personnel Management shall prepare and submit to the Committee on Government Reform of the House of Representatives and the Committee on Governmental Affairs of the Senate a report identifying all existing exchange programs.
>
> (3) Specific information.—The report shall, for each such program, include—

(A) a brief description of the program, including its size, eligibility requirements, and terms or conditions for participation;

(B) specific citation to the law or other authority under which the program is established;

(C) the names of persons to contact for more information, and how they may be reached; and

(D) any other information which the Office considers appropriate.

(f) Report on the Establishment of a Governmentwide Information Technology Training Program.—

> (1) In <<NOTE: Deadline.>> general.—Not later January 1, 2003, the Office of Personnel Management, in consultation with the Chief Information Officers Council and the Administrator of General Services, shall review and submit to the Committee on Government Reform of the House of Representatives and the Committee on Governmental Affairs of the Senate a written report on the following:

(A) The adequacy of any existing information technology training programs available to Federal employees on a Governmentwide basis.

(B)(i) If one or more such programs already exist, recommendations as to how they might be improved.

> (ii) If no such program yet exists, recommendations as to how such a program might be designed and established.

(C) With respect to any recommendations under subparagraph (B), how the program under chapter 37 of title 5, United States Code, might be used to help carry them out.

(2) Cost estimate.—The report shall, for any recommended program (or improvements) under paragraph (1)(B), include the estimated costs associated with the implementation and operation of such program as so established (or estimated difference in costs of any such program as so improved).

(g) Technical and Conforming Amendments.—

(1) Amendments to title 5, united states code.—Title 5, United States Code, is amended—

(A) in section 3111, by adding at the end the following:

``(d) Notwithstanding section 1342 of title 31, the head of an agency may accept voluntary service for the United States under chapter 37 of this title and regulations of the Office of Personnel Management.'';

(B) in section 4108, by striking subsection (d); and

(C) in section 7353(b), by adding at the end the following:

``(4) Nothing in this section precludes an employee of a private sector organization, while assigned to an agency under chapter 37, from continuing to receive pay and benefits from such organization in accordance with such chapter.''.

(2) Amendment to title 18, united states code.—Section 209 of title 18, United States Code, is amended by adding at the end the following:

``(g)(1) This section does not prohibit an employee of a private sector organization, while assigned to an agency under chapter 37 of title 5, from continuing to receive pay and benefits from such organization in accordance with such chapter.

``(2) For purposes of this subsection, the term `agency' means an agency (as defined by section 3701 of title 5) and the Office of the Chief Technology Officer of the District of Columbia.''.

(3) Other amendments.—Section 125(c)(1) of Public Law 100- 238 (5 U.S.C. 8432 note) is amended—

(A) in subparagraph (B), by striking ``or'' at the end;

(B) in subparagraph (C), by striking ``and'' at the end and inserting ``or''; and

(C) by adding at the end the following:

``(D) an individual assigned from a Federal agency to a private sector organization under chapter 37 of title 5, United States Code; and''.

SEC. 210. <<NOTE: 44 USC 3501 note.>> SHARE-IN-SAVINGS INITIATIVES.

(a) Defense Contracts.—(1) Chapter 137 of title 10, United States Code, is amended by adding at the end the following new section:

``Sec. 2332. Share-in-savings contracts

``(a) Authority To Enter Into Share-in-Savings Contracts.—(1) The head of an agency may enter into a share-in-savings contract for information technology (as defined in section 11101(6) of title 40) in which the Government awards a contract to improve mission-related or administrative processes or to accelerate the achievement of its mission and share with the contractor in savings achieved through contract performance.

``(2)(A) Except as provided in subparagraph (B), a share-in-savings contract shall be awarded for a period of not more than five years.

``(B) A share-in-savings contract may be awarded for a period greater than five years, but not more than 10 years, if the head of the agency determines in writing prior to award of the contract that—

``(i) the level of risk to be assumed and the investment to be undertaken by the contractor is likely to inhibit the government from obtaining the needed information technology competitively at a fair and reasonable price if the contract is limited in duration to a period of five years or less; and

``(ii) usage of the information technology to be acquired is likely to continue for a period of time sufficient to generate reasonable benefit for the government.

``(3) Contracts awarded pursuant to the authority of this section shall, to the maximum extent practicable, be performance-based contracts that identify objective outcomes and contain performance standards that will be used to measure achievement and milestones that must be met before payment is made.

``(4) Contracts awarded pursuant to the authority of this section shall include a provision containing a quantifiable baseline that is to be the basis upon which a savings share ratio

## CYBER LAW & FISMA COMPLIANCE 265

is established that governs the amount of payment a contractor is to receive under the contract. Before commencement of performance of such a contract, the senior procurement executive of the agency shall determine in writing that the terms of the provision are quantifiable and will likely yield value to the Government.

``(5)(A) The head of the agency may retain savings realized through the use of a share-in-savings contract under this section that are in excess of the total amount of savings paid to the contractor under the contract, but may not retain any portion of such savings that is attributable to a decrease in the number of civilian employees of the Federal Government performing the function. Except as provided in subparagraph (B), savings shall be credited to the appropriation or fund against which charges were made to carry out the contract and shall be used for information technology.

``(B) Amounts retained by the agency under this subsection shall—

``(i) without further appropriation, remain available until expended; and

``(ii) be applied first to fund any contingent liabilities associated with share-in-savings procurements that are not fully funded.

``(b) Cancellation and Termination.—(1) If funds are not made available for the continuation of a share-in-savings contract entered into under this section in a subsequent fiscal year, the contract shall be canceled or terminated. The costs of cancellation or termination may be paid out of—

``(A) appropriations available for the performance of the contract;

``(B) appropriations available for acquisition of the information technology procured under the contract, and not otherwise obligated; or

``(C) funds subsequently appropriated for payments of costs of cancellation or termination, subject to the limitations in paragraph (3).

``(2) The amount payable in the event of cancellation or termination of a share-in-savings contract shall be negotiated with the contractor at the time the contract is entered into.

``(3)(A) Subject to subparagraph (B), the head of an agency may enter into share-in-savings contracts under this section in any given fiscal year even if funds are not made specifically available for the full costs of cancellation or termination of the contract if funds are available and sufficient to make payments with respect to the first fiscal year of the contract and the following conditions are met regarding the funding of cancellation and termination liability:

``(i) The amount of unfunded contingent liability for the contract does not exceed the lesser of—

``(I) 25 percent of the estimated costs of a cancellation or termination; or

``(II) $5,000,000.

``(ii) Unfunded contingent liability in excess of $1,000,000 has been approved by the Director of the Office of Management and Budget or the Director's designee.

``(B) The aggregate number of share-in-savings contracts that may be entered into under subparagraph (A) by all agencies to which this chapter applies in a fiscal year may not exceed 5 in each of fiscal years 2003, 2004, and 2005.

``(c) Definitions.—In this section:

``(1) The term `contractor' means a private entity that enters into a contract with an agency.

``(2) The term `savings' means—

``(A) monetary savings to an agency; or

``(B) savings in time or other benefits realized by the agency, including enhanced revenues (other than enhanced revenues from the collection of fees, taxes, debts, claims, or other amounts owed the Federal Government).

``(3) The term `share-in-savings contract' means a contract under which—
``(A) a contractor provides solutions for—

``(i) improving the agency's mission-related or administrative processes; or

``(ii) accelerating the achievement of agency missions; and

``(B) the head of the agency pays the contractor an amount equal to a portion of the savings derived by the agency from—

``(i) any improvements in mission-related or administrative processes that result from implementation of the solution; or

``(ii) acceleration of achievement of agency missions.

``(d) Termination.—No share-in-savings contracts may be entered into under this section after September 30, 2005.''.

(2) The table of sections at the beginning of such chapter is amended by adding at the end of the following new item:

``2332. Share-in-savings contracts.''.

(b) Other Contracts.—Title III of the Federal Property and Administrative Services Act of 1949 is amended by adding at the end the following:

``SEC. 317. <<NOTE: 41 USC 266a.>> SHARE-IN-SAVINGS CONTRACTS.

``(a) Authority To Enter Into Share-in-Savings Contracts.—(1) The head of an executive agency may enter into a share-in-savings contract for information technology (as defined in section 11101(6) of title 40, United States Code) in which the Government awards a contract to improve mission-related or administrative processes or to accelerate the achievement of its mission and share with the contractor in savings achieved through contract performance.

``(2)(A) Except as provided in subparagraph (B), a share-in-savings contract shall be awarded for a period of not more than five years.

``(B) A share-in-savings contract may be awarded for a period greater than five years, but not more than 10 years, if the head of the agency determines in writing prior to award of the contract that—

``(i) the level of risk to be assumed and the investment to be undertaken by the contractor is likely to inhibit the government from obtaining the needed information technology competitively at a fair and reasonable price if the contract is limited in duration to a period of five years or less; and ``(ii) usage of the information technology to be acquired is likely to continue for a period of time sufficient to generate reasonable benefit for the government.

``(3) Contracts awarded pursuant to the authority of this section shall, to the maximum extent practicable, be performance-based contracts that identify objective outcomes and contain performance standards that will be used to measure achievement and milestones that must be met before payment is made.

``(4) Contracts awarded pursuant to the authority of this section shall include a provision containing a quantifiable baseline that is to be the basis upon which a savings share ratio is established that governs the amount of payment a contractor is to receive under the contract. Before commencement of performance of such a contract, the senior procurement executive of the agency shall determine in writing that the terms of the provision are quantifiable and will likely yield value to the Government.

``(5)(A) The head of the agency may retain savings realized through the use of a share-in-savings contract under this section that are in excess of the total amount of savings paid to the contractor under the contract, but may not retain any portion of such savings that is attributable to a decrease in the number of civilian employees of the Federal Government performing the function. Except as provided in subparagraph (B), savings shall be credited to the appropriation or fund against which charges were made to carry out the contract and shall be used for information technology.

``(B) Amounts retained by the agency under this subsection shall—

``(i) without further appropriation, remain available until expended; and

``(ii) be applied first to fund any contingent liabilities associated with share-in-savings procurements that are not fully funded.

``(b) Cancellation and Termination.—(1) If funds are not made available for the continuation of a share-in-savings contract entered into under this section in a subsequent fiscal year, the contract shall be canceled or terminated. The costs of cancellation or termination may be paid out of—

``(A) appropriations available for the performance of the contract;

``(B) appropriations available for acquisition of the information technology procured under the contract, and not otherwise obligated; or

``(C) funds subsequently appropriated for payments of costs of cancellation or termination, subject to the limitations in paragraph (3).

``(2) The amount payable in the event of cancellation or termination of a share-in-savings contract shall be negotiated with the contractor at the time the contract is entered into.

``(3)(A) Subject to subparagraph (B), the head of an executive agency may enter into share-in-savings contracts under this section in any given fiscal year even if funds are not made specifically available for the full costs of cancellation or termination of the contract if funds are available and sufficient to make payments with respect to the first fiscal year of the contract and the following conditions are met regarding the funding of cancellation and termination liability:

``(i) The amount of unfunded contingent liability for the contract does not exceed the lesser of—

``(I) 25 percent of the estimated costs of a cancellation or termination; or

``(II) $5,000,000.

``(ii) Unfunded contingent liability in excess of $1,000,000 has been approved by the Director of the Office of Management and Budget or the Director's designee.

``(B) The aggregate number of share-in-savings contracts that may be entered into under subparagraph (A) by all executive agencies to which this chapter applies in a fiscal year may not exceed 5 in each of fiscal years 2003, 2004, and 2005.

``(c) Definitions.—In this section:

``(1) The term `contractor' means a private entity that enters into a contract with an agency.

``(2) The term `savings' means—

``(A) monetary savings to an agency; or

``(B) savings in time or other benefits realized by the agency, including enhanced revenues (other than enhanced revenues from the collection of fees, taxes, debts, claims, or other amounts owed the Federal Government).

``(3) The term `share-in-savings contract' means a contract under which—

``(A) a contractor provides solutions for—

>``(i) improving the agency's mission-related or administrative processes; or

>``(ii) accelerating the achievement of agency missions; and

``(B) the head of the agency pays the contractor an amount equal to a portion of the savings derived by the agency from—

>``(i) any improvements in mission-related or administrative processes that result from implementation of the solution; or

>``(ii) acceleration of achievement of agency missions.

``(d) Termination.—No share-in-savings contracts may be entered into under this section after September 30, 2005.''.

(c) Development of Incentives.—The Director of the Office of Management and Budget shall, in consultation with the Committee on Governmental Affairs of the Senate, the Committee on Government Reform of the House of Representatives, and executive agencies, develop techniques to permit an executive agency to retain a portion of the savings (after payment of the contractor's share of the savings) derived from share-in-savings contracts as funds are appropriated to the agency in future fiscal years.

(d) Regulations.—Not <<NOTE: Deadline.>> later than 270 days after the date of the enactment of this Act, the Federal Acquisition Regulation shall be revised to implement the provisions enacted by this section. Such revisions shall—

> 1. provide for the use of competitive procedures in the selection and award of share-in-savings contracts to—

(A) ensure the contractor's share of savings reflects the risk involved and market conditions; and

(B) otherwise yield greatest value to the government; and

(2) allow appropriate regulatory flexibility to facilitate the use of share-in-savings contracts by executive agencies, including the use of innovative provisions for technology refreshment and nonstandard Federal Acquisition Regulation contract clauses.

(e) Additional Guidance.—The Administrator of General Services shall—

(1) identify potential opportunities for the use of share- in-savings contracts; and

(2) in consultation with the Director of the Office of Management and Budget, provide guidance to executive agencies for determining mutually beneficial savings share ratios and baselines from which savings may be measured.

(f) OMB <<NOTE: Deadline.>> Report to Congress.—In consultation with executive agencies, the Director of the Office of Management and Budget shall, not later than 2 years after the date of the enactment of this Act, submit to Congress a report containing—

(1) a description of the number of share-in-savings contracts entered into by each executive agency under by this section and the amendments made by this section, and, for each contract identified—

(A) the information technology acquired;
(B) the total amount of payments made to the contractor; and
(C) the total amount of savings or other measurable benefits realized;

(2) a description of the ability of agencies to determine the baseline costs of a project against which savings can be measured; and

(3) any recommendations, as the Director deems appropriate, regarding additional changes in law that may be necessary to ensure effective use of share-in-savings contracts by executive agencies.

(g) GAO <<NOTE: Deadline.>> Report to Congress.—The Comptroller General shall, not later than 6 months after the report required under subsection

(f) is submitted to Congress, conduct a review of that report and submit to Congress a report containing—

(1) the results of the review;

(2) an independent assessment by the Comptroller General of the effectiveness of the use of share-in-savings contracts in improving the mission-related and administrative processes of the executive agencies and the achievement of agency missions; and

(3) a recommendation on whether the authority to enter into share-in-savings contracts should be continued.

(h) Repeal of Share-in-Savings Pilot Program.—

(1) Repeal.—Section 11521 of title 40, United States Code, is repealed.
(2) Conforming amendments to pilot program authority. –

(A) Section 11501 of title 40, United States Code, is amended—

(i) in the section heading, by striking ``programs'' and inserting ``program'';

(ii) in subsection (a)(1), by striking ``conduct pilot programs'' and inserting ``conduct a pilot program pursuant to the requirements of section 11521 of this title'';

(iii) in subsection (a)(2), by striking ``each pilot program'' and inserting ``the pilot program'';

(iv) in subsection (b), by striking ``Limitations.—'' and all that follows through ``$750,000,000.'' and inserting the following: ``Limitation on Amount.—The total amount obligated for contracts entered into under the pilot program conducted under this chapter may not exceed $375,000,000.''; and

(v) in subsection (c)(1), by striking ``a pilot'' and inserting ``the pilot''.

(B) The following provisions of chapter 115 of such title are each amended by striking ``a pilot'' each place it appears and inserting ``the pilot'':

(i) Section 11502(a).
(ii) Section 11502(b).

(iii) Section 11503(a).
(iv) Section 11504.

(C) Section 11505 of such chapter is amended by striking ``programs'' and inserting ``program''.

(3) Additional conforming amendments.—

(A) Section 11522 of title 40, United States Code, is redesignated as section 11521.

(B) The chapter heading for chapter 115 of such title is amended by striking ``PROGRAMS'' and inserting ``PROGRAM''.

(C) The subchapter heading for subchapter I and for subchapter II of such chapter are each amended by striking ``PROGRAMS'' and inserting ``PROGRAM''.

(D) The item relating to subchapter I in the table of sections at the beginning of such chapter is amended to read as follows:

``SUBCHAPTER I—CONDUCT OF PILOT PROGRAM''.

(E) The item relating to subchapter II in the table of sections at the beginning of such chapter is amended to read as follows:

``SUBCHAPTER II—SPECIFIC PILOT PROGRAM''.

(F) The item relating to section 11501 in the table of sections at the beginning of such is amended by striking ``programs'' and inserting ``program''.

(G) The table of sections at the beginning of such chapter is amended by striking the item relating to section 11521 and redesignating the item relating to section 11522 as section 11521.

(H) The item relating to chapter 115 in the table of chapters for subtitle III of title 40, United States Code, is amended to read as follows:

``115. INFORMATION TECHNOLOGY ACQUISITION PILOT PROGRAM.........11501''.

(i) Definitions.—In this section, the terms ``contractor'', ``savings'', and ``share-in-savings contract'' have the meanings given those terms in section 317 of the Federal Property and Administrative Services Act of 1949 (as added by subsection (b)).

SEC. 211. <<NOTE: 44 USC 3501 note.>> AUTHORIZATION FOR ACQUISITION OF INFORMATION TECHNOLOGY BY STATE AND LOCAL GOVERNMENTS THROUGH FEDERAL SUPPLY SCHEDULES.

(a) Authority To Use Certain Supply Schedules.—Section 502 of title 40, United States Code, is amended by adding at the end the following new subsection:

``(c) Use of Certain Supply Schedules. –

``(1) In general.—The Administrator may provide for the use by State or local governments of Federal supply schedules of the General Services Administration for automated data processing equipment (including firmware), software, supplies, support equipment, and services (as contained in Federal supply classification code group 70).

``(2) Voluntary use.—In any case of the use by a State or local government of a Federal supply schedule pursuant to paragraph (1), participation by a firm that sells to the Federal Government through the supply schedule shall be voluntary with respect to a sale to the State or local government through such supply schedule.

``(3) Definitions.—In this subsection:

``(A) The term `State or local government' includes any State, local, regional, or tribal government, or any instrumentality thereof (including any local educational agency or institution of higher education).

``(B) The term `tribal government' means—

``(i) the governing body of any Indian tribe, band, nation, or other organized group or community located in the continental United States (excluding the State of Alaska) that is recognized as eligible for the special programs and services provided by the United States to Indians because of their status as Indians, and

``(ii) any Alaska Native regional or village corporation established pursuant to the Alaska Native Claims Settlement Act (43 U.S.C. 1601 et seq.).

``(C) The term `local educational agency' has the meaning given that term in section 8013 of the Elementary and Secondary Education Act of 1965 (20 U.S.C. 7713).

``(D) The term `institution of higher education' has the meaning given that term in section 101(a) of the Higher Education Act of 1965 (20 U.S.C. 1001(a)).''.

(b) Procedures.—Not <<NOTE: Deadline.>> later than 30 days after the date of the enactment of this Act, the Administrator of General Services shall establish procedures to implement section 501(c) of title 40, United States Code (as added by subsection (a)).

(c) Report.—Not <<NOTE: Deadline.>> later than December 31, 2004, the Administrator shall submit to the Committee on Government Reform of the House of Representatives and the Committee on Governmental Affairs of the Senate a report on the implementation and effects of the amendment made by subsection (a).

## SEC. 212. <<NOTE: 44 USC 3501 note.>> INTEGRATED REPORTING STUDY AND PILOT PROJECTS.

(a) Purposes.—The purposes of this section are to—

(1) enhance the interoperability of Federal information systems;

(2) assist the public, including the regulated community, in electronically submitting information to agencies under Federal requirements, by reducing the burden of duplicate collection and ensuring the accuracy of submitted information; and

(3) enable any person to integrate and obtain similar information held by 1 or more agencies under 1 or more Federal requirements without violating the privacy rights of an individual.

(b) Definitions.—In this section, the term—

(1) ``agency'' means an Executive agency as defined under section 105 of title 5, United States Code; and

(2) ``person'' means any individual, trust, firm, joint stock company, corporation (including a government corporation), partnership, association, State, municipality, commission, political subdivision of a State, interstate body, or agency or component of the Federal Government.

(c) Report.—

(1) In <<NOTE: Deadline.>> general.—Not later than 3 years after the date of enactment of this Act, the Director shall oversee a study, in consultation with agencies, the regulated community, public interest organizations, and the public, and submit a report to the Committee on Governmental Affairs of the Senate and the Committee on Government Reform of the House of Representatives on progress toward integrating Federal information systems across agencies.

(2) Contents.—The report under this section shall—

(A) address the integration of data elements used in the electronic collection of information within databases established under Federal statute without reducing the quality, accessibility, scope, or utility of the information contained in each database;

(B) address the feasibility of developing, or enabling the development of, software, including Internet-based tools, for use by reporting persons in assembling, documenting, and validating the accuracy of information electronically submitted to agencies under nonvoluntary, statutory, and regulatory requirements;

(C) address the feasibility of developing a distributed information system involving, on a voluntary basis, at least 2 agencies, that—

(i) provides consistent, dependable, and timely public access to the information holdings of 1 or more agencies, or some portion of such holdings, without requiring public users to know which agency holds the information; and

(ii) allows the integration of public information held by the participating agencies;

(D) address the feasibility of incorporating other elements related to the purposes of this section at the discretion of the Director; and

(E) make any recommendations that the Director deems appropriate on the use of integrated reporting and information systems, to reduce the burden on reporting and strengthen public access to databases within and across agencies.

(d) Pilot Projects To Encourage Integrated Collection and Management of Data and Interoperability of Federal Information Systems.—

(1) In general.—In order to provide input to the study under subsection (c), the Director shall designate, in consultation with agencies, a series of no more than 5 pilot projects that integrate data elements. The Director shall consult with agencies, the regulated community, public interest organizations, and the public on the implementation of the pilot projects.

(2) Goals of pilot projects. –

(A) In general.—Each goal described under subparagraph (B) shall be addressed by at least 1 pilot project each.

(B) Goals.—The goals under this paragraph are to—

(i) reduce information collection burdens by eliminating duplicative data elements within 2 or more reporting requirements;

(ii) create interoperability between or among public databases managed by 2 or more agencies using technologies and techniques that facilitate public access; and

(iii) develop, or enable the development of, software to reduce errors in electronically submitted information.

(3) Input.—Each pilot project shall seek input from users on the utility of the pilot project and areas for improvement.

To the extent practicable, the Director shall consult with relevant agencies and State, tribal, and local governments in carrying out the report and pilot projects under this section.

(e) Protections.—The activities authorized under this section shall afford protections for—

(1) confidential business information consistent with section 552(b)(4) of title 5, United States Code, and other relevant law;

(2) personal privacy information under sections 552(b) (6) and (7)(C) and 552a of title 5, United States Code, and other relevant law;

(3) other information consistent with section 552(b)(3) of title 5, United States Code, and other relevant law; and

(4) confidential statistical information collected under a confidentiality pledge, solely for statistical purposes, consistent with the Office of Management and Budget's Federal Statistical Confidentiality Order, and other relevant law.

**SEC. 213. <<NOTE: 44 USC 3501 note.>> COMMUNITY TECHNOLOGY CENTERS.**

(a) Purposes.—The purposes of this section are to—

(1) study and enhance the effectiveness of community technology centers, public libraries, and other institutions that provide computer and Internet access to the public; and

(2) promote awareness of the availability of on-line government information and services, to users of community technology centers, public libraries, and other public facilities that provide access to computer technology and Internet access to the public.

(b) Study <<NOTE: Deadline.>> and Report.—Not later than 2 years after the effective date of this title, the Administrator shall—

(1) ensure that a study is conducted to evaluate the best practices of community technology centers that have received Federal funds; and

(2) submit a report on the study to—

(A) the Committee on Governmental Affairs of the Senate;

(B) the Committee on Health, Education, Labor, and Pensions of the Senate;

(C) the Committee on Government Reform of the House of Representatives; and

(D) the Committee on Education and the Workforce of the House of Representatives.

(c) Contents.—The report under subsection (b) may consider—

(1) an evaluation of the best practices being used by successful community technology centers;

(2) a strategy for—

(A) continuing the evaluation of best practices used by community technology centers; and

(B) establishing a network to share information and resources as community technology centers evolve;

(3) the identification of methods to expand the use of best practices to assist community technology centers, public libraries, and other institutions that provide computer and Internet access to the public;

(4) a database of all community technology centers that have received Federal funds, including—

(A) each center's name, location, services provided, director, other points of contact, number of individuals served; and

(B) other relevant information;

(5) an analysis of whether community technology centers have been deployed effectively in urban and rural areas throughout the Nation; and

(6) recommendations of how to—

(A) enhance the development of community technology centers; and

(B) establish a network to share information and resources.

(d) Cooperation.—All agencies that fund community technology centers shall provide to the Administrator any information and assistance necessary for the completion of the study and the report under this section.

(e) Assistance.—

(1) In general.—The Administrator, in consultation with the Secretary of Education, shall work with other relevant Federal agencies, and other interested persons in the private and nonprofit sectors to—

(A) assist in the implementation of recommendations; and

(B) identify other ways to assist community technology centers, public libraries, and other institutions that provide computer and Internet access to the public.

(2) Types of assistance.—Assistance under this subsection may include—

(A) contribution of funds;

(B) donations of equipment, and training in the use and maintenance of the equipment; and

(C) the provision of basic instruction or training material in computer skills and Internet usage.

(f) Online Tutorial.—

   (1) In general.—The Administrator, in consultation with the Secretary of Education, the Director of the Institute of Museum and Library Services, other relevant agencies, and the public, shall develop an online tutorial that—

(A) explains how to access Government information and services on the Internet; and

(B) provides a guide to available online resources.

   (2) Distribution.—The Administrator, with assistance from the Secretary of Education, shall distribute information on the tutorial to community technology centers, public libraries, and other institutions that afford Internet access to the public.

(g) Promotion of Community Technology Centers.—The Administrator, with assistance from the Department of Education and in consultation with other agencies and organizations, shall promote the availability of community technology centers to raise awareness within each community where such a center is located.

(h) Authorization of Appropriations.—There are authorized to be appropriated for the study of best practices at community technology centers, for the development and dissemination of the online tutorial, and for the promotion of community technology centers under this section—

   (1) $2,000,000 in fiscal year 2003;
   (2) $2,000,000 in fiscal year 2004; and
   (3) such sums as are necessary in fiscal years 2005 through 2007.

**SEC. 214. <<NOTE: 44 USC 3501 note.>> ENHANCING CRISIS MANAGEMENT THROUGH ADVANCED INFORMATION TECHNOLOGY.**

(a) Purpose.—The purpose of this section is to improve how information technology is used in coordinating and facilitating information on disaster preparedness, response, and recovery, while ensuring the availability of such information across multiple access channels.

(b) In General. –

(1) Study <<NOTE: Deadline.>> on enhancement of crisis response.—Not later than 90 days after the date of enactment of this Act, the Administrator, in consultation with the Federal Emergency Management Agency, shall ensure that a study is conducted on using information technology to enhance crisis preparedness, response, and consequence management of natural and manmade disasters.

(2) Contents.—The study under this subsection shall address—

(A) a research and implementation strategy for effective use of information technology in crisis response and consequence management, including the more effective use of technologies, management of information technology research initiatives, and incorporation of research advances into the information and communications systems of—

(i) the Federal Emergency Management Agency; and

(ii) other Federal, State, and local agencies responsible for crisis preparedness, response, and consequence management; and

(B) opportunities for research and development on enhanced technologies into areas of potential improvement as determined during the course of the study.

(3) Report.—Not <<NOTE: Deadline.>> later than 2 years after the date on which a contract is entered into under paragraph (1), the Administrator shall submit a report on the study, including findings and recommendations to—

(A) the Committee on Governmental Affairs of the Senate; and
(B) the Committee on Government Reform of the House of Representatives.

(4) Interagency cooperation.—Other Federal departments and agencies with responsibility for disaster relief and emergency assistance shall fully cooperate with the Administrator in carrying out this section.

(5) Authorization of appropriations.—There are authorized to be appropriated for research under this subsection, such sums as are necessary for fiscal year 2003.

(c) Pilot Projects.—Based on the results of the research conducted under subsection (b), the Administrator, in consultation with the Federal Emergency Management Agency, shall initiate pilot projects or report to Congress on other activities that further the goal of maximizing the utility of information technology in disaster management.

The Administrator shall cooperate with other relevant agencies, and, if appropriate, State, local, and tribal governments, in initiating such pilot projects.

SEC. 215. <<NOTE: 44 USC 3501 note.>> DISPARITIES IN ACCESS TO THE INTERNET.

(a) Study <<NOTE: Deadlines.>> and Report.—

(1) Study.—Not later than 90 days after the date of enactment of this Act, the Administrator of General Services shall request that the National Academy of Sciences, acting through the National Research Council, enter into a contract to conduct a study on disparities in Internet access for online Government services.

(2) Report.—Not later than 2 years after the date of enactment of this Act, the Administrator of General Services shall submit to the Committee on Governmental Affairs of the Senate and the Committee on Government Reform of the House of Representatives a final report of the study under this section, which shall set forth the findings, conclusions, and recommendations of the National Research Council.

(b) Contents.—The report under subsection (a) shall include a study of—

(1) how disparities in Internet access influence the effectiveness of online Government services, including a review of—

(A) the nature of disparities in Internet access;
(B) the affordability of Internet service;
(C) the incidence of disparities among different groups within the population; and
(D) changes in the nature of personal and public Internet access that may alleviate or aggravate effective access to online Government services;

(2) how the increase in online Government services is influencing the disparities in Internet access and how technology development or diffusion trends may offset such adverse influences; and

(3) related societal effects arising from the interplay of disparities in Internet access and the increase in online Government services.

(c) Recommendations.—The report shall include recommendations on actions to ensure that online Government initiatives shall not have the unintended result of increasing any deficiency in public access to Government services.

(d) Authorization of Appropriations.—There are authorized to be appropriated $950,000 in fiscal year 2003 to carry out this section.

## SEC. 216. <<NOTE: 44 USC 3501 note.>> COMMON PROTOCOLS FOR GEOGRAPHIC INFORMATION SYSTEMS.

(a) Purposes.—The purposes of this section are to—

   (1) reduce redundant data collection and information; and

   (2) promote collaboration and use of standards for government geographic information.

(b) Definition.—In this section, the term ``geographic information'' means information systems that involve locational data, such as maps or other geospatial information resources.

(c) In General.—

   (1) Common protocols.—The Administrator, in consultation with the Secretary of the Interior, working with the Director and through an interagency group, and working with private sector experts, State, local, and tribal governments, commercial and international standards groups, and other interested parties, shall facilitate the development of common protocols for the development, acquisition, maintenance, distribution, and application of geographic information. If practicable, the Administrator shall incorporate intergovernmental and public private geographic information partnerships into efforts under this subsection.

   (2) Interagency group.—The interagency group referred to under paragraph (1) shall include representatives of the National Institute of Standards and Technology and other agencies.

(d) Director.—The Director shall oversee—

   (1) the interagency initiative to develop common protocols;

   (2) the coordination with State, local, and tribal governments, public private partnerships, and other interested persons on effective and efficient ways to align geographic information and develop common protocols; and

   (3) the adoption of common standards relating to the protocols.

(e) Common Protocols.—The common protocols shall be designed to—

(1) maximize the degree to which unclassified geographic information from various sources can be made electronically compatible and accessible; and

(2) promote the development of interoperable geographic information systems technologies that shall—

(A) allow widespread, low-cost use and sharing of geographic data by Federal agencies, State, local, and tribal governments, and the public; and

(B) enable the enhancement of services using geographic data.

(f) Authorization of Appropriations.—There are authorized to be appropriated such sums as are necessary to carry out this section, for each of the fiscal years 2003 through 2007.

TITLE <<NOTE: Federal Information Security Management Act of 2002.>>
III—INFORMATION SECURITY
SEC. 301. INFORMATION SECURITY.

(a) Short <<NOTE: 44 USC 101 note.>> Title.—This title may be cited as the ``Federal Information Security Management Act of 2002''.

(b) Information Security.—

(1) In general.—Chapter 35 of title 44, United States Code, is amended by adding at the end the following new subchapter:

``SUBCHAPTER III—INFORMATION SECURITY
``Sec. 3541. Purposes
``The purposes of this subchapter are to—

``(1) provide a comprehensive framework for ensuring the effectiveness of information security controls over information resources that support Federal operations and assets;

``(2) recognize the highly networked nature of the current Federal computing environment and provide effective governmentwide management and oversight of the related information security risks, including coordination of information security efforts throughout the civilian, national security, and law enforcement communities;

``(3) provide for development and maintenance of minimum controls required to protect Federal information and information systems;

``(4) provide a mechanism for improved oversight of Federal agency information security programs;

``(5) acknowledge that commercially developed information security products offer advanced, dynamic, robust, and effective information security solutions, reflecting market solutions for the protection of critical information infrastructures important to the national defense and economic security of the nation that are designed, built, and operated by the private sector; and

``(6) recognize that the selection of specific technical hardware and software information security solutions should be left to individual agencies from among commercially developed products.

## ``Sec. 3542. Definitions

``(a) In General.—Except as provided under subsection (b), the definitions under section 3502 shall apply to this subchapter.

``(b) Additional Definitions.—As used in this subchapter:

> ``(1) The term `information security' means protecting information and information systems from unauthorized access, use, disclosure, disruption, modification, or destruction in order to provide—

``(A) integrity, which means guarding against improper information modification or destruction, and includes ensuring information nonrepudiation and authenticity;

``(B) confidentiality, which means preserving authorized restrictions on access and disclosure, including means for protecting personal privacy and proprietary information; and

``(C) availability, which means ensuring timely and reliable access to and use of information.

> ``(2)(A) The term `national security system' means any information system (including any telecommunications system) used or operated by an agency or by a contractor of an agency, or other organization on behalf of an agency—

``(i) the function, operation, or use of which—

> ``(I) involves intelligence activities;

> ``(II) involves cryptologic activities related to national security;

> ``(III) involves command and control of military forces;

> ``(IV) involves equipment that is an integral part of a weapon or weapons system; or

> ``(V) subject to subparagraph (B), is critical to the direct fulfillment of military or intelligence missions; or

``(ii) is protected at all times by procedures established for information that have been specifically authorized under criteria established by an Executive order or an Act of Congress to be kept classified in the interest of national defense or foreign policy.

``(B) Subparagraph (A)(i)(V) does not include a system that is to be used for routine administrative and business applications (including payroll, finance, logistics, and personnel management applications).

``(3) The term 'information technology' has the meaning given that term in section 11101 of title 40.

``Sec. 3543. Authority and functions of the Director

``(a) In General.—The Director shall oversee agency information security policies and practices, including—

``(1) developing and overseeing the implementation of policies, principles, standards, and guidelines on information security, including through ensuring timely agency adoption of and compliance with standards promulgated under section 11331 of title 40;

``(2) requiring agencies, consistent with the standards promulgated under such section 11331 and the requirements of this subchapter, to identify and provide information security protections commensurate with the risk and magnitude of the harm resulting from the unauthorized access, use, disclosure, disruption, modification, or destruction of—

``(A) information collected or maintained by or on behalf of an agency; or

``(B) information systems used or operated by an agency or by a contractor of an agency or other organization on behalf of an agency;

``(3) coordinating the development of standards and guidelines under section 20 of the National Institute of Standards and Technology Act (15 U.S.C. 278g-3) with agencies and offices operating or exercising control of national security systems (including the National Security Agency) to assure, to the maximum extent feasible, that such standards and guidelines are complementary with standards and guidelines developed for national security systems;

``(4) overseeing agency compliance with the requirements of this subchapter, including through any authorized action under section 11303 of title 40, to enforce accountability for compliance with such requirements;

``(5) reviewing at least annually, and approving or disapproving, agency information security programs required under section 3544(b);

``(6) coordinating information security policies and procedures with related information resources management policies and procedures;

``(7) overseeing the operation of the Federal information security incident center required under section 3546; and

``(8) reporting to Congress no later than March 1 of each year on agency compliance with the requirements of this subchapter, including—

>  ``(A) a summary of the findings of evaluations required by section 3545;
>
>  ``(B) an assessment of the development, promulgation, and adoption of, and compliance with, standards developed under section 20 of the National Institute of Standards and Technology Act (15 U.S.C. 278g-3) and promulgated under section 11331 of title 40;
>
>  ``(C) significant deficiencies in agency information security practices;
>
>  ``(D) planned remedial action to address such deficiencies; and
>
>  ``(E) a summary of, and the views of the Director on, the report prepared by the National Institute of Standards and Technology under section 20(d) (10) of the National Institute of Standards and Technology Act (15 U.S.C. 278g-3).

``(b) National Security Systems.—Except for the authorities described in paragraphs (4) and (8) of subsection (a), the authorities of the Director under this section shall not apply to national security systems.

``(c) Department of Defense and Central Intelligence Agency Systems. –

(1) The authorities of the Director described in paragraphs (1) and (2) of subsection (a) shall be delegated to the Secretary of Defense in the case of systems described in paragraph (2) and to the Director of Central Intelligence in the case of systems described in paragraph (3).

``(2) The systems described in this paragraph are systems that are operated by the Department of Defense, a contractor of the Department of Defense, or another entity on behalf of the Department of Defense that processes any information the unauthorized access, use, disclosure, disruption, modification, or destruction of which would have a debilitating impact on the mission of the Department of Defense.

``(3) The systems described in this paragraph are systems that are operated by the Central Intelligence Agency, a contractor of the Central Intelligence Agency, or another entity on behalf of the Central Intelligence Agency that processes any information the unauthorized access, use, disclosure, disruption, modification, or destruction of which would have a debilitating impact on the mission of the Central Intelligence Agency.

**``Sec. 3544. Federal agency responsibilities**

``(a) In General.—The head of each agency shall—

``(1) be responsible for—

``(A) providing information security protections commensurate with the risk and magnitude of the harm resulting from unauthorized access, use, disclosure, disruption, modification, or destruction of—

> ``(i) information collected or maintained by or on behalf of the agency; and

> ``(ii) information systems used or operated by an agency or by a contractor of an agency or other organization on behalf of an agency;

``(B) complying with the requirements of this subchapter and related policies, procedures, standards, and guidelines, including—

> ``(i) information security standards promulgated under section 11331 of title 40; and

> ``(ii) information security standards and guidelines for national security systems issued in accordance with law and as directed by the President; and

``(C) ensuring that information security management processes are integrated with agency strategic and operational planning processes;

``(2) ensure that senior agency officials provide information security for the information and information systems that support the operations and assets under their control, including through—

``(A) assessing the risk and magnitude of the harm that could result from the unauthorized access, use, disclosure, disruption, modification, or destruction of such information or information systems;

``(B) determining the levels of information security appropriate to protect such information and information systems in accordance with standards promulgated under section 11331 of title 40, for information security classifications and related requirements;

``(C) implementing policies and procedures to cost- effectively reduce risks to an acceptable level; and

``(D) periodically testing and evaluating information security controls and techniques to ensure that they are effectively implemented;

``(3) delegate to the agency Chief Information Officer established under section 3506 (or comparable official in an agency not covered by such section) the authority to ensure compliance with the requirements imposed on the agency under this subchapter, including—

``(A) designating a senior agency information security officer who shall—

``(i) carry out the Chief Information Officer's responsibilities under this section;

``(ii) possess professional qualifications, including training and experience, required to administer the functions described under this section;

``(iii) have information security duties as that official's primary duty; and

``(iv) head an office with the mission and resources to assist in ensuring agency compliance with this section;

``(B) developing and maintaining an agency wide information security program as required by subsection (b);

``(C) developing and maintaining information security policies, procedures, and control techniques to address all applicable requirements, including those issued under section 3543 of this title, and section 11331 of title 40;

``(D) training and overseeing personnel with significant responsibilities for information security with respect to such responsibilities; and

``(E) assisting senior agency officials concerning their responsibilities under paragraph (2);

``(4) ensure that the agency has trained personnel sufficient to assist the agency in complying with the requirements of this subchapter and related policies, procedures, standards, and guidelines; and

``(5) ensure that the agency Chief Information Officer, in coordination with other senior agency officials, reports annually to the agency head on the effectiveness of the agency information security program, including progress of remedial actions.

``(b) Agency Program.—Each agency shall develop, document, and implement an agency wide information security program, approved by the Director under section 3543(a)(5), to provide information security for the information and information systems that support the operations and assets of the agency, including those provided or managed by another agency, contractor, or other source, that includes—

>``(1) periodic assessments of the risk and magnitude of the harm that could result from the unauthorized access, use, disclosure, disruption, modification, or destruction of information and information systems that support the operations and assets of the agency;

``(2) policies and procedures that—

>``(A) are based on the risk assessments required by paragraph (1);
>
>``(B) cost-effectively reduce information security risks to an acceptable level;
>
>``(C) ensure that information security is addressed throughout the life cycle of each agency information system; and
>
>``(D) ensure compliance with—
>
>``(i) the requirements of this subchapter;
>
>``(ii) policies and procedures as may be prescribed by the Director, and information security standards promulgated under section 11331 of title 40;
>
>``(iii) minimally acceptable system configuration requirements, as determined by the agency; and

``(iv) any other applicable requirements, including standards and guidelines for national security systems issued in accordance with law and as directed by the President;

``(3) subordinate plans for providing adequate information security for networks, facilities, and systems or groups of information systems, as appropriate;

``(4) security awareness training to inform personnel, including contractors and other users of information systems that support the operations and assets of the agency, of—

``(A) information security risks associated with their activities; and ``(B) their responsibilities in complying with agency policies and procedures designed to reduce these risks;

``(5) periodic testing and evaluation of the effectiveness of information security policies, procedures, and practices, to be performed with a frequency depending on risk, but no less than annually, of which such testing—

``(A) shall include testing of management, operational, and technical controls of every information system identified in the inventory required under section 3505(c); and

``(B) may include testing relied on in a evaluation under section 3545;

``(6) a process for planning, implementing, evaluating, and documenting remedial action to address any deficiencies in the information security policies, procedures, and practices of the agency;

``(7) procedures for detecting, reporting, and responding to security incidents, consistent with standards and guidelines issued pursuant to section 3546(b), including—

``(A) mitigating risks associated with such incidents before substantial damage is done;

``(B) notifying and consulting with the Federal information security incident center referred to in section 3546; and

``(C) notifying and consulting with, as appropriate—

``(i) law enforcement agencies and relevant Offices of Inspector General;

``(ii) an office designated by the President for any incident involving a national security system; and

``(iii) any other agency or office, in accordance with law or as directed by the President; and

``(8) plans and procedures to ensure continuity of operations for information systems that support the operations and assets of the agency.

``(c) Agency Reporting.—Each agency shall—

``(1) report annually to the Director, the Committees on Government Reform and Science of the House of Representatives, the Committees on Governmental Affairs and Commerce, Science, and Transportation of the Senate, the appropriate authorization and appropriations committees of Congress, and the Comptroller General on the adequacy and effectiveness of information security policies, procedures, and practices, and compliance with the requirements of this subchapter, including compliance with each requirement of subsection (b);

``(2) address the adequacy and effectiveness of information security policies, procedures, and practices in plans and reports relating to—

``(A) annual agency budgets;

``(B) information resources management under subchapter 1 of this chapter;

``(C) information technology management under subtitle III of title 40;

``(D) program performance under sections 1105 and 1115 through 1119 of title 31, and sections 2801 and 2805 of title 39;

``(E) financial management under chapter 9 of title 31, and the Chief Financial Officers Act of 1990 (31 U.S.C. 501 note; Public Law 101-576) (and the amendments made by that Act);

``(F) financial management systems under the Federal Financial Management Improvement Act (31 U.S.C. 3512 note); and

``(G) internal accounting and administrative controls under section 3512 of title 31, (known as the `Federal Managers Financial Integrity Act'); and

``(3) report any significant deficiency in a policy, procedure, or practice identified under paragraph (1) or (2)—

``(A) as a material weakness in reporting under section 3512 of title 31; and

``(B) if relating to financial management systems, as an instance of a lack of substantial compliance under the Federal Financial Management Improvement Act (31 U.S.C. 3512 note).

``(d) Performance Plan.—(1) In addition to the requirements of subsection (c), each agency, in consultation with the Director, shall include as part of the performance plan required under section 1115 of title 31 a description of—

``(A) the time periods, and

``(B) the resources, including budget, staffing, and training, that are necessary to implement the program required under subsection (b).

``(2) The description under paragraph (1) shall be based on the risk assessments required under subsection (b)(2)(1).

``(e) Public Notice and Comment.—Each agency shall provide the public with timely notice and opportunities for comment on proposed information security policies and procedures to the extent that such policies and procedures affect communication with the public.

``Sec. 3545. Annual independent evaluation

``(a) In General.—(1) Each year each agency shall have performed an independent evaluation of the information security program and practices of that agency to determine the effectiveness of such program and practices.

``(2) Each evaluation under this section shall include—

``(A) testing of the effectiveness of information security policies, procedures, and practices of a representative subset of the agency's information systems;

``(B) an assessment (made on the basis of the results of the testing) of compliance with—

> ``(i) the requirements of this subchapter; and
>
> ``(ii) related information security policies, procedures, standards, and guidelines; and

``(C) separate presentations, as appropriate, regarding information security relating to national security systems.

> ``(b) Independent Auditor.—Subject to subsection (c)—

``(1) for each agency with an Inspector General appointed under the Inspector General Act of 1978, the annual evaluation required by this section shall be performed by the Inspector General or by an independent external auditor, as determined by the Inspector General of the agency; and

> ``(2) for each agency to which paragraph (1) does not apply, the head of the agency shall engage an independent external auditor to perform the evaluation.

``(c) National Security Systems.—For each agency operating or exercising control of a national security system, that portion of the evaluation required by this section directly relating to a national security system shall be performed—

> ``(1) only by an entity designated by the agency head; and

``(2) in such a manner as to ensure appropriate protection for information associated with any information security vulnerability in such system commensurate with the risk and in accordance with all applicable laws.

``(d) Existing Evaluations.—The evaluation required by this section may be based in whole or in part on an audit, evaluation, or report relating to programs or practices of the applicable agency.

``(e) Agency <<NOTE: Deadline.>> Reporting. —

``(1) Each year, not later than such date established by the Director, the head of each agency shall submit to the Director the results of the evaluation required under this section.

``(2) To the extent an evaluation required under this section directly relates to a national security system, the evaluation results submitted to the Director shall contain only a summary and assessment of that portion of the evaluation directly relating to a national security system.

``(f) Protection of Information.—Agencies and evaluators shall take appropriate steps to ensure the protection of information which, if disclosed, may adversely affect information security. Such protections shall be commensurate with the risk and comply with all applicable laws and regulations.

``(g) OMB Reports to Congress. —

``(1) The Director shall summarize the results of the evaluations conducted under this section in the report to Congress required under section 3543(a)(8).

``(2) The Director's report to Congress under this subsection shall summarize information regarding information security relating to national security systems in such a manner as to ensure appropriate protection for information associated with any information security vulnerability in such system commensurate with the risk and in accordance with all applicable laws.

``(3) Evaluations and any other descriptions of information systems under the authority and control of the Director of Central Intelligence or of National Foreign Intelligence Programs systems under the authority and control of the Secretary of Defense shall be made available to Congress only through the appropriate oversight committees of Congress, in accordance with applicable laws.

``(h) Comptroller <<NOTE: Reports.>> General.—The Comptroller General shall periodically evaluate and report to Congress on—

``(1) the adequacy and effectiveness of agency information security policies and practices; and

``(2) implementation of the requirements of this subchapter.

``Sec. 3546. Federal information security incident center

``(a) In General.—The Director shall ensure the operation of a central Federal information security incident center to—

``(1) provide timely technical assistance to operators of agency information systems regarding security incidents, including guidance on detecting and handling information security incidents;

``(2) compile and analyze information about incidents that threaten information security;

``(3) inform operators of agency information systems about current and potential information security threats, and vulnerabilities; and

``(4) consult with the National Institute of Standards and Technology, agencies or offices operating or exercising control of national security systems (including the National Security Agency), and such other agencies or offices in accordance with law and as directed by the President regarding information security incidents and related matters.

``(b) National Security Systems.—Each agency operating or exercising control of a national security system shall share information about information security incidents, threats, and vulnerabilities with the Federal information security incident center to the extent consistent with standards and guidelines for national security systems, issued in accordance with law and as directed by the President.

``Sec. 3547. National security systems

``The head of each agency operating or exercising control of a national security system shall be responsible for ensuring that the agency—

``(1) provides information security protections commensurate with the risk and magnitude of the harm resulting from the unauthorized access, use, disclosure, disruption, modification, or destruction of the information contained in such system;

``(2) implements information security policies and practices as required by standards and guidelines for national security systems, issued in accordance with law and as directed by the President; and

``(3) complies with the requirements of this subchapter.

``**Sec. 3548. Authorization of appropriations**

``There are authorized to be appropriated to carry out the provisions of this subchapter such sums as may be necessary for each of fiscal years 2003 through 2007.

``**Sec. 3549. Effect on existing law**

``Nothing in this subchapter, section 11331 of title 40, or section 20 of the National Standards and Technology Act (15 U.S.C. 278g-3) may be construed as affecting the authority of the President, the Office of Management and Budget or the Director thereof, the National Institute of Standards and Technology, or the head of any agency, with respect to the authorized use or disclosure of information, including with regard to the protection of personal privacy under section 552a of title 5, the disclosure of information under section 552 of title 5, the management and disposition of records under chapters 29, 31, or 33 of title 44, the management of information resources under subchapter I of chapter 35 of this title, or the disclosure of information to the Congress or the Comptroller General of the United States. While this subchapter is in effect, subchapter II of this chapter shall not apply.''.

1. Clerical amendment.—The table of sections at the beginning of such chapter 35 is amended by adding at the end the following:

``**SUBCHAPTER III—INFORMATION SECURITY**

``Sec.

``3541. Purposes.

``3542. Definitions.

``3543. Authority and functions of the Director.

``3544. Federal agency responsibilities.

``3545. Annual independent evaluation.

``3546. Federal information security incident center.

``3547. National security systems.

``3548. Authorization of appropriations.

``3549. Effect on existing law.''.

(c) Information Security Responsibilities of Certain Agencies. -

1. National <<NOTE: 44 USC 3501 note.>> security responsibilities.—(A) Nothing in this Act (including any amendment made by this Act) shall supersede any authority of the Secretary of Defense, the Director of Central Intelligence, or other agency head, as authorized by law and as directed by the President, with regard to the operation, control, or management of national security systems, as defined by section 3542(b)(2) of title 44, United States Code.

(B) Section 2224 of title 10, United States Code, is amended—

(i) in subsection (b), by striking ``(b) Objectives and Minimum Requirements.—(1)'' and inserting ``(b) Objectives of the Program.—'';

(ii) in subsection (b), by striking paragraph (2); and

(iii) in subsection (c), in the matter preceding paragraph (1), by inserting ``, including through compliance with subchapter III of chapter 35 of title 44'' after ``infrastructure''.

1. Atomic <<NOTE: 44 USC 3501 note.>> energy act of 1954.—Nothing in this Act shall supersede any requirement made by or under the Atomic Energy Act of 1954 (42 U.S.C. 2011 et seq.). Restricted data or formerly restricted data shall be handled, protected, classified, downgraded, and declassified in conformity with the Atomic Energy Act of 1954 (42 U.S.C. 2011 et seq.).

## SEC. 302. MANAGEMENT OF INFORMATION TECHNOLOGY.

(a) In General.—Section 11331 of title 40, United States Code, is amended to read as follows:

``Sec. 11331. Responsibilities for Federal information systems standards

``(a) Standards and Guidelines.—

``(1) Authority to prescribe.—Except as provided under paragraph (2), the Secretary of Commerce shall, on the basis of standards and guidelines developed by the National Institute of Standards and Technology pursuant to paragraphs (2) and (3) of section 20(a) of the National Institute of Standards and Technology Act (15 U.S.C. 278g-3(a)), prescribe standards and guidelines pertaining to Federal information systems.

``(2) National security systems.—Standards and guidelines for national security systems (as defined under this section) shall be developed, prescribed, enforced, and overseen as otherwise authorized by law and as directed by the President.

``(b) Mandatory Requirements.—

``(1) Authority to make mandatory.—Except as provided under paragraph (2), the Secretary shall make standards prescribed under subsection (a)(1) compulsory and binding to the extent determined necessary by the Secretary to improve the efficiency of operation or security of Federal information systems.

``(2) Required mandatory standards.—(A) Standards prescribed under subsection (a)(1) shall include information security standards that—

``(i) provide minimum information security requirements as determined under section 20(b) of the National Institute of Standards and Technology Act (15 U.S.C. 278g-3(b)); and

``(ii) are otherwise necessary to improve the security of Federal information and information systems.

``(B) Information security standards described in subparagraph (A) shall be compulsory and binding.

``(c) Authority to Disapprove or Modify.—The President may disapprove or modify the standards and guidelines referred to in subsection (a)(1) if the President determines such action to be in the public interest. The President's authority to disapprove or modify such standards and guidelines may not be delegated. <<NOTE: Federal Register, publication.>> Notice of such disapproval or modification shall be published promptly in the Federal Register. Upon receiving notice of such disapproval or modification, the Secretary of Commerce shall immediately rescind or modify such standards or guidelines as directed by the President.

``(d) Exercise of Authority.—To ensure fiscal and policy consistency, the Secretary shall exercise the authority conferred by this section subject to direction by the President and in coordination with the Director of the Office of Management and Budget.

``(e) Application of More Stringent Standards.—The head of an executive agency may employ standards for the cost-effective information security for information systems within or under the supervision of that agency that are more stringent than the standards the Secretary prescribes under this section if the more stringent standards—

> ``(1) contain at least the applicable standards made compulsory and binding by the Secretary; and

> ``(2) are otherwise consistent with policies and guidelines issued under section 3543 of title 44.

``(f) Decisions <<NOTE: Deadline.>> on Promulgation of Standards.—The decision by the Secretary regarding the promulgation of any standard under this section shall occur not later than 6 months after the submission of the proposed standard to the Secretary by the National Institute of Standards and Technology, as provided under section 20 of the National Institute of Standards and Technology Act (15 U.S.C. 278g- 3).

``(g) Definitions.—In this section:

> ``(1) Federal information system.—The term `Federal information system' means an information system used or operated by an executive agency, by a contractor of an executive agency, or by another organization on behalf of an executive agency.

> ``(2) Information security.—The term `information security' has the meaning given that term in section 3542(b)(1) of title 44.

``(3) National security system.—The term `national security system' has the meaning given that term in section 3542(b)(2) of title 44.''.

(b) Clerical Amendment.—The item relating to section 11331 in the table of sections at the beginning of chapter 113 of such title is amended to read as follows:

``11331. Responsibilities for Federal information systems standards.''.

## SEC. 303. NATIONAL INSTITUTE OF STANDARDS AND TECHNOLOGY.

Section 20 of the National Institute of Standards and Technology Act (15 U.S.C. 278g-3), is amended by striking the text and inserting the following:

``(a) In General.—The Institute shall—

``(1) have the mission of developing standards, guidelines, and associated methods and techniques for information systems;

``(2) develop standards and guidelines, including minimum requirements, for information systems used or operated by an agency or by a contractor of an agency or other organization on behalf of an agency, other than national security systems (as defined in section 3542(b)(2) of title 44, United States Code); and

``(3) develop standards and guidelines, including minimum requirements, for providing adequate information security for all agency operations and assets, but such standards and guidelines shall not apply to national security systems.

``(b) Minimum Requirements for Standards and Guidelines. —The standards and guidelines required by subsection (a) shall include, at a minimum—

``(1)(A) standards to be used by all agencies to categorize all information and information systems collected or maintained by or on behalf of each agency based on the objectives of providing appropriate levels of information security according to a range of risk levels;

``(B) guidelines recommending the types of information and information systems to be included in each such category; and

``(C) minimum information security requirements for information and information systems in each such category;

``(2) a definition of and guidelines concerning detection and handling of information security incidents; and

``(3) guidelines developed in conjunction with the Department of Defense, including the National Security Agency, for identifying an information system as a national security system consistent with applicable requirements for national security systems, issued in accordance with law and as directed by the President.

``(c) Development of Standards and Guidelines.—In developing standards and guidelines required by subsections (a) and (b), the Institute shall—

``(1) consult with other agencies and offices and the private sector (including the Director of the Office of Management and Budget, the Departments of Defense and Energy, the National Security Agency, the General Accounting Office, and the Secretary of Homeland Security) to assure—

``(A) use of appropriate information security policies, procedures, and techniques, in order to improve information security and avoid unnecessary and costly duplication of effort; and

``(B) that such standards and guidelines are complementary with standards and guidelines employed for the protection of national security systems and information contained in such systems;

``(2) provide the public with an opportunity to comment on proposed standards and guidelines;

``(3) <<NOTE: Deadlines.>> submit to the Secretary of Commerce for promulgation under section 11331 of title 40, United States Code—

``(A) standards, as required under subsection (b)(1)(A), no later than 12 months after the date of the enactment of this section; and

``(B) minimum information security requirements for each category, as required under subsection (b)(1)(C), no later than 36 months after the date of the enactment of this section;

``(4) <<NOTE: Deadline.>> issue guidelines as required under subsection (b)(1)(B), no later than 18 months after the date of the enactment of this section;

``(5) to the maximum extent practicable, ensure that such standards and guidelines do not require the use or procurement of specific products, including any specific hardware or software;

``(6) to the maximum extent practicable, ensure that such standards and guidelines provide for sufficient flexibility to permit alternative solutions to provide equivalent levels of protection for identified information security risks; and

``(7) to the maximum extent practicable, use flexible, performance-based standards and guidelines that permit the use of off-the-shelf commercially developed information security products.

``(d) Information Security Functions.—The Institute shall—

``(1) submit standards developed pursuant to subsection (a), along with recommendations as to the extent to which these should be made compulsory and binding, to the Secretary of Commerce for promulgation under section 11331 of title 40, United States Code;

``(2) provide technical assistance to agencies, upon request, regarding—

``(A) compliance with the standards and guidelines developed under subsection (a);

``(B) detecting and handling information security incidents; and

``(C) information security policies, procedures, and practices;

``(3) conduct research, as needed, to determine the nature and extent of information security vulnerabilities and techniques for providing cost-effective information security;

``(4) develop and periodically revise performance indicators and measures for agency information security policies and practices;

``(5) evaluate private sector information security policies and practices and commercially available information technologies to assess potential application by agencies to strengthen information security;

``(6) assist the private sector, upon request, in using and applying the results of activities under this section;

``(7) evaluate security policies and practices developed for national security systems to assess potential application by agencies to strengthen information security;

``(8) periodically assess the effectiveness of standards and guidelines developed under this section and undertake revisions as appropriate;

``(9) solicit and consider the recommendations of the Information Security and Privacy Advisory Board, established by section 21, regarding standards and guidelines developed under subsection (a) and submit such recommendations to the Secretary of Commerce with such standards submitted to the Secretary; and

``(10) prepare an annual public report on activities undertaken in the previous year, and planned for the coming year, to carry out responsibilities under this section.

``(e) Definitions.—As used in this section—

``(1) the term `agency' has the same meaning as provided in section 3502(1) of title 44, United States Code;

``(2) the term `information security' has the same meaning as provided in section 3542(b)(1) of such title;

``(3) the term `information system' has the same meaning as provided in section 3502(8) of such title;

``(4) the term `information technology' has the same meaning as provided in section 11101 of title 40, United States Code; and

``(5) the term `national security system' has the same meaning as provided in section 3542(b)(2) of title 44, United States Code.

``(f) Authorization of Appropriations.—There are authorized to be appropriated to the Secretary of Commerce $20,000,000 for each of fiscal years 2003, 2004, 2005, 2006, and 2007 to enable the National Institute of Standards and Technology to carry out the provisions of this section.''.

**SEC. 304. INFORMATION SECURITY AND PRIVACY ADVISORY BOARD.**

Section 21 of the National Institute of Standards and Technology Act (15 U.S.C. 278g-4), is amended—

(1) in subsection (a), by striking ``Computer System Security and Privacy Advisory Board" and inserting ``Information Security and Privacy Advisory Board";

(2) in subsection (a)(1), by striking ``computer or telecommunications" and inserting ``information technology";

(3) in subsection (a)(2)—

(A) by striking ``computer or telecommunications technology" and inserting ``information technology"; and

(B) by striking ``computer or telecommunications equipment" and inserting ``information technology";

(4) in subsection (a)(3)—

(A) by striking ``computer systems" and inserting ``information system"; and

(B) by striking ``computer systems security" and inserting ``information security";

(5) in subsection (b)(1) by striking ``computer systems security" and inserting ``information security";

(6) in subsection (b) by striking paragraph (2) and inserting the following:

``(2) to advise the Institute, the Secretary of Commerce, and the Director of the Office of Management and Budget on information security and privacy issues pertaining to Federal Government information systems, including through review of proposed standards and guidelines developed under section 20; and";

(7) in subsection (b)(3) by inserting ``annually" after ``report";

(8) by inserting after subsection (e) the following new subsection:

``(f) The Board shall hold meetings at such locations and at such time and place as determined by a majority of the Board.";

(9) by redesignating subsections (f) and (g) as subsections

(g) and (h), respectively; and

(10) by striking subsection (h), as redesignated by paragraph (9), and inserting the following:

``(h) As used in this section, the terms `information system' and `information technology' have the meanings given in section 20.''.

## SEC. 305. TECHNICAL AND CONFORMING AMENDMENTS.

(a) Computer Security Act.—Section 11332 of title 40, United States Code, and the item relating to that section in the table of sections for chapter 113 of such title, are repealed.

(b) Floyd D. Spence National Defense Authorization Act for Fiscal Year 2001.—The Floyd D. Spence National Defense Authorization Act for Fiscal Year 2001 (Public Law 106-398) is amended by striking section 1062 (44 U.S.C. 3531 note).

(c) Paperwork Reduction Act.—(1) Section 3504(g) of title 44, United States Code, is amended—

(A) by adding ``and'' at the end of paragraph (1);
(B) in paragraph (2)—

(i) by striking ``sections 11331 and 11332(b) and

(c) of title 40'' and inserting ``section 11331 of title 40 and subchapter II of this chapter''; and

(ii) by striking ``; and'' and inserting a period; and

(C) by striking paragraph (3). (2) Section 3505 of such title is amended by adding at the end—

``(c) Inventory of Major Information Systems.—(1) The head of each agency shall develop and maintain an inventory of major information systems (including major national security systems) operated by or under the control of such agency.

``(2) The identification of information systems in an inventory under this subsection shall include an identification of the interfaces between each such system and all other systems or networks, including those not operated by or under the control of the agency.

``(3) Such inventory shall be—

``(A) updated at least annually;
``(B) made available to the Comptroller General; and
``(C) used to support information resources management, including—

``(i) preparation and maintenance of the inventory of information resources under section 3506(b)(4);

``(ii) information technology planning, budgeting, acquisition, and management under section 3506(h), subtitle III of title 40, and related laws and guidance;

``(iii) monitoring, testing, and evaluation of information security controls under subchapter II;

``(iv) preparation of the index of major information systems required under section 552(g) of title 5, United States Code; and

``(v) preparation of information system inventories required for records management under chapters 21, 29, 31, and 33.

``(4) The Director shall issue guidance for and oversee the implementation of the requirements of this subsection.''.

(3) Section 3506(g) of such title is amended—

(A) by adding ``and'' at the end of paragraph (1);
(B) in paragraph (2)—

(i) by striking ``section 11332 of title 40'' and inserting ``subchapter II of this chapter''; and

(ii) by striking ``; and'' and inserting a period; and

(C) by striking paragraph (3).

## TITLE IV—AUTHORIZATION OF APPROPRIATIONS AND EFFECTIVE DATES

### SEC. 401. AUTHORIZATION OF APPROPRIATIONS.

Except for those purposes for which an authorization of appropriations is specifically provided in title I or II, including the amendments made by such titles, there are authorized to be appropriated such sums as are necessary to carry out titles I and II for each of fiscal years 2003 through 2007.

**SEC. 402. EFFECTIVE DATES.**

(a) Titles <<NOTE: 44 USC 3601 note.>> I and II.—

> (1) In general.—Except as provided under paragraph (2), titles I and II and the amendments made by such titles shall take effect 120 days after the date of enactment of this Act.
>
> (2) Immediate enactment.—Sections 207, 214, and 215 shall take effect on the date of enactment of this Act.

(b) Titles <<NOTE: 44 USC 3541 note.>> III and IV.—Title III and this title shall take effect on the date of enactment of this Act.

TITLE <<NOTE: Confidential Information Protection and Statistical Efficiency Act of 2002.>> V—CONFIDENTIAL INFORMATION PROTECTION AND STATISTICAL EFFICIENCY

SEC. 501. <<NOTE: 44 USC 3501 note.>> SHORT TITLE.

This title may be cited as the ``Confidential Information Protection and Statistical Efficiency Act of 2002''.

SEC. 502. <<NOTE: 44 USC 3501 note.>> DEFINITIONS.

As used in this title:

1. The term ``agency'' means any entity that falls within the definition of the term ``executive agency'' as defined in section 102 of title 31, United States Code, or ``agency'', as defined in section 3502 of title 44, United States Code.
2. The term ``agent'' means an individual—

    A. (i) who is an employee of a private organization or a researcher affiliated with an institution of higher learning (including a person granted special sworn status by the Bureau of the Census under section 23(c)of title 13, United States Code), and with whom a contract or other agreement is executed, on a temporary basis, by an executive agency to perform exclusively statistical activities under the control and supervision of an officer or employee of that agency;

(ii) who is working under the authority of a government entity with which a contract or other agreement is executed by an executive agency to perform exclusively statistical activities under the control of an officer or employee of that agency;

(iii) who is a self-employed researcher, a consultant, a contractor, or an employee of a contractor, and with whom a contract or other agreement is executed by an executive agency to perform a statistical activity under the control of an officer or employee of that agency; or

(iv) who is a contractor or an employee of a contractor, and who is engaged by the agency to design or maintain the systems for handling or storage of data received under this title; and

A. who agrees in writing to comply with all provisions of law that affect information acquired by that agency.

1. The term ``business data'' means operating and financial data and information about businesses, tax-exempt organizations, and government entities.
2. The term ``identifiable form'' means any representation of information that permits the identity of the respondent to whom the information applies to be reasonably inferred by either direct or indirect means.
3. The term ``nonstatistical purpose''—

A. means the use of data in identifiable form for any purpose that is not a statistical purpose, including any administrative, regulatory, law enforcement, adjudicatory, or other purpose that affects the rights, privileges, or benefits of a particular identifiable respondent; and

A. includes the disclosure under section 552 of title 5, United States Code (popularly known as the Freedom of Information Act) of data that are acquired for exclusively statistical purposes under a pledge of confidentiality.

1. The term ``respondent'' means a person who, or organization that, is requested or required to supply information to an agency, is the subject of information requested or required to be supplied to an agency, or provides that information to an agency.

1. The term ``statistical activities''—

A. means the collection, compilation, processing, or analysis of data for the purpose of describing or making estimates concerning the whole, or relevant groups or components within, the economy, society, or the natural environment; and
B. includes the development of methods or resources that support those activities, such as measurement methods, models, statistical classifications, or sampling

frames.

1. The term ``statistical agency or unit" means an agency or organizational unit of the executive branch whose activities are predominantly the collection, compilation, processing, or analysis of information for statistical purposes.

(9) The term ``statistical purpose"—

A. means the description, estimation, or analysis of the characteristics of groups, without identifying the individuals or organizations that comprise such groups; and
B. includes the development, implementation, or maintenance of methods, technical or administrative procedures, or information resources that support the purposes described in subparagraph (A).

**SEC. 503. <<NOTE: 44 USC 3501 note.>> COORDINATION AND OVERSIGHT OF POLICIES.**

a. In General.—The Director of the Office of Management and Budget shall coordinate and oversee the confidentiality and disclosure policies established by this title. The Director may promulgate rules or provide other guidance to ensure consistent interpretation of this title by the affected agencies.

a. Agency Rules.—Subject to subsection (c), agencies may promulgate rules to implement this title. Rules governing disclosures of information that are authorized by this title shall be promulgated by the agency that originally collected the information.

a. Review and Approval of Rules.—The Director shall review any rules proposed by an agency pursuant to this title for consistency with the provisions of this title and chapter 35 of title 44, United States Code, and such rules shall be subject to the approval of the Director.

a. Reports.—

1. The head of each agency shall provide to the Director of the Office of Management and Budget such reports and other information as the Director requests.
2. Each Designated Statistical Agency referred to in section 522 shall report annually to the Director of the Office of Management and Budget, the Committee on Government Reform of the House of Representatives, and the Committee on Governmental Affairs of the Senate on the actions it has taken to implement sections 523 and 524. The report shall include copies of each written agreement entered into pursuant to section 524(a) for the applicable year.
3. The Director of the Office of Management and Budget shall include a summary of reports submitted to the Director under paragraph (2) and actions taken by the Director to advance the purposes of this title in the annual report to the Congress on statistical programs prepared under section 3504(e)(2) of title 44, United States Code.

**SEC. 504. <<NOTE: 44 USC 3501 note.>> EFFECT ON OTHER LAWS.**

a. Title 44, United States Code.—This title, including amendments made by this title, does not diminish the authority under section 3510 of title 44, United States Code, of the Director of the Office of Management and Budget to direct, and of an agency to make, disclosures that are not inconsistent with any applicable law.

a. Title 13 and Title 44, United States Code.—This title, including amendments made by this title, does not diminish the authority of the Bureau of the Census to provide information in accordance with sections 8, 16, 301, and 401 of title 13, United States Code, and section 2108 of title 44, United States Code.

a. Title 13, United States Code.—This title, including amendments made by this

# CYBER LAW & FISMA COMPLIANCE 315

title, shall not be construed as authorizing the disclosure for nonstatistical purposes of demographic data or information collected by the Census Bureau pursuant to section 9 of title 13, United States Code.

a. Various Energy Statutes.—Data or information acquired by the Energy Information Administration under a pledge of confidentiality and designated by the Energy Information Administration to be used for exclusively statistical purposes shall not be disclosed in identifiable form for nonstatistical purposes under—

1. section 12, 20, or 59 of the Federal Energy Administration Act of 1974 (15 U.S.C. 771, 779, 790h);
2. section 11 of the Energy Supply and Environmental Coordination Act of 1974 (15 U.S.C. 796); or
3. section 205 or 407 of the Department of the Energy Organization Act of 1977 (42 U.S.C. 7135, 7177).

a. Section 201 of Congressional Budget Act of 1974.—This title, including amendments made by this title, shall not be construed to limit any authorities of the Congressional Budget Office to work (consistent with laws governing the confidentiality of information the disclosure of which would be a violation of law) with databases of Designated Statistical Agencies (as defined in section 522), either separately or, for data that may be shared pursuant to section 524 of this title or other authority, jointly in order to improve the general utility of these databases for the statistical purpose of analyzing pension and health care financing issues.
b. Preemption of State Law.—Nothing in this title shall preempt applicable State law regarding the confidentiality of data collected by the States.
c. Statutes Regarding False Statements.—Notwithstanding section 512, information collected by an agency for exclusively statistical purposes under a pledge of confidentiality may be provided by the collecting agency to a

law enforcement agency for the prosecution of submissions to the collecting agency of false statistical information under statutes that authorize criminal penalties (such as section 221 of title 13, United States Code) or civil penalties for the provision of false statistical information, unless such disclosure or use would otherwise be prohibited under Federal law.

d. Construction.—Nothing in this title shall be construed as restricting or diminishing any confidentiality protections or penalties for unauthorized disclosure that otherwise apply to data or information collected for statistical purposes or nonstatistical purposes, including, but not limited to, section 6103 of the Internal Revenue Code of 1986 (26 U.S.C. 6103).

i. Authority of Congress.—Nothing in this title shall be construed to affect the authority of the Congress, including its committees, members, or agents, to obtain data or information for a statistical purpose, including for oversight of an agency's statistical activities.

**Subtitle A—Confidential Information Protection**

SEC. 511. <<NOTE: 44 USC 3501 note.>> FINDINGS AND PURPOSES.

(a) Findings.—The Congress finds the following:

1. Individuals, businesses, and other organizations have varying degrees of legal protection when providing information to the agencies for strictly statistical purposes.
2. Pledges of confidentiality by agencies provide assurances to the public that information about individuals or organizations or provided by individuals or organizations for exclusively statistical purposes will be held in confidence and will not be used against such individuals or organizations in any agency action.
3. Protecting the confidentiality interests of individuals or organizations who provide information under a pledge of confidentiality for Federal statistical programs serves both the interests of the public and the needs of society.
4. Declining trust of the public in the protection of information provided under

a pledge of confidentiality to the agencies adversely affects both the accuracy and completeness of statistical analyses.
5. Ensuring that information provided under a pledge of confidentiality for statistical purposes receives protection is essential in continuing public cooperation in statistical programs.

(b) Purposes.—The purposes of this subtitle are the following:

1. To ensure that information supplied by individuals or organizations to an agency for statistical purposes under a pledge of confidentiality is used exclusively for statistical purposes.
2. To ensure that individuals or organizations who supply information under a pledge of confidentiality to agencies for statistical purposes will neither have that information disclosed in identifiable form to anyone not authorized by this title nor have that information used for any purpose other than a statistical purpose.
3. To safeguard the confidentiality of individually identifiable information acquired under a pledge of confidentiality for statistical purposes by controlling access to, and uses made of, such information.

**SEC. 512. <<NOTE: 44 USC 3501 note. >> LIMITATIONS ON USE AND DISCLOSURE OF DATA AND INFORMATION.**

a. Use of Statistical Data or Information.—Data or information acquired by an agency under a pledge of confidentiality and for exclusively statistical purposes shall be used by officers, employees, or agents of the agency exclusively for statistical purposes.
b. Disclosure of Statistical Data or Information.—

1. Data or information acquired by an agency under a pledge of confidentiality for exclusively statistical purposes shall not be disclosed by an agency in

identifiable form, for any use other than an exclusively statistical purpose, except with the informed consent of the respondent.
2. A disclosure pursuant to paragraph (1) is authorized only when the head of the agency approves such disclosure and the disclosure is not prohibited by any other law.
3. This section does not restrict or diminish any confidentiality protections in law that otherwise apply to data or information acquired by an agency under a pledge of confidentiality for exclusively statistical purposes.

a. Rule for Use of Data or Information for Nonstatistical Purposes.—A statistical agency or unit shall clearly distinguish any data or information it collects for nonstatistical purposes (as authorized by law) and provide notice to the public, before the data or information is collected, that the data or information could be used for nonstatistical purposes.
b. Designation of Agents.—A statistical agency or unit may designate agents, by contract or by entering into a special agreement containing the provisions required under section 502(2) for treatment as an agent under that section, who may perform exclusively statistical activities, subject to the limitations and penalties described in this title.

**SEC. 513. <<NOTE: 44 USC 3501 note.>> FINES AND PENALTIES.**

Whoever, being an officer, employee, or agent of an agency acquiring information for exclusively statistical purposes, having taken and subscribed the oath of office, or having sworn to observe the limitations imposed by section 512, comes into possession of such information by reason of his or her being an officer, employee, or agent and, knowing that the disclosure of the specific information is prohibited under the provisions of this title, willfully discloses the information in any manner to a person or agency not entitled to receive it, shall be guilty of a class E felony and imprisoned for not more than 5 years, or fined not more than $250,000, or both.

**Subtitle B—Statistical Efficiency**

**SEC. 521. <<NOTE: 44 USC 3501 note.>> FINDINGS AND PURPOSES.**

(a) Findings.—The Congress finds the following:

1. Federal statistics are an important source of information for public and private decision-makers such as policymakers, consumers, businesses, investors, and workers.
2. Federal statistical agencies should continuously seek to improve their efficiency. Statutory constraints limit the ability of these agencies to share data and thus to achieve higher efficiency for Federal statistical programs.
3. The quality of Federal statistics depends on the willingness of businesses to respond to statistical surveys. Reducing reporting burdens will increase response rates, and therefore lead to more accurate characterizations of the economy.
4. Enhanced sharing of business data among the Bureau of the Census, the Bureau of Economic Analysis, and the Bureau of Labor Statistics for exclusively statistical purposes will improve their ability to track more accurately the large and rapidly changing nature of United States business. In particular, the statistical agencies will be able to better ensure that businesses are consistently classified in appropriate industries, resolve data anomalies, produce statistical samples that are consistently adjusted for the entry and exit of new businesses in a timely manner, and correct faulty reporting errors quickly and efficiently.
5. The Congress enacted the International Investment and Trade in Services Act of 1990 that allowed the Bureau of the Census, the Bureau of Economic Analysis, and the Bureau of Labor Statistics to share data on foreign-owned companies. The Act not only expanded detailed industry coverage from 135 industries to over 800 industries with no increase in the data collected from respondents but also demonstrated how data sharing can result in the creation of valuable data products.
6. With subtitle A of this title, the sharing of business data among the Bureau of the Census, the Bureau of Economic Analysis, and the Bureau of Labor Statistics continues to ensure the highest level of confidentiality for respondents to statistical surveys.

(b) Purposes.—The purposes of this subtitle are the following:

1. To authorize the sharing of business data among the Bureau of the Census, the Bureau of Economic Analysis, and the Bureau of Labor Statistics for exclusively statistical purposes.
2. To reduce the paperwork burdens imposed on businesses that provide requested information to the Federal Government.
3. To improve the comparability and accuracy of Federal economic statistics by allowing the Bureau of the Census, the Bureau of Economic Analysis, and the Bureau of Labor Statistics to update sample frames, develop consistent classifications of establishments and companies into industries, improve coverage, and reconcile significant differences in data produced by the three agencies.
4. To increase understanding of the United States economy, especially for key industry and regional statistics, to develop more accurate measures of the impact of technology on productivity growth, and to enhance the reliability of the Nation's most important economic indicators, such as the National Income and Product Accounts.

**SEC. 522. <<NOTE: 44 USC 3501 note.>> DESIGNATION OF STATISTICAL AGENCIES.**

For purposes of this subtitle, the term ``Designated Statistical Agency'' means each of the following:

1. The Bureau of the Census of the Department of Commerce.
2. The Bureau of Economic Analysis of the Department of Commerce.
3. The Bureau of Labor Statistics of the Department of Labor.

**SEC. 523. <<NOTE: 44 USC 3501 note.>> RESPONSIBILITIES OF DESIGNATED STATISTICAL AGENCIES.**

The head of each of the Designated Statistical Agencies shall—

1. identify opportunities to eliminate duplication and otherwise reduce reporting burden and cost imposed on the public in providing information for statistical purposes;
2. enter into joint statistical projects to improve the quality and reduce the cost of statistical programs; and
3. protect the confidentiality of individually identifiable information acquired for statistical purposes by adhering to safeguard principles, including—

   a. emphasizing to their officers, employees, and agents the importance of protecting the confidentiality of information in cases where the identity of individual respondents can reasonably be inferred by either direct or indirect means;
   b. training their officers, employees, and agents in their legal obligations to protect the confidentiality of individually identifiable information and in the procedures that must be followed to provide access to such information;
   c. implementing appropriate measures to assure the physical and electronic security of confidential data;
   d. establishing a system of records that identifies individuals accessing confidential data and the project for which the data were required; and
   e. being prepared to document their compliance with safeguard principles to other agencies authorized by law to monitor such compliance.

SEC. 524. <<NOTE: 44 USC 3501 note.>> SHARING OF BUSINESS DATA AMONG DESIGNATED STATISTICAL AGENCIES.

   a. In General.—A Designated Statistical Agency may provide business data in an identifiable form to another Designated Statistical Agency under the terms of a written agreement among the agencies sharing the business data that specifies—

1. the business data to be shared;
2. the statistical purposes for which the business data are to be used;
3. the officers, employees, and agents authorized to examine the business data to be shared; and
4. appropriate security procedures to safeguard the confidentiality of the business data.

a. Responsibilities of Agencies Under Other Laws.—The provision of business data by an agency to a Designated Statistical Agency under this subtitle shall in no way alter the responsibility of the agency providing the data under other statutes (including section 552 of title 5, United States Code (popularly known as the Freedom of Information Act), and section 552b of title 5, United States Code (popularly known as the Privacy Act of 1974)) with respect to the provision or withholding of such information by the agency providing the data.

b. Responsibilities of Officers, Employees, and Agents.—Examination of business data in identifiable form shall be limited to the officers, employees, and agents authorized to examine the individual reports in accordance with written agreements pursuant to this section. Officers, employees, and agents of a Designated Statistical Agency who receive data pursuant to this subtitle shall be subject to all provisions of law, including penalties, that relate—

1. to the unlawful provision of the business data that would apply to the officers, employees, and agents of the agency that originally obtained the information; and
2. to the unlawful disclosure of the business data that would apply to officers, employees, and agents of the agency that originally obtained the information.

a. Notice.—Whenever <<NOTE: Public information.>> a written agreement concerns data that respondents were required by law to report and the respondents were not informed that the data could be shared among the

Designated Statistical Agencies, for exclusively statistical purposes, the terms of such agreement shall be described in a public notice issued by the agency that intends to provide the data. Such notice shall allow a minimum of 60 days for public comment.

**SEC. 525. <<NOTE: 44 USC 3501 note.>> LIMITATIONS ON USE OF BUSINESS DATA PROVIDED BY DESIGNATED STATISTICAL AGENCIES.**

a. Use, Generally.—Business data provided by a Designated Statistical Agency pursuant to this subtitle shall be used exclusively for statistical purposes.
b. Publication.—Publication of business data acquired by a Designated Statistical Agency shall occur in a manner whereby the data furnished by any particular respondent are not in identifiable form.

## SEC. 526. <<NOTE: 44 USC 3501 note.>> CONFORMING AMENDMENTS.

a. Department of Commerce.—Section 1 of the Act of January 27, 1938 (15 U.S.C. 176a) is amended by striking ``The'' and inserting ``Except as provided in the Confidential Information Protection and Statistical Efficiency Act of 2002, the''.
b. Title 13.—Chapter 10 of title 13, United States Code, is amended—(1) by adding after section 401 the following:

``Sec. 402. Providing business data to Designated Statistical Agencies ``The <<NOTE: 44 USC 3601 note.>> Bureau of the Census may provide business data to the Bureau of Economic Analysis and the Bureau of Labor Statistics (`Designated Statistical Agencies') if such information is required for an authorized statistical purpose and the provision is the subject of a written agreement with that Designated Statistical Agency, or their successors, as defined in the Confidential Information Protection and Statistical Efficiency Act of 2002.''; and (2) in the table of sections for the chapter by adding after the item relating to section 401 the following:

``402. Providing business data to Designated Statistical Agencies.''.

Approved December 17, 2002.

**See the full text here:**

https://Convocourses.com/courses/cyberlaw

https://www.congress.gov/

# Public Law 113-283 Federal Information Security Modernization Act of 2014

113th Congress

**An Act**

To amend chapter 35 of title 44, United States Code, to provide for reform to Federal information security.

<<NOTE: Dec. 18, 2014 - [S. 2521]>>

<<NOTE: Federal Information Security Modernization Act of 2014. 44 USC 101 note.>>

*Be it enacted by the Senate and House of Representatives of the United States of America in Congress assembled,*

**SECTION 1. SHORT TITLE.**

This Act may be cited as the ``Federal Information Security Modernization Act of 2014''.

**SEC. 2. FISMA REFORM.**

(a) I General.—Chapter 35 of title 44, United States Code, is amended by striking subchapters II and III and inserting the following:

<<NOTE: 44 USC prec. 3531, 3531-3538, 3541 prec., 3541-3549.>>

``SUBCHAPTER II—INFORMATION SECURITY

<<NOTE: 44 USC prec. 3551.>>

``Sec. 3551. Purposes

<<NOTE: 44 USC 3551.>>

``The purposes of this subchapter are to—

``(1) provide a comprehensive framework for ensuring the effectiveness of information security controls over information resources that support Federal operations and assets;

``(2) recognize the highly networked nature of the current Federal computing environment and provide effective governmentwide management and oversight of the related information security risks, including coordination of information security efforts throughout the civilian, national security, and law enforcement communities;

``(3) provide for development and maintenance of minimum controls required to protect Federal information and information systems;

``(4) provide a mechanism for improved oversight of Federal agency information security programs, including through automated security tools to continuously diagnose and improve security;

``(5) acknowledge that commercially developed information security products offer advanced, dynamic, robust, and effective information security solutions, reflecting market solutions for the protection of critical information infrastructures important to the national defense and economic security of the nation that are designed, built, and operated by the private sector; and

``(6) recognize that the selection of specific technical hardware and software information security solutions should be left to individual agencies from among commercially developed products.

``Sec. 3552. Definitions

<<NOTE: 44 USC 3552.>>

``(a) In General.—Except as provided under subsection (b), the definitions under section 3502 shall apply to this subchapter.

``(b) Additional Definitions.—As used in this subchapter:

``(1) The term `binding operational directive' means a compulsory direction to an agency that—

>``(A) is for purposes of safeguarding Federal information and information systems from a known or reasonably suspected information security threat, vulnerability, or risk;

>``(B) shall be in accordance with policies, principles, standards, and guidelines issued by the Director; and

>``(C) may be revised or repealed by the Director if the direction issued on behalf of the Director is not in accordance with policies and principles developed by the Director.

``(2) The term `incident' means an occurrence that—

<<NOTE: Applicability.>>

>``(A) actually or imminently jeopardizes, without lawful authority, the integrity, confidentiality, or availability of information or an information system; or

>``(B) constitutes a violation or imminent threat of violation of law, security policies, security procedures, or acceptable use policies.

``(3) The term `information security' means protecting information and information systems from unauthorized access, use, disclosure, disruption, modification, or destruction in order to provide—

>``(A) integrity, which means guarding against improper information modification or destruction, and includes ensuring information nonrepudiation and authenticity;

``(B) confidentiality, which means preserving authorized restrictions on access and disclosure, including means for protecting personal privacy and proprietary information; and

``(C) availability, which means ensuring timely and reliable access to and use of information.

``(4) The term `information technology' has the meaning given that term in section 11101 of title 40.

``(5) The term `intelligence community' has the meaning given that term in section 3(4) of the National Security Act of 1947 (50 U.S.C. 3003(4)).

``(6)(A) The term `national security system' means any information system (including any telecommunications system) used or operated by an agency or by a contractor of an agency, or other organization on behalf of an agency-

``(i) the function, operation, or use of which—

``(I) involves intelligence activities;

``(II) involves cryptologic activities related to national security;

``(III) involves command and control of military forces;

``(IV) involves equipment that is an integral part of a weapon or weapons system; or

``(V) subject to subparagraph (B), is critical to the direct fulfillment of military or intelligence missions; or

``(ii) is protected at all times by procedures established for information that have been specifically authorized under criteria established by an Executive order or an Act of Congress to be kept classified in the interest of national defense or foreign policy.

``(B) Subparagraph (A)(i)(V) does not include a system that is to be used for routine administrative and business applications (including payroll, finance, logistics, and personnel management applications).

``(7) The term `Secretary' means the Secretary of Homeland Security.

``**Sec. 3553. <<NOTE: 44 USC 3553.>> Authority and functions of the Director and the Secretary**

``(a) Director.—The Director shall oversee agency information security policies and practices, including—

``(1) developing and overseeing the implementation of policies, principles, standards, and guidelines on information security, including through ensuring timely agency adoption of and compliance with standards promulgated under section 11331 of title 40;

``(2) requiring agencies, consistent with the standards promulgated under such section 11331 and the requirements of this subchapter, to identify and provide information security protections commensurate with the risk and magnitude of the harm resulting from the unauthorized access, use, disclosure, disruption, modification, or destruction of—

``(A) information collected or maintained by or on behalf of an agency; or

``(B) information systems used or operated by an agency or by a contractor of an agency or other organization on behalf of an agency;

``(3) ensuring that the Secretary carries out the authorities and functions under subsection (b);

``(4) coordinating the development of standards and guidelines under section 20 of the National Institute of Standards and Technology Act (15 U.S.C. 278g-3) with agencies and offices operating or exercising control of national security systems (including the National Security Agency) to assure, to the maximum extent feasible, that such standards and guidelines are complementary with standards and guidelines developed for national security systems;

``(5) overseeing agency compliance with the requirements of this subchapter, including through any authorized action under section 11303 of title 40, to enforce accountability for compliance with such requirements; and

``(6) coordinating information security policies and procedures with related information resources management policies and procedures.

``(b) <<NOTE: Consultation.>> Secretary.—The Secretary, in consultation with the Director, shall administer the implementation of agency information security policies and practices for information systems, except for national security systems and information systems described in paragraph (2) or (3) of subsection (e), including—

``(1) assisting the Director in carrying out the authorities and functions under paragraphs (1), (2), (3), (5), and (6) of subsection (a);

``(2) developing and overseeing the implementation of binding operational directives to agencies to implement the policies, principles, standards, and guidelines developed by the Director under subsection (a)(1) and the requirements of this subchapter, which may be revised or repealed by the Director if the operational directives issued on behalf of the Director are not in accordance with policies, principles, standards, and guidelines developed by the Director, including—

``(A) requirements for reporting security incidents to the Federal information security incident center established under section 3556;

``(B) requirements for the contents of the annual reports required to be submitted under section 3554(c)(1);

``(C) requirements for the mitigation of exigent risks to information systems; and

``(D) <<NOTE: Consultation.>> other operational requirements as the Director or Secretary, in consultation with the Director, may determine necessary;

``(3) monitoring agency implementation of information security policies and practices;

``(4) convening meetings with senior agency officials to help ensure effective implementation of information security policies and practices;

``(5) coordinating Government-wide efforts on information security policies and practices, including consultation with the Chief Information Officers Council established under section 3603 and the Director of the National Institute of Standards and Technology;

``(6) providing operational and technical assistance to agencies in implementing policies, principles, standards, and guidelines on information security, including implementation of standards promulgated under section 11331 of title 40, including by—

``(A) operating the Federal information security incident center established under section 3556;

``(B) upon request by an agency, deploying technology to assist the agency to continuously diagnose and mitigate against cyber threats and vulnerabilities, with or without reimbursement;

``(C) compiling and analyzing data on agency information security; and

``(D) developing and conducting targeted operational evaluations, including threat and vulnerability assessments, on the information systems; and

``(7) <<NOTE: Consultation.>> other actions as the Director or the Secretary, in consultation with the Director, may determine necessary to carry out this subsection.

``(c) <<NOTE: Consultation.>> Report.—Not later than March 1 of each year, the Director, in consultation with the Secretary, shall submit to Congress a report on the effectiveness of information security policies and practices during the preceding year, including—

''(1) a summary of the incidents described in the annual reports required to be submitted under section 3554(c)(1), including a summary of the information required under section 3554(c)(1)(A)(iii);

''(2) a description of the threshold for reporting major information security incidents;

''(3) a summary of the results of evaluations required to be performed under section 3555;

''(4) <<NOTE: Assessment.>> an assessment of agency compliance with standards promulgated under section 11331 of title 40; and

''(5) <<NOTE: Assessment.>> an assessment of agency compliance with data breach notification policies and procedures issued by the Director.

''(d) National Security Systems.—Except for the authorities and functions described in subsection (a)(5) and subsection (c), the authorities and functions of the Director and the Secretary under this section shall not apply to national security systems.

''(e) Department of Defense and Intelligence Community Systems.—(1) The authorities <<NOTE: Delegated authority.>> of the Director described in paragraphs

''(1) and (2) of subsection (a) shall be delegated to the Secretary of Defense in the case of systems described in paragraph (2) and to the Director of National Intelligence in the case of systems described in paragraph (3).

''(2) The systems described in this paragraph are systems that are operated by the Department of Defense, a contractor of the Department of Defense, or another entity on behalf of the Department of Defense that processes any information the unauthorized access, use, disclosure, disruption, modification, or destruction of which would have a debilitating impact on the mission of the Department of Defense.

``(3) The systems described in this paragraph are systems that are operated by an element of the intelligence community, a contractor of an element of the intelligence community, or another entity on behalf of an element of the intelligence community that processes any information the unauthorized access, use, disclosure, disruption, modification, or destruction of which would have a debilitating impact on the mission of an element of the intelligence community.

``(f) Consideration.—

``(1) In general.—In carrying out the responsibilities under subsection (b), the Secretary shall consider any applicable standards or guidelines developed by the National Institute of Standards and Technology and issued by the Secretary of Commerce under section 11331 of title 40.

``(2) Directives.—The Secretary shall—

``(A) <<NOTE: Consultation.>> consult with the Director of the National Institute of Standards and Technology regarding any binding operational directive that implements standards and guidelines developed by the National Institute of Standards and Technology; and

``(B) ensure that binding operational directives issued under subsection (b)(2) do not conflict with the standards and guidelines issued under section 11331 of title 40.

``(3) Rule of construction.—Nothing in this subchapter shall be construed as authorizing the Secretary to direct the Secretary of Commerce in the development and promulgation of standards and guidelines under section 11331 of title 40.

``(g) <<NOTE: President. Coordination.>> Exercise of Authority. —To ensure fiscal and policy consistency, the Secretary shall exercise the authority under this section subject to direction by the President, in coordination with the Director.

``Sec. 3554. <<NOTE: 44 USC 3554.>> Federal agency responsibilities

``(a) In General.—The head of each agency shall—

``(1) be responsible for—

``(A) providing information security protections commensurate with the risk and magnitude of the harm resulting from unauthorized access, use, disclosure, disruption, modification, or destruction of—

> ``(i) information collected or maintained by or on behalf of the agency; and
>
> ``(ii) information systems used or operated by an agency or by a contractor of an agency or other organization on behalf of an agency;

``(B) complying with the requirements of this subchapter and related policies, procedures, standards, and guidelines, including—

> ``(i) information security standards promulgated under section 11331 of title 40;
>
> ``(ii) operational directives developed by the Secretary under section 3553(b);
>
> ``(iii) policies and procedures issued by the Director; and
>
> ``(iv) <<NOTE: President.>> information security standards and guidelines for national security systems issued in accordance with law and as directed by the President; and

``(C) ensuring that information security management processes are integrated with agency strategic, operational, and budgetary planning processes;

``(2) ensure that senior agency officials provide information security for the information and information systems that support the operations and assets under their control, including through—

``(A) assessing the risk and magnitude of the harm that could result from the unauthorized access, use, disclosure, disruption, modification, or destruction of such information or information systems;

``(B) determining the levels of information security appropriate to protect such information and information systems in accordance with standards promulgated under section 11331 of title 40, for information security classifications and related requirements;

``(C) implementing policies and procedures to cost-effectively reduce risks to an acceptable level; and

``(D) periodically testing and evaluating information security controls and techniques to ensure that they are effectively implemented;

``(3) <<NOTE: Delegated authority.>> delegate to the agency Chief Information Officer established under section 3506 (or comparable official in an agency not covered by such section) the authority to ensure compliance with the requirements imposed on the agency under this subchapter, including—

``(A) designating a senior agency information security officer who shall—

``(i) carry out the Chief Information Officer's responsibilities under this section;

``(ii) possess professional qualifications, including training and experience, required to administer the functions described under this section;

``(iii) have information security duties as that official's primary duty; and ``(iv) head an office with the mission and resources to assist in ensuring agency compliance with this section;

``(B) developing and maintaining an agency wide information security program as required by subsection (b);

``(C) developing and maintaining information security policies, procedures, and control techniques to address all applicable requirements, including those issued under section 3553 of this title and section 11331 of title 40;

``(D) training and overseeing personnel with significant responsibilities for information security with respect to such responsibilities; and

``(E) assisting senior agency officials concerning their responsibilities under paragraph (2);

``(4) ensure that the agency has trained personnel sufficient to assist the agency in complying with the requirements of this subchapter and related policies, procedures, standards, and guidelines;

``(5) <<NOTE: Coordination. Reports. Deadline.>> ensure that the agency Chief Information Officer, in coordination with other senior agency officials, reports annually to the agency head on the effectiveness of the agency information security program, including progress of remedial actions;

``(6) ensure that senior agency officials, including chief information officers of component agencies or equivalent officials, carry out responsibilities under this subchapter as directed by the official delegated authority under paragraph (3); and

``(7) ensure that all personnel are held accountable for complying with the agency-wide information security program implemented under subsection (b).

``(b) Agency Program.—Each agency shall develop, document, and implement an agency-wide information security program to provide information security for the information and information systems that support the operations and assets of the agency, including those provided or managed by another agency, contractor, or other source, that includes—

``(1) <<NOTE: Risk assessments.>> periodic assessments of the risk and magnitude of the harm that could result from the unauthorized access, use, disclosure, disruption, modification, or destruction of information and information systems that support the operations and assets of the agency, which may include using automated tools consistent with standards and guidelines promulgated under section 11331 of title 40;

``(2) <<NOTE: Procedures.>> policies and procedures that—

``(A) are based on the risk assessments required by paragraph (1);

``(B) cost-effectively reduce information security risks to an acceptable level;

``(C) ensure that information security is addressed throughout the life cycle of each agency information system; and

``(D) ensure compliance with—

``(i) the requirements of this subchapter;

``(ii) policies and procedures as may be prescribed by the Director, and information security standards promulgated under section 11331 of title 40;

``(iii) minimally acceptable system configuration requirements, as determined by the agency; and

``(iv) <<NOTE: President.>> any other applicable requirements, including standards and guidelines for national security systems issued in accordance with law and as directed by the President;

``(3) subordinate plans for providing adequate information security for networks, facilities, and systems or groups of information systems, as appropriate;

``(4) security awareness training to inform personnel, including contractors and other users of information systems that support the operations and assets of the agency, of—

``(A) information security risks associated with their activities; and

``(B) their responsibilities in complying with agency policies and procedures designed to reduce these risks;

``(5) <<NOTE: Evaluation.>> periodic testing and evaluation of the effectiveness of information security policies, procedures, and practices, to be performed with a frequency depending on risk, but no less than annually, of which such testing—

``(A) shall include testing of management, operational, and technical controls of every information system identified in the inventory required under section 3505(c);

``(B) may include testing relied on in an evaluation under section 3555; and

``(C) shall include using automated tools, consistent with standards and guidelines promulgated under section 11331 of title 40;

``(6) a process for planning, implementing, evaluating, and documenting remedial action to address any deficiencies in the information security policies, procedures, and practices of the agency;

``(7) <<NOTE: Procedures.>> procedures for detecting, reporting, and responding to security incidents, which—

``(A) shall be consistent with the standards and guidelines described in section 3556(b);

``(B) may include using automated tools; and

``(C) <<NOTE: Notification. Consultation.>> shall include—

``(i) mitigating risks associated with such incidents before substantial damage is done;

``(ii) notifying and consulting with the Federal information security incident center established in section 3556; and

``(iii) notifying and consulting with, as appropriate—

``(I) law enforcement agencies and relevant Offices of Inspector General and Offices of General Counsel;

``(II) <<NOTE: President.>> an office designated by the President for any incident involving a national security system;

``(III) for a major incident, the committees of Congress described in subsection (c)(1)—

``(aa) <<NOTE: Deadline.>> not later than 7 days after the date on which there is a reasonable basis to conclude that the major incident has occurred; and

``(bb) after the initial notification under item (aa), within a reasonable period of time after additional information relating to the incident is discovered, including the summary required under subsection (c)(1)(A)(i); and

``(IV) <<NOTE: President.>> any other agency or office, in accordance with law or as directed by the President; and

``(8) <<NOTE: Plans. Procedures.>> plans and procedures to ensure continuity of operations for information systems that support the operations and assets of the agency.

``(c) Agency Reporting.—

``(1) Annual report.—

``(A) In general.—Each agency shall submit to the Director, the Secretary, the Committee on Government Reform, the Committee on

Homeland Security, and the Committee on Science of the House of Representatives, the Committee on Homeland Security and Governmental Affairs and the Committee on Commerce, Science, and Transportation of the Senate, the appropriate authorization and appropriations committees of Congress, and the Comptroller General a report on the adequacy and effectiveness of information security policies, procedures, and practices, including—

> ``(i) a description of each major information security incident or related sets of incidents, including summaries of—

> ``(I) the threats and threat actors, vulnerabilities, and impacts relating to the incident;

> ``(II) <<NOTE: Risk assessments. Deadline.>> the risk assessments conducted under section 3554(a)(2)(A) of the affected information systems before the date on which the incident occurred;

> ``(III) the status of compliance of the affected information systems with applicable security requirements at the time of the incident; and

> ``(IV) the detection, response, and remediation actions;

> ``(ii) the total number of information security incidents, including a description of incidents resulting in significant compromise of information security, system impact levels, types of incident, and locations of affected systems;

> ``(iii) a description of each major information security incident that involved a breach of personally identifiable information, as defined by the Director, including—

> ``(I) the number of individuals whose information was affected by the major information security incident; and

> ``(II) a description of the information that was breached or exposed; and

``(iv) <<NOTE: Consultation.>> any other information as the Director or the Secretary, in consultation with the Director, may require.

``(B) Unclassified report. –

``(i) In general.—Each report submitted under subparagraph (A) shall be in unclassified form, but may include a classified annex.

``(ii) Access to information.—The head of an agency shall ensure that, to the greatest extent practicable, information is included in the unclassified version of the reports submitted by the agency under subparagraph (A).

``(2) Other plans and reports.—Each agency shall address the adequacy and effectiveness of information security policies, procedures, and practices in management plans and reports.

``(d) <<NOTE: Consultation.>> Performance Plan. –

(1) In addition to the requirements of subsection (c), each agency, in consultation with the Director, shall include as part of the performance plan required under section 1115 of title 31 a description of—

``(A) the time periods; and

``(B) the resources, including budget, staffing, and training, that are necessary to implement the program required under subsection (b).

``(2) The description under paragraph (1) shall be based on the risk assessments required under subsection (b)(1).

``(e) Public Notice and Comment.—Each agency shall provide the public with timely notice and opportunities for comment on proposed information security policies and procedures to the extent that such policies and procedures affect communication with the public.

``Sec. 3555. <<NOTE: 42 USC 3555.>> Annual independent evaluation

``(a) In General.—(1) Each year each agency shall have performed an independent evaluation of the information security program and practices of that agency to determine the effectiveness of such program and practices.

``(2) Each evaluation under this section shall include—

``(A) <<NOTE: Testing.>> testing of the effectiveness of information security policies, procedures, and practices of a representative subset of the agency's information systems;

``(B) <<NOTE: Assessment.>> an assessment of the effectiveness of the information security policies, procedures, and practices of the agency; and

``(C) separate presentations, as appropriate, regarding information security relating to national security systems.

``(b) Independent Auditor.—Subject to subsection (c)—

``(1) for each agency with an Inspector General appointed under the Inspector General Act of 1978, the annual evaluation required by this section shall be performed by the Inspector General or by an independent external auditor, as determined by the Inspector General of the agency; and

``(2) for each agency to which paragraph (1) does not apply, the head of the agency shall engage an independent external auditor to perform the evaluation.

``(c) National Security Systems.—For each agency operating or exercising control of a national security system, that portion of the evaluation required by this section directly relating to a national security system shall be performed—

``(1) only by an entity designated by the agency head; and

``(2) in such a manner as to ensure appropriate protection for information associated with any information security vulnerability in such system commensurate with the risk and in accordance with all applicable laws.

``(d) Existing Evaluations.—The evaluation required by this section may be based in whole or in part on an audit, evaluation, or report relating to programs or practices of the applicable agency.

``(e) Agency Reporting.—(1) Each year, not later than such date established by the Director, the head of each agency shall submit to the Director the results of the evaluation required under this section.

``(2) <<NOTE: Assessment.>> To the extent an evaluation required under this section directly relates to a national security system, the evaluation results submitted to the Director shall contain only a summary and assessment of that portion of the evaluation directly relating to a national security system.

``(f) Protection of Information.—Agencies and evaluators shall take appropriate steps to ensure the protection of information which, if disclosed, may adversely affect information security. Such protections shall be commensurate with the risk and comply with all applicable laws and regulations.

``(g) OMB Reports to Congress.—(1) The Director shall summarize the results of the evaluations conducted under this section in the report to Congress required under section 3553(c).

``(2) The Director's report to Congress under this subsection shall summarize information regarding information security relating to national security systems in such a manner as to ensure appropriate protection for information associated with any information security vulnerability in such system commensurate with the risk and in accordance with all applicable laws.

``(3) <<NOTE: Evaluations.>> Evaluations and any other descriptions of information systems under the authority and control of the Director of National Intelligence or of National Foreign Intelligence Programs systems under the authority and control of the Secretary of Defense shall be made available to Congress only through the appropriate oversight committees of Congress, in accordance with applicable laws.

``(h) <<NOTE: Evaluation. Reports.>> Comptroller General.—The Comptroller General shall periodically evaluate and report to Congress on—

``(1) the adequacy and effectiveness of agency information security policies and practices; and

``(2) implementation of the requirements of this subchapter.

``(i) <<NOTE: Testing.>> Assessment Technical Assistance. —The Comptroller General may provide technical assistance to an Inspector General or the head of an agency, as applicable, to assist the Inspector General or head of an agency in carrying out the duties under this section, including by testing information security controls and procedures.

``(j) <<NOTE: Consultation.>> Guidance.—The Director, in consultation with the Secretary, the Chief Information Officers Council established under section 3603, the Council of the Inspectors General on Integrity and Efficiency, and other interested parties as appropriate, shall ensure the development of guidance for evaluating the effectiveness of an information security program and practices.

``Sec. 3556. <<NOTE: 44 USC 3556.>> Federal information security incident center

``(a) In General.—The Secretary shall ensure the operation of a central Federal information security incident center to—

``(1) provide timely technical assistance to operators of agency information systems regarding security incidents, including guidance on detecting and handling information security incidents;

``(2) <<NOTE: Analysis.>> compile and analyze information about incidents that threaten information security;

``(3) inform operators of agency information systems about current and potential information security threats, and vulnerabilities;

``(4) provide, as appropriate, intelligence and other information about cyber threats, vulnerabilities, and incidents to agencies to assist in risk assessments conducted under section 3554(b); and

``(5) <<NOTE: Consultation. President.>> consult with the National Institute of Standards and Technology, agencies or offices operating or exercising control of national security systems (including the National Security Agency), and such other agencies or offices in accordance with law and as directed by the President regarding information security incidents and related matters.

> ``(b) National Security Systems.—Each agency operating or exercising control of a national security system shall share information about information security incidents, threats, and vulnerabilities with the Federal information security incident center to the extent consistent with standards and guidelines for national security systems, issued in accordance with law and as directed by the President.

``Sec. 3557. <<NOTE: 44 USC 3557.>> National security systems

``The head of each agency operating or exercising control of a national security system shall be responsible for ensuring that the agency—

> ``(1) provides information security protections commensurate with the risk and magnitude of the harm resulting from the unauthorized access, use, disclosure, disruption, modification, or destruction of the information contained in such system;
>
> ``(2) <<NOTE: President.>> implements information security policies and practices as required by standards and

guidelines for national security systems, issued in accordance with law and as directed by the President; and

``(3) <<NOTE: Compliance.>> complies with the requirements of this subchapter.

``**Sec. 3558. <<NOTE: 44 USC 3558.>> Effect on existing law**

``Nothing in this subchapter, section 11331 of title 40, or section 20 of the National Standards and Technology Act (15 U.S.C. 278g-3) may be construed as affecting the authority of the President, the Office of Management and Budget or the Director thereof, the National Institute of Standards and Technology, or the head of any agency, with respect to the authorized use or disclosure of information, including with regard to the protection of personal privacy under section 552a of title 5, the disclosure of information under section 552 of title 5, the management and disposition of records under chapters 29, 31, or 33 of title 44, the management of information resources under subchapter I of chapter 35 of this title, or the disclosure of information to the Congress or the Comptroller General of the United States.''.

(b) <<NOTE: 44 USC 3554 note.>> Major Incident.—The Director of the Office of Management and Budget shall—

(1) <<NOTE: Guidance.>> develop guidance on what constitutes a major incident for purposes of section 3554(b) of title 44, United States Code, as added by subsection (a); and

(2) <<NOTE: Briefings. Deadline.>> provide to Congress periodic briefings on the status of the developing of the guidance until the date on which the guidance is issued.

(c) <<NOTE: Time period. Assessment.>> Continuous Diagnostics.—During the 2-year period beginning on the date of enactment of this Act, the Director of the Office of Management and Budget, with the assistance of the Secretary of Homeland Security, shall include in each report submitted under section 3553(c) of title 44, United States Code, as added by subsection (a), an assessment of the adoption by agencies of continuous diagnostics technologies, including through the Continuous Diagnostics and Mitigation program, and other advanced security tools to provide information security, including challenges to the adoption of such technologies or security tools.

(d) <<NOTE: 44 USC 3553 note. Notification.>> Breaches.—

> (1) Requirements.—The Director of the Office of Management and Budget shall ensure that data breach notification policies and guidelines are updated periodically and require—

(A) except as provided in paragraph (4), notice by the affected agency to each committee of Congress described in section 3554(c)(1) of title 44, United States Code, as added by subsection (a), the Committee on the Judiciary of the Senate, and the Committee on the Judiciary of the House of Representatives, which shall—

> > i. <<NOTE: Deadline.>> be provided expeditiously and not later than 30 days after the date on which the agency discovered the unauthorized acquisition or access; and
> > ii. (ii) include—

I. information about the breach, including a summary of any information that the agency knows on the date on which notification is provided about how the breach occurred;

II. <<NOTE: Estimate. Risk assessment.>> an estimate of the number of individuals affected by the breach, based on information that the agency knows on the date on which notification is provided, including an assessment of the risk of harm to affected individuals;

III. a description of any circumstances necessitating a delay in providing notice to affected individuals; and

IV. <<NOTE: Estimate.>> an estimate of whether and when the agency will provide notice to affected individuals; and

(B) notice by the affected agency to affected individuals, pursuant to data breach notification policies and guidelines, which shall be provided as expeditiously as practicable and without unreasonable delay after the agency discovers the unauthorized acquisition or access.

> (2) National security; law enforcement; remediation. –The Attorney General, the head of an element of the intelligence community (as such term is defined under section 3(4) of the National Security Act of 1947 (50 U.S.C. 3003(4)), or the Secretary of Homeland Security may delay the notice to affected individuals under paragraph (1)(B) if the notice would disrupt a law enforcement investigation, endanger national security, or hamper security remediation actions.
>
> (3) <<NOTE: Time period. Effective date.>> Reports.—

(A) Director of omb.—During the first 2 years beginning after the date of enactment of this Act, the Director of the Office of Management and Budget shall, on an annual basis—

    i. <<NOTE: Assessment.>> assess agency implementation of data breach notification policies and guidelines in aggregate; and

    ii. (ii) include the assessment described in clause (i) in the report required under section 3553(c) of title 44, United States Code.

(B) Secretary of homeland security.—During the first 2 years beginning after the date of enactment of this Act, the Secretary of Homeland Security shall include an assessment of the status of agency implementation of data breach notification policies and guidelines in the requirements under section 3553(b)(2)(B) of title 44, United States Code.

(4) <<NOTE: Notification.>> Exception.—Any element of the intelligence community (as such term is defined under section 3(4) of the National Security Act of 1947 (50 U.S.C. 3003(4)) that is required to provide notice under paragraph (1)(A) shall only provide such notice to appropriate committees of Congress.

(5) Rule of construction.—Nothing in paragraph (1) shall be construed to alter any authority of a Federal agency or department.

(e) Technical and Conforming Amendments.—

(1) Table of sections.—The table of sections for chapter 35 of title 44, United States Code is amended by striking the matter relating to subchapters II and III <<NOTE: 44 USC prec.

3501.>> and inserting the following:

``subchapter ii—information security

``3551. Purposes.

``3552. Definitions.

``3553. Authority and functions of the Director and the Secretary.

``3554. Federal agency responsibilities.

``3555. Annual independent evaluation.

``3556. Federal information security incident center.

``3557. National security systems.

``3558. Effect on existing law.''.

(2) Cybersecurity research and development act. —Section 8(d)(1) of the Cybersecurity Research and Development Act (15 U.S.C. 7406) is amended by striking ``section 3534'' and inserting ``section 3554''.

(3) Homeland security act of 2002.—The Homeland Security Act of 2002 (6 U.S.C. 101 et seq.) is amended—

(A) in section 223 (6 U.S.C. 143)

i. in the section heading, by inserting ``federal and'' before ``non-federal'';

ii. (ii) in the matter preceding paragraph (1), by striking ``the Under Secretary for Intelligence and Analysis, in cooperation with the Assistant Secretary for Infrastructure Protection'' and inserting ``the Under Secretary appointed under section 103(a)(1)(H)'';

iii. (iii) in paragraph (2), by striking the period at the end and inserting ``; and''; and

iv. (iv) by adding at the end the following:

``(3) fulfill the responsibilities of the Secretary to protect Federal information systems under subchapter II of chapter 35 of title 44, United States Code.'';

(B) in section 1001(c)(1)(A) (6 U.S.C. 511(c)(1)(A)), by striking ``section 3532(3)'' and inserting ``section 3552(b)(5)''; and

(C) in the table of contents in section 1(b), by striking the item relating to section 223 and inserting the following:

``**Sec. 223. Enhancement of Federal and non-Federal cybersecurity.**''.

(4) National institute of standards and technology act.—Section 20 of the National Institute of Standards and Technology Act (15 U.S.C. 278g-3) is amended—

(A) in subsection (a)(2), by striking ``section 3532(b)(2)'' and inserting ``section 3552(b)(5)''; and

(B) in subsection (e)—

i. in paragraph (2), by striking ``section 3532(1)'' and inserting ``section 3552(b)(2)''; and

ii. (ii) in paragraph (5), by striking ``section 3532(b)(2)'' and inserting ``section 3552(b)(5)''.

(5) Title 10.—Title 10, United States Code, is amended—

(A) <<NOTE: 10 USC 2222.>> in section 2222(j)(5), by striking ``section 3542(b)(2)'' and inserting ``section 3552(b)(5)'';

(B) in section 2223(c)(3), by striking ``section 3542(b)(2)'' and inserting ``section 3552(b)(5)''; and

(C) in section 2315, by striking ``section 3542(b)(2)'' and inserting ``section 3552(b)(5)''.

(f) Other Provisions.—

(1) <<NOTE: Reports. Deadline.>> Circular a-130.—Not later than 1 year after the date of enactment of this Act, the Director of the Office of Management and Budget shall amend or revise Office of Management and Budget Circular A-130 to eliminate inefficient or wasteful reporting. The <<NOTE: Deadline. Briefings.>> Director of the Office of Management and Budget shall provide quarterly briefings to Congress on the status of the amendment or revision required under this paragraph.

(2) ISPAB.—Section 21(b) of the National Institute of Standards and Technology Act (15 U.S.C. 278g-4(b)) is amended—

(A) in paragraph (2), by inserting ``, the Secretary of Homeland Security,'' after ``the Institute''; and

(B) in paragraph (3), by inserting ``the Secretary of Homeland Security,'' after ``the Secretary of Commerce,''.

Approved December 18, 2014.

# GLOSSARY OF KEY TERMS AND ACRONYMS

1. Automated Tools for Security Assessments: Technology-based tools that automate the process of assessing the security posture of information systems, identifying vulnerabilities, and detecting unauthorized activities.
2. BODs (Binding Operational Directives): Cybersecurity directives issued by DHS to federal agencies for mitigating known vulnerabilities.
3. Continuous Monitoring: The ongoing process of detecting, reporting, and responding to security threats in real-time or near-real-time to ensure the security and resilience of information systems.
4. Cybersecurity Framework: A guide developed by NIST to help organizations manage cybersecurity risk.
5. Cybersecurity Posture: The overall status and preparedness of an organization's cybersecurity defenses, including its capabilities to protect against, detect, and respond to cyber threats.
6. E-Government Act: Enacted in 2002, it includes Title III, which is the original FISMA legislation, aimed at improving the management of electronic government services and processes.
7. Enhanced Security Requirements: Additional or stricter security protocols and measures applied to information systems, especially those handling sensitive or national security information, to provide heightened protection.
8. Federal Information Systems: Information systems used or operated by an agency of the U.S. government or by a contractor or other organization on behalf of a government

agency.
9. FISIC (Federal Information Security Incident Center): a centralized body for overseeing federal cybersecurity incident management.
10. FISMA 2002: Federal Information Security Management Act of 2002; established to improve the security of federal information and data systems.
11. FISMA 2014: Federal Information Security Modernization Act of 2014; updates FISMA 2002 to address evolving cybersecurity threats and practices.
12. Incident Response: The process of managing and responding to a cybersecurity event or breach to minimize its impact.
13. Incident Response and Recovery: The set of policies and procedures for addressing and managing the aftermath of a security breach or cyberattack, with the aim of minimizing damage and recovering normal operations as quickly as possible.
14. Information Security: The practice of protecting information and information systems from unauthorized access, use, disclosure, disruption, modification, or destruction.
15. Major Incident: A cybersecurity event that has a significant impact on an agency's operations, assets, or individuals.
16. National Security Systems: Information systems that involve intelligence activities, cryptologic activities related to national security, command and control of military forces, or are integral to a weapon or weapons system.
17. Operational Efficiency: The capability of an organization to deliver products or services in a cost-effective manner while ensuring the security and integrity of its operations.
18. Risk Management: The process of identifying, assessing,

and prioritizing risks to organizational operations (including mission, functions, image, and reputation), organizational assets, individuals, other organizations, and the Nation, followed by coordinated application of resources to minimize, monitor, and control the probability and/or impact of unfortunate events.
19. Risk Management Framework (RMF): A structured process for managing information security risk, developed by NIST.
20. Security Controls: Safeguards or countermeasures to protect information systems from threats and vulnerabilities, as outlined in NIST SP 800-53.
21. Strategic Alignment: The process of aligning an organization's information security strategy with its broader mission and objectives, ensuring that security measures support overall goals.

**Acronyms**

1. CDM: Continuous Diagnostics and Mitigation
2. CISA: Cybersecurity and Infrastructure Security Agency
3. DHS: Department of Homeland Security
4. DoD: Department of Defense
5. FISIC: Federal Information Security Incident Center
6. FISMA 2014: Federal Information Security Modernization Act of 2014
7. GAO: Government Accountability Office
8. IAM: Identity and Access Management
9. IDPS: Intrusion Detection and Prevention Systems
10. NCCIC: National Cybersecurity and Communications Integration Center
11. NIST: National Institute of Standards and Technology
12. OMB: Office of Management and Budget

13. SIEM: Security Information and Event Management
14. S-CERT: United States Computer Emergency Readiness Team

# REFERENCES

"Federal Information Security Modernization Act | CISA." Www.cisa.gov, www.cisa.gov/topics/cyber-threats-and-advisories/federal-information-security-modernization-act#:~:text=Overview.

"The Federal Information Security Management Act of 2002: A Potemkin Village." Fordham Law Review, vol. 79, 2010, p. 369.

Blakey, J. Russell. "The Foreign Investment Risk Review Modernization Act: The Double-Edged Sword of U.S. Foreign Investment Regulations." Loyola of Los Angeles Law Review, vol. 53, 2019, p. 981.

Department of Homeland Security (DHS). Cybersecurity and Infrastructure Security Agency (CISA). (2023). Cybersecurity Strategy. (https://www.cisa.gov/cybersecurity-strategic-plan)

E-Government Act of 2002 (including the Federal Information Security Management Act of 2002), Public Law 107-347, https://www.congress.gov/107/plaws/publ347/PLAW-107publ347.pdf

Federal Information Security Modernization Act (FISMA) of 2014, Public Law No: 113-283, https://www.congress.gov/bill/113th-congress/house-bill/1163

Federal Information Security Modernization Act of 2014 Annual Report to Congress Fiscal Year 2017.White,

Daniel M. https://www.whitehouse.gov/wp content/uploads/2017/11/FY2017FISMAReportCongress.pdf[1]

Federal Information Security Modernization Act of 2014." Wikipedia, 19 Dec. 2021, en.wikipedia.org/wiki/Federal_Information_Security_Modernization_Act_of_2014. https://en.wikipedia.org/wiki/Federal_Information_Security_Modernization_Act_of_2014

https://csrc.nist.gov/pubs/sp/1800/40/iprd

https://nvlpubs.nist.gov/nistpubs/SpecialPublications/NIST.SP.800-12r1.pdf

https://stevevincent.info/ITS4350_2018_1.htm

https://www.researchgate.net/publication/262728749_Federal_Information_Security_Management_Act_I

https://www.sciencedirect.com/topics/computer-science/federal-information-system

https://www.securityarchitecture.com/fisma-2014-codifies-many-aspects-of-current-federal-security-practice/

https://www.techtarget.com/searchsecurity/definition/Federal-Information-Security-Management-Act

National Institute of Standards and Technology. (2018). Risk Management Framework for Information Systems and Organizations: A System Life Cycle Approach for Security and Privacy (NIST Special Publication 800-37

---

1. https://www.whitehouse.gov/wp

Rev. 2). https://nvlpubs.nist.gov/nistpubs/SpecialPublications/NIST.SP.800-37r2.pdf

National Institute of Standards and Technology. (2020). Security and Privacy Controls for Information Systems and Organizations (NIST Special Publication 800-53 Rev. 5). https://nvlpubs.nist.gov/nistpubs/SpecialPublications/NIST.SP.800-53r5.pdf

NIST Cybersecurity Framework, Framework for Improving Critical Infrastructure Cybersecurity, https://www.nist.gov/cyberframework

NIST Special Publication 800-53, Security and Privacy Controls for Federal Information Systems and Organizations, https://nvlpubs.nist.gov/nistpubs/SpecialPublications/NIST.SP.800-53r5.pdf

OMB Memorandum M-14-03, Enhancing the Security of Federal Information and Information Systems, https://obamawhitehouse.archives.gov/sites/default/files/omb/memoranda/2014/m-14-03.pdf

United States Congress. (2014). Federal Information Security Modernization Act of 2014. Public Law No. 113-283, 128 Stat. 3073.